Praise f

This is the kind of book that you keep by your bedside and read over and over. Each time you pick it up, you're invited into the private life of another person's tale of transformation. It's a classic inspirational collection to be revisited time and time again and a work of great importance. In this time of dramatic change, when so many of us must redefine ourselves based on a new reality, Elise shows us we can experience our greatest selves.

–Marci Shimoff, Author of Happy for No Reason, Love for No Reason, and Chicken Soup for the Woman's Soul.

Interesting and inspirational, Epiphany is for thoughtful readers, in whom it is likely to trigger self-examination and the effort to listen to one's own inner voice.

–Booklist

Curl up on the couch and warm your heart with Elise Ballard's uplifting book – a WOW-read!

–Health Magazine

Elise Ballard's collection of "universal lightbulb" accounts explores pivotal moments that will inspire everyone.

–Psychology Today

For those who have experienced some sort of "aha!" revelation, I highly recommend Elise Ballard's book, Epiphany, offering examples of epiphany moments from folks like Deepak Chopra, Maya Angelou, Ali McGraw and Desmond Tutu – it's the book to give as a gift this year!

–Huffington Post

Have you ever experienced an epiphany, a life-changing moment or realization?

Elise Ballard has, and she was so stunned by its effect on her life that she started asking others if they had ever experienced these kinds of breakthroughs. What began as simple curiosity led to an unexpected and exciting journey, spanning several years and the breadth of human experience. The result of her interviews is *Epiphany*, a collection of more than fifty revelations that changed lives forever.

Inspiring, thought-provoking, and eye-opening, *Epiphany* shares deeply intimate stories of people from all walks of life, from public figures like Maya Angelou, Deepak Chopra, Ali MacGraw, and Barry Manilow, to personal acquaintances and lifelong friends, to new contacts made in the most unexpected and serendipitous of circumstances.

Whether discovering purpose in life, awakening to new possibilities, or finding a new direction after a catastrophic setback, each person's epiphany is a gift, providing new insight into these remarkable lives and a window into the universal truths that connect us all.

ABOUT THE AUTHOR

ELISE BALLARD is an award-winning producer, writer and journalist. She started her career working as an actress in New York, Austin and Los Angeles before moving into writing, filmmaking and production work. Her critically acclaimed directorial debut, *Lord of the Wiens: A Dachumentary*, a movie about the annual wiener dog races in Buda, Texas, became a cult hit. She divides her time between her hometown of Dallas and Los Angeles.

To view her Epiphany! video interviews, TEDx talks, read related articles, share your epiphanies, and get information on speaking engagements and workshops, please visit www.EpiphanyChannel. com. Connect with her @EliseBallard and on Facebook.com/ EliseBallard.

www.EpiphanyChannel.com

ALSO AVAILABLE AS AN EBOOK.

Cover Design by Misa Erder

Author Photograph by Tim French

epiphany

TRUE STORIES OF SUDDEN INSIGHT
TO INSPIRE, ENCOURAGE, AND TRANSFORM

ELISE BALLARD

Epiphany is a registered trademark of Temerity Entertainment/Elise Ballard.

First published in the United States by Harmony Books, an imprint of the
Crown Publishing Group, a division of Random House, Inc., New York.

Library of Congress Cataloging-in-Publication Data for the Hardcover Edition

Ballard, Elise.
    Epiphany : true stories of sudden insight to inspire, encourage, and transform /
by Elise Ballard.
    1. Epiphanies.   2. Insight.   3. Change (Psychology)   4. Intuition.   I. Title.
    BF449.5.B35 2011
    153—dc22   2010029439

ISBN 978-0692265451 (pbk)

ISBN 978-0-307-71610-1 (hc)

Printed in the United States of America

Cover design by Misa Erder

Author photo by Tim French

This book is dedicated to:

Mom, Dad and Faye.

All of the magnificent people who have generously shared
their epiphany stories with me.

My teachers and devoted teachers everywhere who help to
shape us and move us forward.

The epiphany was like life opened a doorway, and my job was

to walk through it. I didn't know what I was going to find.

I didn't know what was going to happen.

But in life, you don't ever know what's going to happen.

What I do know is that as life continues to open these doors,

I feel safe enough and trusting enough to

walk through them.

—KRISTIN NEFF

CONTENTS

EPIPHANY

epiphany : a moment of great or sudden revelation; an intuitive grasp of reality through something usually simple and striking; an illuminating discovery, realization, or disclosure

PREFACE

Since the original publication of this book, I have been interviewed, asked to speak about and to conduct workshops on epiphanies—delving deep into what these moments are, what they contain for us, and how we can best cultivate and utilize them in our lives.

To be honest, I never knew this would happen. I always laughingly say I'm an "accidental epiphany expert" because I never planned on becoming a go-to person for epiphanies or being sought out for interviews and speaking, much less *teaching*, about these moments. I was an actress and documentary filmmaker who had an epiphany that propelled me into changing my life when nothing else had. I was so fascinated that a flash of revelation had sparked such drastic, desperately needed change in my life, that I was compelled to ask others if they'd had moments like these. Thus began my journey of the *Epiphany* project and what I now consider to be my greatest epiphany in life. The four elements of an epiphany: **Listening, Belief, Action,** and **Serendipity (see Introduction)** continually recur for me in relation to this project. The categories into which I divide the epiphanies covered are **New Directions, Awakenings, Miracles, Healings, Comings of Age** and **Callings.** But these are more for the ease of the reader than a rule or scientific categorization, and every epiphany presented could probably fall within each category, including my ongoing revelations from this *Epiphany* journey.

Through the process of working with the stories and information I've gathered and by talking and teaching about what I've learned, I've discovered even more about the power of our epiphanies and why they are so important to us. They are an invaluable tool to which we all have access. My work on epiphanies has become about not only presenting interesting true stories of fascinating moments and change in different people's lives, but it's also meant to help people become aware of these revelatory moments and find concrete ways to utilize and cultivate their own epiphanies to enhance and create change in their lives.

Why People Have Epiphanies

Everyone has epiphanies—from children to centenarians; from atheists to religious leaders; from street urchins to billionaires—people of all ages, from all belief systems and from all walks of life. These moments are completely democratic. They are a birthright of being human. They can creep in the most quiet, personal ways, or explode in dramatic, miraculous fashion. Researchers can't exactly pinpoint why or how people have these sudden revelations, and we certainly can't force life-changing epiphanies to happen. However, I did discover several patterns that happen every time someone has a powerful epiphany. In addition to the aforementioned, **Listening, Belief, Action** and **Serendipity**, there is always a quality present that I call **Reverence**, a deep respect for the experience and what was learned.

Why do people have epiphanies? *Because they are ready for them.* They may be praying for one or just in contemplation or they may be in absolute crisis, but overall, in varying degrees, they are *ready*–**and because you are reading this right now, you probably are too.**

We want to learn to cultivate an environment in our lives and within ourselves so that we're always ready and open for epiphanies, rather than having them only once we are in a crisis. We don't want life to have to "bring us to our knees," so to speak, for us to start paying attention. These moments are unique gifts to help guide and direct us to our best lives. We want to live in tune with our inner voices and wisdom so that epiphanies come easily, and we get the message. Learning to live like this can shift many areas of our lives that need it, and our epiphanies can become more like slight adjustments of direction than blinding flashes of life-changing insight.

Utilizing Epiphanies for Success and Building Blocks for Life

Before I embarked on this project, I wasn't sure that each of us actually had a "purpose" or unique "path" in life. Now I believe that is absolutely the case. We all come in to the world with specific gifts and talents meant to be fully developed and utilized in the world, and when we hook into these gifts and talents (our strengths that usually make our hearts sing and time disappear), we're led to living our most fulfilled lives. We're energized instead of depleted in our careers, personal lives, and communities. If you'll note as you read the numerous stories in this book, most of the people, even those who had experienced extreme loss and set-backs, demonstrate this. All seem to be thriving professionally and personally, and are reaching out to serve in bigger ways.

Ultimately, epiphanies are wake-up calls to our gifts and talents as well as to what is holding us back in life. They guide us to finding our purposes, to healings and to overcoming our blocks. **Increased self-knowledge, stronger relationships, heightened creativity, ongoing productivity,** and **shortening** and **sustaining pathways to success** are just some of the benefits of honoring and working with epiphanies that I have seen over and over again through my research and interviews.

I have also discovered a powerful set of commonalities in **how successful people view and use their epiphanies.** The most successful people I interviewed in terms of prestige and career success **honor their epiphanies.** They all know *exactly* what their greatest epiphany in life is—they didn't pause for an instant to think about what it might be when I asked them about it. They have never glossed over it or forgotten about it. They know the story and all the details, and they know what it meant to them then and what it means to them today. People such as Maya Angelou, Desmond Tutu and Dr. Mehmet Oz had amazing, succinct, powerful stories that they told me, often spontaneously, in answer to my unexpected question.

In each case, the person's greatest epiphany was an experience on which he or she had built the rest of his or her life. These people use their moments of revelations as baseboards and building blocks for life. They realize their epiphanies are gifts of wisdom—sometimes hard-earned, but sometimes not. Sometimes people just "get it" in a flash, know what it means for them and act on it. I also found highly successful people to be some of the most willing and generous about sharing their stories, and I believe it's because of this awareness of the wisdom that they were passing on. It's an attitude of, "This is what happened to me and changed my life for the better and got me on my path, so here you go... if it helps, go forth and share." **This is why I encourage everyone to share their story, at least with their loved ones, and to ask them about theirs. You never know who you will help by doing so and every epiphany contains wisdom that we all can learn from, which is only one of the four major gifts that can directly result from sharing our stories.**

Four Gifts of Sharing Your Epiphany Stories

1. **WISDOM** — Our epiphanies contain some of our greatest wisdom and most of them become building blocks for our lives. Imparting and receiving wisdom and knowledge are some of the most important aspects of our growth as human beings.

2. **INSIGHT** — Many times our epiphanies come to us in very personal, intimate ways. When you ask someone about their epiphanies and when you share these stories with someone, you will gain insight into them, and many times into yourself, in new and deeper ways.

3. **INTIMACY** — Sharing stories of personal, hard-won wisdom and insight can develop a level of intimacy and compassion with others you have never before experienced.

4. **HEALING/INSPIRATION/ENCOURAGEMENT** — The elements of wisdom, insight and intimacy can result in healing, inspiration, encouragement, and more—for both the teller and the listener. You never know how what you do or say will affect or help

another person and deepen our life experiences. By discussing and sharing your epiphany stories, you can affect others in numerous positive and powerful ways.

The Ripple Effect

We've all heard of "the ripple effect." A **ripple effect** is a situation where, like the ever-expanding ripples across water when an object is dropped into it, an effect from an initial state can be followed outwards incrementally. When you act on your epiphanies, they inevitably ripple out in the world and lead you to make some of your greatest contributions in life. These moments provide a clear context and precise way of tracing and witnessing the ripple effect phenomena. As G.W. Bailey beautifully puts it in his interview, "One human being's experience can have such an impact on so many people. And it's not that they're trying to have an impact. I'm not talking about Paul on the road to Damascus and the angel comes to visit him and he feels compelled to change the world... It's just that when one life changes, many lives are changed because all the people connected to that one life are affected."

I'd also like to highlight another small but important point. Most people I interviewed who have very satisfying and successful careers and had their epiphanies as children, teens or young adults (many of these accounts appear in the Callings section), usually had at least one parent or adult notice their gifts and desires and wholeheartedly support them. Not in a crazy stage parent kind of way, but in a grounded, loving, mature way. This can make all the difference in a young person's life and enable them to ripple out in the world in huge ways.

Acting on epiphanies can lead to major contributions to the world or to minor ones, but if you examine them, they always ultimately result in some kind of contribution to yourself or to others. It is actually very simple and straightforward on many levels, but often we aren't aware of how we are affecting the world around us. Many times we take these revelations for granted and don't consider them as being the powerful, special and invaluable tools that they are for us all.

The Essence of Epiphanies

Life can become pretty magical and miraculous when you're consciously cultivating epiphanies. When we take epiphanies down to their essences, they really amount to one thing:

Love. Love of self, of others, of one's work or calling; love of community; love of the Divine; and love of the world-at-large. When you are taking action on your epiphanies, what you ripple out to everyone around you is love. And I think we all agree, the world can never get enough of that.

Often I get the question: **"How do I know I've had an epiphany and what do I do about it when I have had one?"** This is how I answer it: "An epiphany is a moment of sudden or great revelation that usually changes your life in some way. If the moment or happening you are considering changed your perspective so drastically that you are thinking and wondering about it, it probably was an epiphany. But neither I nor anyone else can tell you whether or not you had an epiphany. You must be the sole judge of that in the end. And what you can do about it is **take action** to incorporate what you have learned into your life."

Sometimes people aren't sure how to take action. I have exercises and suggestions to help with this at the end of the book, and by reading others' stories, you will see a myriad of ways to take action in life. But here is one simple thing I suggest you always do with any epiphany: **Look for the love**. Always be looking for the love that is the foundation of every epiphany. If you simply focus on that discovery, it will guide you to what action to take. It will lead you to healing and understanding. It is the love epiphanies reveal that will eventually inspire, encourage and transform your life.

What Is Your Greatest Epiphany in Life?

This is what I've been asking people from all different professions, nationalities, ages, beliefs, and walks of life—from well-known figures to my fifth-grade teacher to a former street urchin in Tanzania. *Epiphany* contains the stories of the revelations that changed their lives forever.

True epiphanies change not just us but also the other people in our lives—and sometimes the world. This book includes epiphanies that have led to achievements in science, medicine, education, sports, government, religion, music, technology, books, entertainment, world outreach, personal growth, healing, child rearing, and many other areas of life.

Epiphanies are incredible gifts. They reveal some of our greatest wisdom and many universal truths. Some of the narratives here "turned the kaleidoscope" for me. They might contain insights that I've heard before, but somehow in the way the stories are shared, it caused a shift and I now understand them in a completely new, personal way. I have found that every one of the stories in this book has enhanced my life in some way, and I hope the same is true for you.

*   *   *

One morning several years ago, I woke up and realized my life had completely changed. I sat up in bed and looked around me with a mix of bewilderment, shock, and wonder. Scanning the unfamiliar belongings filling the downtown loft I found myself in, it dawned on me just how drastically different my life had become in a few short weeks. Here I was, subletting and living alone for the first time in my life while my husband of almost eight years and our beloved cat were still in our home a few miles away. "I really am getting a divorce," I thought and the thin veil of denial lifted and a heavy suffocating blanket of reality began to sink into its place. And suddenly I recalled how it happened. I remembered the *exact* moment that led me to a stranger's home and an unrecognizable life. A couple of months before, in one singular, solitary moment, everything began to change for me.

*   *   *

To say my husband and I were in a struggling marriage is probably the understatement of the century—we were both miserably unhappy and had been for a while. We were living in Austin, Texas, at the time, and I was the lead actress in a play by Lawrence Wright called *Sonny's Last Shot*, about the trials and tribulations of Texas politics. I played a West Texas woman who is very much in love with her husband, a rancher and state congressman. My character desperately wants to have a baby. When she discovers that she is infertile, she is devastated—only to find out next from her husband that he has had a one-night stand with a fellow legislator and has gotten the woman pregnant.

Toward the end of the play, my character goes to the "other woman" and asks her to put the baby up for adoption. In the last scene, my character and her husband have adopted the baby. (This happens *after* he appropriately grovels and begs for forgiveness. He was a good guy; he just screwed up this one time.) He ends up Speaker of the House, and everyone ends up happily ever after.

When preparing for a role, I like to do as much research as possible into the character's background and circumstances. To play this woman, I researched fertility ailments and treatments and, of course, adoption. I told the prop master that I would provide the adoption agency brochure for my character to hand to the "other woman" onstage. I will never forget the moment I printed that brochure. I'd done hours of research online about how different kinds of adoptions work and read all these testimonials from different families about it, and had finally found an appropriate-looking brochure to print. As I watched the blank paper getting pulled into the printer and the wet colors of the brochure slowly emerging toward me, I was suddenly struck by a realization. And the word is *struck*—I was *hit*. Suddenly I could see everything clearly. In that moment I knew that one of the major reasons I was staying in my marriage was because, being in my thirties, I feared that if I left, I might never have a child of my own.

The fear was so real and deep and terrifying that until that flash of insight, I hadn't been able to admit it to myself. This fear of mine had, in fact, been paralyzing me from doing anything about my situation. As I was watching the images of the adoption brochure appear out of the printer, my "kaleidoscope" turned and the picture of my life looked completely different. In an instant, I was free from my fear of leaving the marriage. I actually felt it lift, as if it snapped free of my body. My research for this role had educated me about the options available to become a parent and, in doing so, had uncovered my fear and released it at the same time. Before that, I knew very little about fertility treatments and almost nothing about adoption and had never really considered it to be an option for me, but now I realized it was something that I absolutely could and would consider if I needed to. I remember actually thinking, "I could do that. I don't have to stay." When the play's run ended, so did my marriage.

A few months later when I found myself looking around in amazement at my new life, I remembered the moment at the printer and thought, "That was an *epiphany*." The power of that one moment was fascinating to me. It seemed almost miraculous that in literally one moment, I both faced a paralyzing fear *and* gained freedom from it.

That defining moment drastically changed me, and also taught me a great life lesson about how I had previously dealt with fear—namely, by avoiding it. In this case, not only had acquiring knowledge revealed my fear, but it also had eliminated it, and even empowered me. I decided to make this experience my model: now when anything scares me or I don't understand something, I try to educate myself about it as much as possible. Knowledge and understanding, information and education, are the keys to eliminating fear. In other words, the cliché is profoundly true: knowledge really is power.

After processing what my epiphany meant to me, I was curious to know if other people had experienced the same sort of momentous breakthroughs, and I began asking friends, family, and acquaintances if they thought they had ever had an epiphany. Their answers captivated me, so I decided to ask everyone I could about their epiphany and film their answers. I thought perhaps I could edit the interviews into a movie or at least create a website for them. I even briefly worked with a production company interested in developing the concept into a reality show. But as I was filming and then transcribing and editing the interviews, I realized how powerful these stories were in written form. The seed for this book was planted.

A question I get asked a lot is, "What do you mean by *epiphany*, exactly?" Everyone from Oprah to Mutual of Omaha is talking about realizations and awakenings, and many times these are referred to as "aha moments." But to me, that term is a little more casual and speaks more to everyday insights. By *epiphanies* I mean the major, life-changing revelations that have had the greatest impact on our lives.

After all, the word *epiphany* originated in ancient Greece to describe our great revelations from the gods, and it has a deep, archetypal resonance. The history of the word is fascinating. *Epiphany*, when it's capitalized, is the name of the Christian church celebration of the three wise men or magi coming to see the baby Jesus in Bethlehem. This is usually celebrated on January 6, which in the Western church calendar starts an Epiphany season that lasts until the first day of Lent. It is a season of new beginnings; after the visit of the magi, church feast days and readings recount the baptism of Jesus by John the Baptist, and Jesus' first public miracle at Cana, where he turned water into wine. *Epiphany*, from the Greek *epiphaneia*, means "appearance" or "manifestation," and was first seen in English around 1310. For about three hundred years, it meant the religious feast day and nothing else.

By the mid-1600s, *epiphany*—with a lowercase *e*—was being used to refer to other manifestations of Christ and to appearances of divine beings in other religions. Since the nineteenth century, the meanings of *epiphany* began expanding. Writers such as Thomas De Quincey (who wrote of "bright epiphanies of the Grecian intellect") and William Wordsworth, then later James Joyce (who wrote that epiphanies "are the most delicate and evanescent of moments") and John Updike, helped broaden the definition of *epiphany* to include the secular realm. Today it carries a range of meanings, including "an intuitive grasp of reality," "an illuminating discovery, realization, disclosure, or insight," or simply "a revealing scene or moment." My definition of an epiphany is "a moment of sudden or great realization about life that usually changes you in some way."

I started asking the people I interviewed for their definitions and was enchanted and inspired by some of the answers I received:

An epiphany is a realization; an opening; a portal to the Divine; growing up; a magic moment that impacts you and changes you forever and you can remember it as vividly as you experienced it; a moment that changes the lens through which you view your life; our soul scratching around our head and giving us a signal to guide our lives with; a moment of descending light, open knowledge, and choice; a drastic shift in energy and change of perspective that happens in the form of a moment of clarity; something that gives you the strength to take a different direction or move forward and opens up everything; a sense of wonderment; a clarifying direction; that moment where you know your life is never going to be the same.

One of my favorites is Maya Angelou's answer:

"It probably has a million definitions. It's the occurrence when the mind, the body, the heart, and the soul focus together and see an old thing in a new way."

Given these definitions, it should be no surprise that our greatest epiphanies tend to be deeply personal stories. Many people admitted that they had never told anyone about their epiphany, not even their loved ones. Two of my closest friends astounded me when they told me about miracles in their lives that they'd never shared before. When I asked why they hadn't, they replied that they just don't really talk about it—the experience seemed too deep and private. And many people, until asked, had never even thought they'd had an epiphany. Once remembered, their epiphanies were some of the most profound and emotional.

We don't often speak about our epiphanies because they are held so close to our hearts. There simply aren't opportunities in our society to share such delicate moments, and often we're embarrassed by them. We don't always take the time to think about extraordinary moments in our lives and what they really mean. We miss the experience of awe that comes from listening closely to others, to ourselves, and to the signs in the world around us.

Through this project, I've learned it's important not only to know others' stories but also to honor and tell our own. When we do, we often discover things about ourselves or find a deeper meaning behind an epiphany. This happened over and over again when I interviewed people. Until they were telling their stories, they had not fully realized what certain points and moments truly meant to them. Many times they also realized or remembered other epiphanies in their lives that they had forgotten or buried, and only now could they see how their epiphanies had similar themes and built upon one another. Examining our epiphanies can be quite helpful in gaining insight into our lives and seeing where we've grown and where we still may want to grow.

I've found that, just as most great spiritual teachings seem to share similar essential values and messages, those I spoke with seemed to share wisdom and lessons that are universal in nature even though they experienced their epiphanies in very different ways. The goal of this project has always been to see what we can learn from one another. How are we the same? How are we different? Can we benefit from hearing these stories? This project explores the mystery that each of us is unique and different, yet we are all also very much the same. We have widely varying backgrounds, professions, beliefs, religions, experiences, and stories, yet our greatest revelations center on core truths and wisdoms.

Every epiphany included the following:

1. LISTENING. Whether they were calmly contemplating the sky, meditating or praying, clinging to hope in a crisis, desperate to heal, or searching for an answer, people were *listening* and *paying attention* to signs and what was going on around them. I say "listening" because many of the epiphanies, especially the more miraculous ones, almost all had to do with hearing a voice, either an inner voice or one from a Higher Power.

2. BELIEF. When people had an epiphany, they never doubted for one instant that whatever happened was real for them. They had absolute *faith* and *trust* in their experience and themselves,

knowing the action they were taking because of their epiphany was right for them, regardless of what anyone else thought.

3. ACTION. Every single person whose epiphany positively changed his or her life took *action*. All of them took the first step toward whatever the epiphany compelled them to do, even if they had no idea what would happen after that.

4. SERENDIPITY. After people began to take action on their epiphanies, *circumstances* seemed to fall into place so that they could take the next step. It is as if the world conspires to support your decisions and actions, to confirm that you are on the right track. Many (not all) of the people I talked to felt the hand of God or some other mysterious, benevolent force in their lives after their epiphanies.

While many epiphanies do seem to occur out of crisis, a time when we are compelled to be more acutely aware of our life and its meaning, I know that doesn't have to be the case. We can purposefully be listening and paying attention all the time, not just when we are in pain or having difficulties. We can have faith and believe in ourselves instead of always doubting and disregarding what we feel is true for us. We can always choose to take action. We can notice and trust serendipity in our lives, acknowledging that the world seems to be supporting the actions we're taking. If we feel good about those actions, then we're probably on the right track. By always practicing these things, we could be experiencing epiphanies all the time, from very tiny ones to life-transforming ones…and life gets pretty exciting and interesting when we do.

The epiphanies contained here are a testament to that. For the most part, I spoke with each individual either in person or on the phone, and interviews ran anywhere from five minutes to over an hour, the average being twenty to thirty minutes. These interviews have been edited directly from our conversations. I tried not to change the way people said things and to keep the stories in each individual's unique voice. If they are filmed (some of them are, and you can view them on the website EpiphanyChannel.

com), you can experience people's essence and voice directly; I wanted you to experience their essence on the page as well.

The people who share their stories in *Epiphany* are not all world-famous, but some are. I consider every one successful, and by that I mean they are not only respected professionally, but also seem to have fulfilling personal lives and are comfortable in their own skin. The people included are my friends, friends of friends, colleagues, people I've met along the way, and people I admire whom I simply cold-called to interview. They range in age from twenty-three to ninety-one, and they are from widely varying walks of life. To highlight some of the most common themes that emerged from these epiphanies, I've grouped them in sections such as "Callings" and "New Directions," but as you'll see, most could fit in several or all categories.

These stories have moved me to tears of joy and sadness. They have made me laugh out loud. They have rendered me speechless. Some have forced me to think in new ways or ponder them over time. Many times I find meaning in an epiphany one way when I first hear it, and then later it takes on a new significance as I recognize something that I didn't before. As with all good stories, that is what they are meant to do, and they can be revisited time and time again. Without exception, I would find myself thinking about every single one of the epiphanies at some point later—sometimes soon after, sometimes months, even years later—and know I will for years to come.

Most of all, these stories have taught me to wonder at the magnificence and resilience of the human spirit. It's not only what these people have accomplished and how they've triumphed and learned, but also the beautiful, generous spirit in which they shared their stories and hard-won wisdom. No one received compensation for participating in this project. People told their stories simply because I wanted to hear them, hoping that perhaps others could learn from what they had lived. As the people I interviewed who started nonprofits all said, the majority of people are extremely generous if you give them an opportunity.

There are so many amazing people around you who help weave the tapestry of your life. Notice them. Observe. Inquire. Act. Wonderful riches are to be mined from everyone around us, from those we meet in random everyday encounters to the people closest to us. So many of the people who have helped me throughout my life turned out to have riveting and important stories to share with me. Because I had never asked, I had no idea about their epiphanies. I had known them for years, but what they shared with me has given me greater insight into them and into my own life.

People will share their stories generously if they know that their experiences are respected and needed. Many people said they wanted to ask their parents or grandparents about their epiphanies, but couldn't anymore. So do it. Share your epiphanies and ask the people in your life about theirs. Even ask people out in the world whom you admire for whatever reason, or write in and tell me who they are so I can! And I invite you to come experience still more stories—and share your own—on our website, EpiphanyChannel.com.

This project has been the greatest epiphany of my life. It has left me changed and has led me both to learning and to healing. That's been my experience. And now, I want you to have yours.

RESOURCE

resource : a source of information or expertise

I have always viewed *Epiphany* as not only being a collection of interviews and stories to serve as a source of inspiration and motivation, but also as a resource to further research these people, their stories, and any of their organizations, books, healing modalities, advice or work that may be of help or interest to you.

In addition, this book started as a film idea, and as a lover of behind-the-scenes work, it was important for me that you be able to somewhat experience the inner workings of this project too. If nothing else, it's sometimes fun to see the face behind the story!

Therefore, each person in this book has a bio, a "behind-the-scenes" section called "The Interview," and website links for further research, as well as a photo and any videos available with the aforementioned information on their individual pages at www.EpiphanyChannel.com/People.

If there is an EpiphanyChannel video of an interview, the end of "The Interview" section says "View the Interview" with its link.

All Epiphany Project related videos can be found on www.EpiphanyChannel.com or on YouTube at www.youtube.com/epiphanychannel.

About The Epiphany Project Videos: www.epiphanychannel.com/project

AWAKENINGS

awakening : an act or moment of becoming suddenly aware of something; making conscious or alert; rousing into activity; rebirth, arousal, renewal

When one life changes, many lives are changed.

—G.W. BAILEY

G.W. BAILEY is a stage, film, and television actor, internationally known for his many roles, including Capt. Harris in the *Police Academy* film series, Sgt. Rizzo from the M*A*S*H television series, and his role as Lt. Provenza on the hit TNT television series *Major Crimes* and *The Closer.* He is also the executive director of the nonprofit Sunshine Kids Foundation, which provides trips and activities for hundreds of young cancer patients annually. He is a father and grandfather and resides in Los Angeles, California. (www.SunshineKids.org)

THE INTERVIEW

When this project started taking off, I called G.W. right away. He is a consummate storyteller and always has wonderful stories to tell. Once again, my friend delivered. Even though he had been shooting earlier on *The Closer* and had to attend an event for his organization, the Sunshine Kids, that afternoon, he squeezed in some time to talk with me about his epiphany. He says he is moved to both laughter and tears whenever he shares this story, and so was I when I heard his poignant account.

View the Interview:

www.epiphanychannel.com/people/gw-bailey

*   *   *

I think about an epiphany as something that happens, say, as you are coming around a corner and suddenly an event takes place that changes your life—it is completely unexpected and unanticipated.

Consequently, it also changes the lives of many others because we are all connected. That moment for me happened to take place in Breckenridge, Colorado, about twenty-five years ago.

My goddaughter, Brandy, was diagnosed with cancer at age twelve. I was very close to her and to her little sister and parents, whom I've known since college. When she was diagnosed we were all, of course, devastated by it. Brandy had a very difficult first year fighting the disease because she was homebound and isolated, which is terrible for anyone, especially a teenager.

Through a series of circumstances, after this first year of battling cancer Brandy was invited on a ski trip with a group of kids—all of whom had cancer—with an organization called Sunshine Kids that was about three years old at the time. On this ski trip, something amazing happened for her. The experience completely changed her approach to her disease. For the first time, she was around a lot of other kids who were just like her. Nobody cared about whether you were bald or not; nobody cared about scars or amputations or central lines; and they were able to share a lot of stories and common experiences. Suddenly she wasn't isolated in her experience anymore, and it was wonderful. She was so excited when she got back and told me all about it.

That summer, Sunshine Kids had another trip, but this time it was a family trip. So Brandy and her family went to Breckenridge, Colorado, with families of kids from all over the country for a week of activities. On the first day of this trip, Brandy called me and wanted me to come join them. I'm an actor by profession, and at the time (in the 1980s) I was doing a series of movies that were enormously popular with teenagers called *Police Academy*. I'd also done a couple of other light, silly movies that kids had liked, so my career was going very well in the feature business, and she wanted me to come up because I was her B-movie star, quasi-celebrity godfather. I told her I was so sorry but I couldn't come, I was just too busy. She kept on and on, and I told her again that it wasn't possible but as soon as she got back I'd have her come to Los Angeles and make it up to her, but I just couldn't come to Colorado right now. So we hung up, and about five minutes later she called back. And very slowly and determinedly she said, "You are my godfather, and I want you here." Pause. She meant it. I sighed and kidded her about manipulating me and told her I'd just get to come for a day, that it was going to be an ordeal getting there and would cost a lot, and she replied in typical teenage Brandy fashion, "Whatever." So of course I laughed and begrudgingly said I'd come—I couldn't deny her anything. I got there the next day.

Brandy had given me their activity schedule, so I knew they'd be at the volunteer fire department when I arrived. They were having a battle with the water hoses, and the kids were all dressed up in fireman outfits and hats and all that stuff. When I got to the fire station, you could hear all the commotion of the kids playing outside in the back, so I walked toward the noise of the children, went out the back door, and rounded a corner. And what I saw forever changed my life.

I had seen one child with cancer. I had seen a couple of children with cancer. But I had *never* seen *thirty* children with cancer all together in the same place. They were all laughing—all having this exuberant celebration of their lives. I had this overwhelming emotional response I still can't describe properly. It was all these kids—all ages, all sizes—and it was just like...what is this?

No one had seen me yet, so I turned around and went back out to my rental car, and I sat in it for ten or fifteen minutes. And I cried. I cried for her. I cried for all of them.

I ended up staying the entire week in Breckenridge, and then flew straight to Houston to meet with Rhoda, the founder of Sunshine Kids. I knew I had to be involved and be a part of this organization that helped these kids to celebrate their lives in spite of their illness. That was twenty-five years ago. I started as a volunteer at events, filling coolers, blowing up balloons, and also helped put events together and raised money. Eventually I became the executive director of the Sunshine Kids Foundation, which I still am today.

When I started, we only had the ski trip in the winter and the family trip in the summer, so we were only reaching forty to fifty kids a year. Sunshine Kids now has twelve national events and hundreds of regional and local events impacting thousands of kids and their families a year. Hundreds of volunteers and our staff work to help give a little bit of these kids' childhoods back to them that's been somewhat taken away because of their battle with their disease.

Through this epiphany, I have gained a great appreciation of time. I realized how important and precious our time here is. We lost Brandy when she was seventeen, and though many children that have been Sunshine Kids are now doctors and nurses and countless other professions as they've grown up and beaten their disease, I've also had to bury too many children over the years— though even one is too many. If there's anything to be learned out of all of this, it's that life goes on... it has to. And you have to celebrate life while you're here, and celebrate our children—all children everywhere.

Rounding that corner that day in Breckenridge, Colorado, changed my life. It's changed my family's life. This idea of epiphanies is fascinating to me because one human being's experience can have such an impact on so many people. And it's not that they're trying to have an impact. I'm not talking about Paul on the road to Damascus and the angel comes to visit him, and he feels compelled to change the world. That's not at all what I'm talking about. It's just that when one life changes, many lives are changed because all of the people connected to that one life are affected.

We are loved by Love itself.
There is nothing good that we can't do.
— MAYA ANGELOU

DR. MAYA ANGELOU was a celebrated African American poet, memoirist, novelist, educator, dramatist, actress, producer, historian, filmmaker, and civil rights activist. In 1970 her autobiography, *I Know Why the Caged Bird Sings*, was published to international acclaim and enormous popular success. The list of her published verse, nonfiction, and fiction now includes more than thirty bestselling titles. Her screenplay *Georgia, Georgia*, the first by an African American woman ever to be filmed, was nominated for a Pulitzer Prize, as was her volume of poetry *Just Give Me a Cool Drink of Water 'Fore I Diiie*. She was a member of the Harlem Writers Guild in the late 1950s, was active in the civil rights movement, and served as northern coordinator of Dr. Martin Luther King Jr.'s Southern Christian Leadership Conference. Dr. Angelou served on two presidential committees, was awarded the Presidential Medal of Arts in 2000 and the Lincoln Medal in 2008, received three Grammy Awards, and was awarded more than thirty honorary degrees. She was a professor at Wake Forest University from 1991-2014, the recipient of the first lifetime Reynolds Professorship of American Studies there. Dr. Maya Angelou passed away on May 29, 2014, leaving behind one son, Guy, many loved ones and an indelible legacy. (www.MayaAngelou.com)

THE INTERVIEW

Many people requested Maya Angelou as one of the people whose greatest epiphany they'd like to know about, and her interview remains one of the most extraordinary experiences of my life.

I was a little tongue-tied when I first heard that famous, mellifluous *voice* on the other end of the phone, but of course Dr. Angelou was warm, calm, and composed, and at the same time quite passionate, when she told her stories. She truly is a master of the spoken and written word, and having the honor of experiencing that powerful mastery and what she shared still moves me.

•   •   •

The truth is everybody probably has 250 epiphanies. The way you're changed at ten prepares you to be changed again at fifteen, but you couldn't have been changed at fifteen had you not had that change at ten. You see what I mean? Epiphany builds upon epiphany.

When my son was born, I was seventeen. And I came home from the hospital and my mother put him in the bed with me. I was so afraid I'd roll over on this *beautiful* baby. But she said, "It's all right. You'll be all right." I thought I might smother him or something. I was just scared.

Sometime in the middle of the night, my mother awakened me, and she said, "Don't move. Just look." And I had put my arm up and put my hand on the mattress, and put the blanket over my arm so that my baby was lying in a tent.

And my mom softly said to me, "See, baby? When you mean right, you do right."

A few years later, when I was maybe twenty-two or so, I was studying voice, and the voice teacher lived in my house and rented from me. He taught a number of accomplished actresses and singers, and they all studied in my house. So I knew them slightly. But they were all white, and they were accomplished, and many of them were forty years old and had been written about in the San Francisco newspaper, where I lived at the time.

Once a month, the voice teacher asked us to come together and read from a book called *Lessons in Truth*. We all would read a page, or a half a page, whatever he assigned. And at one point, I was reading and read the line, "God loves me."

And he stopped me and said, "Read it again."

So I read it again: *"God loves me."*

He said, "Again."

And suddenly I became embarrassed. I was young and black, and everybody else was white and accomplished. And I felt he was really embarrassing me. Putting me on the spot. So I read it with ferocity—forcefully: *"GOD. LOVES. ME."*

And, at that moment, I knew it. *I knew it!*

I thought, "God? That which made bees and mountains and water? *That? Loves me?* Maya Angelou? Well then, there's nothing I can't do. *I can do anything good."*

Even now, telling you this some fifty years later, it still brings goose bumps to me. I could weep with joy at the knowledge that I am loved by Love itself.

Every one of us has to pick our own way
through the land mines of life—no one can or should do it for us.
Sometimes the most extravagant pain is the gateway to
something incandescent.

—ALI MACGRAW

ALI MACGRAW is an internationally known, award-winning actress, author, and activist. She starred in the critically acclaimed and international blockbuster hit films *Goodbye Columbus, The Getaway,* and *Love Story* (for which she received a Golden Globe award and an Academy Award nomination), the epic miniseries *The Winds of War,* and the popular TV series *Dynasty,* among many others. Her autobiography, *Moving Pictures,* was an international bestseller, and her yoga video *Ali MacGraw: Yoga Mind and Body* was a bestseller upon release and is still popular more than a decade later. She is the mother of filmmaker Joshua Evans and currently lives in New Mexico. She travels extensively, appearing in documentaries and working on behalf of numerous social, animal, and environmental causes. In 2008 she received the Luminaria Award from the Santa Fe Community Foundation, and the New Mexico Governor's Award for Contribution to the Arts.

THE INTERVIEW

I was on a plane reading the March 2010 issue of *Vanity Fair* when I came across this terrific article on Ali MacGraw and felt I had to try to contact her. When we finally spoke on the phone, she was just as wonderful as everyone says. Her epiphany had happened six months before and she had not discussed it with many people, so I feel very honored that she was willing to share it here.

*   *   *

Epiphany is a word that appeals to me a lot. To my mind, it refers to an overwhelming burst of light that feels like it's changing your life right down to the cells in your body. When I heard the title of your book, I thought, "Yes, I did have one of those." And it surprised me. It came out of nowhere. I did not have it sitting in church. And I've been to church a lot. I did not have it sitting in a temple. I've been there. I've sampled every imaginable religion with respect and curiosity, and sometimes I've been very, very moved. But I never had the gut "hit" that I longed for. There's a huge difference between the brain wanting to believe and the heart and gut knowing and *feeling* that something is true. To be honest, for at least twenty years or more I have been trying to consciously find faith and live in it. Do you dare turn over this situation, whatever it might be, to a Higher Power? I absolutely wanted to, but I could feel myself holding back.

At the end of 2009, for many reasons, my private life was very, very difficult. Quite a few people who mattered to me tremendously were suffering, and I wanted to help. I knew I was powerless to do anything, really, but I couldn't let go of my desire to. I have always been a high-energy, tightly wrapped, very controlling person. This has been the uncomfortable truth of my behavior. I try to fix everything. I want so badly to make everything right for everyone and everything—which is actually incredible arrogance on my part. I think a lot of us are caretakers. Some of it comes from having a good heart; some of it comes from needing to control things. But there comes a point where you have to turn it over to something much bigger than yourself. The question is whether you're able to.

There was one particular person in my life who was going through something really quite frightening, and I clearly couldn't make it okay. This person means so much to me that I was going through tremendous sorrow—heaviness, tears, frustrations, and anger. I was wound even more tightly than usual.

Since I believe that the cleanest, healthiest body is the best way we can choose to live, I go to a cutting-edge medical facility periodically for detox, and I went there during this time. One of the tools at this facility involves working with sound and light, and I went into the session having no idea what to expect. I don't know what in the world they were doing exactly with this incomprehensible mixture of light and sound, but I was *stunned* by what happened to me.

During that session, I had the most dramatic, crystal-clear, light-drenched experience. It was like a shatteringly brilliant hit in my third eye and heart that made me feel that I finally could, and absolutely *had* to, connect with a Higher Power. Instantly I felt as if elephants had stepped off my chest. There was suddenly a lightness and a lack of that pressure you sometimes feel behind your eyes even when your mouth is smiling.

Nobody who had been to this facility told me this might happen. And maybe it doesn't happen to anybody else. It doesn't matter. But in an absolute moment, I saw something clearly: we have our own paths, and sometimes the things we stumble upon that seem horrendous are part of a larger plan for us. I had a moment of absolute clarity in which I saw that reality is a much bigger picture than my tiny vision can grasp. In the larger reality, sometimes the most extravagant pain is the gateway to something incandescent. I've always thought this intellectually, but that moment allowed me to get it. It was actually the biggest, most completely specific "oh, I get it" moment that I can ever remember. It was as if I heard: "Okay. Are you listening? This is it. This is what you have to do—*you have to live your life in faith.*"

In that moment, I became clear about faith—about the absolute truth of the power of the Light, about the power of Love without judgment. Entrusting the people and things we care about to that Light is the best we can do. We've all read about this concept ad nauseam, but it's another thing to feel it. In a *very* unintellectual way, I had a *very* deep experience of. . . I use the word *God*, but without any connotations that come with an organized religion. It was absolutely in my solar plexus, and in my heart.

My experience is very personal. I've only told my son and a few friends about this. Mine may not be as specific in some ways as other people's epiphanies, but it was enormous for me, and it has altered me. Certainly I am very clear that I know nothing—meaning that my life will always be a work in progress—but I am beginning to learn to live a different way. I know I am changing. I learned something that I know my friends will notice. I am becoming more peaceful, less controlling, and less narrow. I'm ever so slowly stopping my compulsion to fix, fix, fix—and with that has come tremendous relief. I feel as if I'd been wearing an enormous bandage, and suddenly it unwrapped. I am freer, much freer. It's wonderful to look at things in a more peaceful, more permissive way. I am learning the power of true compassion and the importance of stepping back with love. I know now that my idea of what's good for people is not necessarily the whole story. You can wish people well, offer them kindness and supporting prayers. But then you have to permit them to follow their own paths, helping where you can, but knowing that you probably cannot change them. I've realized that is the greatest gift that we have to offer.

Every one of us gets to find our way, hopefully surrounded by love, but we still have to pick out our own way through the land mines of life. By accepting this and relinquishing control, there's just extraordinary beauty.

This change in me has deeply changed my relationship with the person I was so worried about. The tiniest behavior of ours affects those around us. There are little things we can do, *coming from a peaceful place*, that are hugely helpful. So any tool that I can find to attain real, deep peace in myself I know is a gift to the people in my life. I used to be dramatic, self-involved, always Busy with a big capital *B*, filling the air with noise. Now I think that the big gift is serenity—to somehow be more peaceful than not. When I'm peaceful, I've got the strength to actually process distressing information and see if I can be helpful. But I can't do anything useful when I'm coming from chaos—I just sign on to the drama.

Epiphanies, at least in my case, are one of the most *astonishing* gifts. They are life-changing, insofar as they transform our private worlds and our values. They aren't casual things that just slide across our consciousness. They stop us cold in our tracks and we have to examine them. What's inherent in understanding these moments is the concept of hope—hope, solution, direction, and then, on a deeper level, some peace of mind.

*Striving to be the best possible version of yourself and
helping the people around you do the same enriches
your life and comes right back to you.*
—ROGER BIRNBAUM

ROGER BIRNBAUM is the co-founder, co-chairman, and
chief executive officer of Spyglass Entertainment, whose ros-
ter of films has won twenty-eight Oscar nominations and three
Academy Awards, and was co-chairman and CEO of MGM Studios from 2010 to 2012. He has produced more than one hundred films, ranging from *The Sixth Sense*, *Seabiscuit*, *Memoirs
of a Geisha*, *The Insider*, and *Invictus* to *Bruce Almighty*, *Eight
Below*, *Shanghai Knights*, *Twenty-Seven Dresses*, and *Star Trek*.
Birnbaum serves as a trustee on the board and as the co-artis-
tic director of the American Film Institute. He is also the father
of a beautiful daughter and resides in Los Angeles, California.
(www.spyglassentertainment.com)

THE INTERVIEW

Roger and I became instant friends at a buffet-style dinner party
in Los Angeles when I expressed to him my utter dismay at the
disappearance of all the chocolate-dipped macaroons I'd been
eyeing all evening. He had arrived at the dessert table in anticipa-
tion of the coveted macaroons as well. Bonded by our disappoint-
ment, we started talking. This book came up, and he said he had
an epiphany story, so I wanted to hear it. For days I couldn't quit
thinking about his anecdote and this phrase he used, "the best
version of yourself." It really made me step back and consider: did
I even know what the best version of myself *was*? His interview
was conducted in person at his exquisite home in Beverly Hills,

California, and his story was just as captivating as it was the first night I heard it standing over a big, barren platter of chocolate macaroons.

*　　*　　*

My most powerful epiphany occurred when I was thirty or so. A dear friend of mine—let's call him George—had been living in downtown Los Angeles. Someone broke in to rob his loft, and George was murdered. It was a real trauma for me and all his friends. We were still young enough to think that we were immortal—that nothing would ever happen to us. We were all coming into our own. Things were starting to happen for us in our careers and lives...then one of them ended in this senseless, brutal way.

I remember sitting in the memorial service packed with family and friends who took turns standing up to speak about George. Like everybody else, I felt raw. At a time like that, it's so intense—so many emotions come over you—that you're *vibrating*. I was listening to and feeling every word that was spoken. One friend of George's came up and said, "You know, whenever I was with George, he always made me feel like I was being the best possible person I could be. There was no judgment. There was no jealousy. He was a friend who, when he was in my presence, inspired and encouraged me to become the best I could be—either on my own or with his help."

My first thought was simply, "Wow. What an amazing thing." But then I started to question myself: "Am I like that? Or am I one of those people that has to make sure that somebody else is doing much worse in order for me to feel better?" In my heart I knew I wasn't quite that kind of person, but that I also wasn't like George. And at that moment—I remember it as clearly as if it had happened yesterday—I said to myself, "I don't know what kind of person I am, but from this moment on, I'm going to be George's kind of person. I'll strive to be the best possible version of myself, and I will also try to help the person or people around me to do the same."

I think that moment at his memorial was one of the most powerful in my life. The example George set has affected me, and a lot of other people who have entered my life since then: friends, family, and colleagues. Helping each person be the best possible version of who they can be—that will only enrich your life. It comes right back to you. If you're supporting all the people in your life, and if they indeed become their best possible selves, then you're around the best. I've made this one of the guiding tenets of my life.

Many times, tremendous value lies in what we
push aside as worthless.
—FLORENCE HORNE

FLORENCE HORNE was a retired teacher and a researcher on a project with the State Department of Education of New Jersey studying the effects of music and art on learning and development. She was the mother of three sons and was still vibrantly pursuing her many interests, including participating in the Age Looks At Aging photography project, when she passed away in 2011 at the age of ninety-two. (www.AgeLooksAtAging.com)

THE INTERVIEW
I met Florence through my photographer friend Brian Braff, who created a project called Age Looks at Aging. Brian gave still cameras to many of the residents of the Gardens of Santa Monica and Ocean House, two assisted-living communities in Santa Monica, California, and asked them to record with their cameras their experiences of aging. Florence was ninety-one but looked much younger, and was just as "with it" and stimulating as Brian told me. She had only been living in the assisted-living community for a few months when we conducted the interview in her room on the day of the photography exhibit opening. Not only is her photography marvelous and insightful, but the many stories and wisdom she shared with me were beautiful.

View the Interview:
www.epiphanychannel.com/people/florence-horne

*   *   *

I was a very young girl, about ten. As part of a school dramatic performance, I was to play the role of a tiny, dwarfed hunchback in the employ of a king. And this *really* upset me. I wanted to be the princess. Why wasn't I the princess? Why was I picked to do this dwarf hunchback role? It made me feel that I was deformed, deficient, and worthless. But as the play unfolded, the king had many enemies—and when they stormed the king's palace it was I, the little hunchback, who protected the king. I took an arrow that killed me, but I saved the king. When the play was over, I saw that my character, the hunchback, had displayed more nobility of character than the princess had. And that made a deep impression on me.

We're shaped by a lot of things, but this experience was really fundamental to me. It gave me a point of view for evaluating life. It was a way of making a statement. I realized that I could look below the surfaces and not be hung up on appearances—that it was important to always look deeper. Seeing that the hunchback's inner beauty far outshone the princess's appearance taught me that unexpected people or situations or occurrences can quietly take on a role with real impact and power. I understood that what we're inclined to push aside as meaningless or trivial may be the very clue to a deeper, more thoughtful understanding. Many times, tremendous value lies in what we push aside as worthless. It prepared me with the analytical skills that would become a way of life for me.

I had this revelation as a growing ten-year-old, and I still think about it. I still reflect on what it means to be the little one with potential for something greater, with the ability to observe and examine the deeper meaning in each encounter. The experience taught me to search for what is rewarding in any situation. I learned to look for what's in the "role," the various roles we play in life, how it communicates and encourages the same in others. When life's conditions offer a "role" I had not counted on, I try to bring to it my highest level of competence and mindfulness. Many times it becomes an unanticipated source of creativeness and personal growth. What can I find? What can I induce from another person when I have an exchange? I'm enriched when I can elicit something we may share in common or the revelation of something new. I look for the true essence of someone else. Playing this little dwarf, I'd unlocked his essential greatness. And if we can do that, if we can find the truth in every situation and unlock a little of our own as well as someone else's greatness in every exchange, it's very enriching—usually for all parties involved.

Epiphanies come in all sizes, and they make themselves known to you when you are ready to access the underlying meaning of the encounter, the exchange, the event. It's thrilling when you recognize them. The process continues for me to be challenging and spontaneous, requiring adaptation to the moment, and always contains the potential for learning.

No one, no relationship, no role, no thing, nothing
outside of you defines you.
You have to define yourself, and then everyone around
you reaps the benefits of that.

—JULIE HORTON

JULIE HORTON serves as the executive vice president of Real-songs, the music publishing company of renowned songwriter Diane Warren, and oversees the Diane Warren Foundation. She spent fifteen years at the American Society of Composers, Authors, and Publishers (ASCAP) as the west regional head of membership, where she mentored many songwriters who went on to have hits in every market. She is the mother of a daughter and a son and resides with her husband in Los Angeles, California. (www.realsongs.com)

THE INTERVIEW

I originally called Julie to request an interview with Diane Warren at the inception of this project. Julie was very encouraging, which is so important at that stage of creating something. Julie originally said she didn't think she'd ever had an epiphany, but later that day I got a surprise email summarizing this story. This happens quite a bit—once you talk about the subject of epiphanies and get to thinking about it, you discover moments you might have forgotten or buried. What she said and the way she said it were very powerful for me, so I requested her official interview too!

＊　　＊　　＊

In 1994, right after the big earthquake in Los Angeles, my husband and the father of my two young children got sick with leukemia. After a year and a half, we thought he had gone into remission, but it came back and we lost him. I found myself a single parent with two children, seven and a half and ten years old.

I fell apart. I couldn't get out of bed. For half of my life, my husband had been my world. We'd been married sixteen years. My whole identity was wrapped up in who I was to him and who he was to me and to our family. Without him, I felt like I couldn't do it. I wasn't okay in any way. He was my everything, my kids' too, and we'd all been doing so well. And then he was gone.

I cried for days until finally I wore myself out. My eyes were practically swollen shut. Literally at that very moment, when I stopped crying, I remember lying in my bed thinking, "If I could just die, if I could just go crawl in a hole…there's no life for me anymore." And then, in the other room, I heard my kids. My mind suddenly went clear. I don't know how, but I realized I could do this by myself, and thought, "I can lie here, wallow and be miserable, not care about anybody but myself, and leave my kids to take care of themselves. Or I can get up and *do* this." And I did. It was hard. It was very, very hard. But I did it.

I immediately got up and started cleaning the house. I got up and moved forward, and that was it. I didn't ever really look back. Everything from that point was forward. It was very strange. I literally took a garbage bag, went through my husband's bathroom, and threw everything away. I cleaned everything up. It was almost maniacal. That first step started the momentum that kept me moving forward.

I've read stories about so many women who just give up. You know, they don't have anything they can do. They're not educated for a profession, or they've lived with a man their whole life. They have their children, and that's all they focus on—then when their husband dies, they're lost. They had no backup plan. But I had one. I'd always worked, even though I hadn't respected it very much before this. It actually was empowering to me when I became the sole provider and my family's survival depended on me. Everything shifted for me. I realized that I could do it by myself—that I was strong, I had a job that I could grow in, and I could support my family. I could actually make it alone. I also became two parents overnight.

The big realization for me was this: that I was as strong alone as I had been as part of a couple. As much as I loved my husband, I didn't need him to make me whole and my life okay. I'd thought I was only complete as half of two, but realized I was still complete as one.

I had let my relationship with my husband define me. No relationship and no other person, not even my children, define me now. I didn't have a romantic relationship for eight years after my husband died. I am now married again, and this partnership is completely balanced. I'm totally secure in myself because I know I can be alone. I don't need my husband to do what I do. If he left tomorrow, I would be fine, which makes the relationship very strong.

My attitude and actions became more self-centered after my epiphany, and I don't mean that in a bad way; my kids were still a priority, but first I had to care for me. I structured our lives around maintaining my own strength first. If it had been all about them, I would again be using someone else to define myself. And I never wanted that again. My kids caught the rewards of my decision, and they have turned out great. I'm very proud of them and they tell me all the time that they admire me, which for me is the greatest compliment there is.

I learned to be a whole person. No one, no relationship, no role, no thing, nothing outside of you defines you. You have to define yourself, and then everyone around you reaps the benefits of that.

Value your heritage and embrace your distinctiveness.
—ANDREW KO

ANDREW KO is the Vice President for World Wide Education at Samsung Corporation, responsible for promoting and creating innovative programs to improve education through the use of technology. During his career he has also advised commercial banks, corporate restructuring committees, the South Korean government, and international lending agencies including the World Bank, the Asian Development Bank, and the International Monetary Fund. He also assisted with the establishment of the Korean Deposit Insurance Corporation. In 2009 Ko was appointed by Governor Tim Kaine of Virginia to that state's Asian Advisory Board. Through the nonprofit Armed Forces Communications and Electronics Association, Ko has co-chaired the Veteran Retraining Initiative, assisting wounded soldiers returning from Iraq and Afghanistan to get IT jobs after their service. He now resides in South Korea with his wife, Mi Joung, his daughter, Kaylen, and two sons, Anderson and Ayden.

THE INTERVIEW

One rainy January afternoon in Los Angeles, a friend called and invited me to attend a taping of *The Jimmy Kimmel Show* with some friends of hers who were in town on business for Microsoft. Something told me I should go (besides the fact that Barry Manilow and Ozzy Osbourne were guests), and I'm glad I listened to that "something", since that taping is where I met Andrew. We sat by each other at dinner afterward, and once we'd been talking for a while, I knew I wanted his story. I interviewed him by phone a couple of weeks later.

*   *   *

In the early seventies my parents immigrated to America from South Korea. My father was an engineer, my mother a teacher. They came to the U.S. with $100 in their pocket and had to completely start over. My father needed to have an engineering degree from here, so he washed dishes in the evenings, then went to school in the mornings. My mother worked as an assistant in a nursing home, basically cleaning up after elderly people, and then she went to work on an assembly line. It's a very typical immigrant story. They started out in El Paso, Texas, where I was born, but later moved to the suburbs of Maryland, where I was the only Korean in my school. Although my grandmother immigrated to the U.S. to help care for me, I was definitely a latchkey kid.

Growing up, I would come home and take my shoes off before I came in the house, where we spoke only Korean and ate only Korean food, and this was very normal to me. Then when I'd go to school, everything I did was very American. I spoke and read English, and ate things like grilled cheese sandwiches—grilled cheese is definitely *not* a Korean staple. And this was normal to me too, so it was objectively strange, but this double life felt natural.

One of my earliest memories is this: I was five or so and some of my neighborhood friends came over to play. They acted kind of funny when they had to take their shoes off when they came into my house. To do that is a very common, everyday tradition in many Asian countries, but none of my friends knew about it. At that moment I felt like my family was strange. We were different. That was when I realized I wasn't necessarily "American."

Growing up, this feeling stuck with me—and it wasn't negative. I just never really felt *completely* American. There were little things like those standardized tests you take in school, which ask you to mark yourself as white, black, Asian, Pacific Islander. I never knew what that meant. Pacific Islander? I thought, "Where's the one that just says I'm American?" There wasn't that box to check.

Fast-forward to 1997, when I was twenty-six. This was during that awful Asian financial meltdown, when whole countries faced

collapse, and I worked in management consulting. I really felt that
I should go to Korea and help during this crisis. I changed my job
for one that would send me over there to consult with Korean
banks. I was on my way to "help my people." Or so I thought.

Literally, during the final airport approach of that fifteen-
hour flight, I was struck by an overpowering realization: "Oh my
God. I'm not really Korean."

I had only been there once, in high school during the Olympics in 1988—a vacation, really. I couldn't speak the language well
and didn't know how to read or write in Korean. I might "look
like them," but I didn't know their everyday culture. And here I
was, going to go advise these massive banks and their government
on how to restructure their bad loans and toxic assets . . . what was
I thinking? Sure enough, after I landed, it was very much a foreign
country to me. I suffered anxiety for many months, self-conscious
about the fact that I seemed Korean but really wasn't.

What was I, in fact?

I lived and worked in Korea on this project for two and a
half years, and since then have also worked in many other countries. What I have realized, and I guess you could say the biggest epiphany about my life, is this: *I am not American. I am not
Korean. I am both.* I have fully internalized the fact of my blended
background and am very proud of it now. I have the best of both
worlds: I am very much an American because of the way I grew
up, my education, friends, and so on. And I have deep roots back
in Korea: my wife is Korean, and that culture, its cuisine . . . it's all
a big part of my life. I understand now that being an American
is about *who I am on the inside* and transcends, yet includes, my
family's background and culture, what I look like, and the language I speak.

When I got back from living in Korea and had this realization, I
started getting involved with politics. Asian American communities
are, generally speaking, very hardworking and introverted. They
don't speak out a lot. But I think that's the beauty of this country—
we have that right. We can call the authorities out. If we're unhappy

with the current administration or something else, we have the ability to do something about it. That wasn't true in South Korea until
quite recently. I've lived and worked in numerous countries that
do not have very open systems, politically or economically, much
less decent living conditions. Some lack clean running water and
suffer staggering pollution. The corruption I've seen in some places
makes American scandals seem almost naive. Of course, the U.S. is
far from perfect—but honestly, for every imperfection we complain
about here, I could probably give you ten examples of how much
worse it is in other countries. And the wonderful thing here is that
what we don't like, we can actually *do* something about. In other
places it's a lot harder and sometimes pretty dangerous. I think a
lot of people don't appreciate how great we have it here and how
amazing America is.

This realization makes me want to do my part to make our
country even better. I want to give back—not just for myself or my
kids but also for other people who have similar backgrounds to
mine. So I've gotten involved in politics. I have focused my ener-
gies primarily on the Asian communities and have helped start a
couple of organizations locally.

I look back in hindsight at my parents. They were both well
educated, with jobs in Korea, and when they came over here they
were broke. They lived in the basement of a poor Texas widow's
house. I've joked that they probably wouldn't do it all over again,
but I think they absolutely would. Still, it took a lot of courage for
them. They knew that in the U.S. if you work hard, you have a
good shot at being successful. My parent raised me as an American but also as a Korean, with the best of both cultures.

Value your heritage and embrace your distinctiveness. I have.
I realize now that I don't have to belong to one clique or one
group. I can belong to many. I know now that that's what being
American is.

*Don't worry about making it all perfect, because
it's never going to be perfect.
Not-so-perfect is still special. It's even beautiful.*

—RACHEL BLAYLOCK

RACHEL BLAYLOCK is a homemaker, wife, and mother of three. She studied as an actress, began taking minor roles in Dallas, Texas, then moved to Manhattan to "make it." She then entered a two-year acting program and became pregnant with her first child before completing it, and has spent the past six years raising three children with little attention to acting. She has now moved back to Texas with her husband and children to be closer to family, and considers it highly probable that she will be "discovered" on a Texas street corner by Steven Spielberg or the like, because that is the irony of life.

THE INTERVIEW

Rachel is married to one of my best childhood friends. When I was in New York pitching this project, I visited the Blaylocks and showed them the promotional video for the website to get their feedback. We started talking and Rachel said, "You know, I think I had an epiphany." And she gave the following account. It's another prime example of what I've experienced *a lot* when I mention this phenomenon: people start to remember, or even to recognize for the first time, their own epiphanies. I went back and filmed her story (complete with her daughter, Nell, and the fateful Father's Day card she talks about) in their New York City apartment right before they relocated back to Dallas, our hometown.

View the Interview:
www.epiphanychannel.com/people/rachel-blaylock

*   *   *

The greatest realization that I ever had seems really basic, and to some it might not seem significant, but it made a huge difference in my life. My husband and I have been married for ten years and we now have three kids, ages six, three, and three months. I am a stay-at-home mom, so basically my life for the past six years has been restricted to diapers and baby gear, spit-up, poop—all the stuff that comes with kids. I moved to New York City in the first place to become famous, and instead I got knocked up three times. It's been great, it's been wonderful, but I cannot count how many times silly things have made me want to take my husband and throttle him.

We have all these kids, and there's always so much to be done. In the midst of caring for them, I'd look over, and my husband would be sitting on the couch reading the paper. Reading the paper! He could just sit down in the middle of this commotion, ignore us all, and read. It drove me nuts. And he's a huge golfer. Loves golf. I hate it. Golf takes up a lot of time and isn't cheap. I would think, "I don't get to do things like that. How come he gets to do that?" Sometimes he'd be late coming home from work, and I'd get a call: "Oh, honey, some guys and I stayed a little late for drinks and I'm not going to be home until such-and-such, so I won't be home to help." I never got to call home and say, "Oh, my plans have changed, so you get to take care of the kids right now." It's always me at home, with the kids, and while it's extremely rewarding and great fun at times, it's also really, really hard. I just didn't feel like my husband really understood or appreciated what I was doing day in and day out. The way I saw it, even though he was trying to understand and trying to pull his weight, the buck always stopped with me, and he could get away with more. He could turn it on and off when he wanted to, but I was always stuck. What's more, he could rest easier, because he knew the kids were taken care of by someone who was trying to get it perfect, so if he slacked a little it wouldn't make that much difference.

These feelings had been building up over the years. Last Father's Day, I needed to buy him a Father's Day card. I walked in the store, and I'm trying to find one that's funny. And I'm staring at and reading all the cards in the Father's Day section—and all of a sudden the cards kind of start popping out at me. One after the other after the other—the dad sitting on the chair, reading the paper; the dad playing golf; the dad asleep on the couch; and on and on.

Then it dawned on me: "Oh my God. It's not just my husband. *It's not just my husband.* It is a lot of husbands, probably even some of my friends who said their husbands are different!" It seemed I'd hit a universal truth—that dads sit on the couch and read the paper; that dads play golf; that dads drink beer while they mow the lawn, et cetera. Obviously, not *all* dads are like that, but there *are* enough out there to warrant cards about it! They are stereotypes, but stereotypes that are true. There they were, all in front of me, all these guys who could be my husband. All these men, just being *themselves*. Then I realized: This is part of marriage. This is part of raising kids. I literally said to myself, "He's the dad, Rachel, and you're the mom, and there's a difference. Being a dad is a completely different thing."

I saw that I'd been expecting John to be a second mom, to take over all the things I do to give me a break. But he's not a second mom. As a man, he has to be able to do things in his own way. I can't expect him to have the same instincts as me. I realized that I was resentful of him for being himself. I also had to admit that I hadn't just wanted him to help. I'd wanted him to do things *my way*, and also wanted him to completely understand and appreciate everything I had to do all the time, which he couldn't, just like I can't entirely appreciate everything that goes on for him in his office at work. I realized I was more jealous of his perceived freedom than anything else. All this, from a bunch of greeting cards!

This realization dissipated a lot of anger in my marriage. Since then, I overlook a lot of things that used to enrage me, and I've cut my husband some slack. Our marriage has improved. I accept my husband for who he is and his role in our family. He really is a wonderful father and a great provider. He adores and spends time with our children and is involved in their lives and does help with dressing, feeding, babysitting, and those kinds of things when he can. He just does things differently than I do and doesn't always have the time or energy to do things the way I want him to sometimes, and I accept that now. I'm also more reconciled to my own role as a wife and a mother. I had this ideal in my head that things should be shared 50/50 in every area of our lives, but I realize now that 50/50 in running a household is different for everyone, and in our home we have varying roles and responsibilities, and that's okay.

I now consider raising young kids as my career. That makes this my absolute "crunch time"—the most professionally intense. Many days do not seem short. But sooner than I think, they will all be over. If I were a CNN war reporter in Afghanistan, going sleepless to follow Christiane Amanpour, that would also be an intense time in my career. It's really not that different—this career just happens to be wife and mother.

Those silly greeting cards helped me realize that I love my life, even though sometimes it seems like a lot of hard and thankless work. I love being a mom and the bottom line is...I love my husband. I just needed to just chill out and quit worrying so much about making it all perfect, because it's never going to be perfect. I've found not-so-perfect is still special. It's even beautiful.

To be blessed, be generous.

—ALEXIS MINKO

ALEXIS MINKO was born in Libreville, Gabon, and was raised primarily there and in Paris, France. He began his career as an attorney working for the United Nations in New York in 2007 and worked with the Security Council of the United Nations on peacekeeping operations for the delegation of Gabon to the UN. He is a proud resident of New York City.

THE INTERVIEW

Alex is nothing short of dashing—tall, thin, and sophisticated, with impeccable manners and a charming accent—the kind of person who walks into a room and everyone notices. Alex was a new friend, but when I told him about this project, he said he wanted to do what he could to help. He exudes generosity in everything he does, and in the most joyous way. We ended up meeting for lunch in New York City, and during the course of our conversation I asked him if he thought he had an epiphany he'd be willing to share. He said he'd share a story with me, but he wasn't sure if it was an epiphany. After the hour had passed, we had both laughed and cried, and I could not believe I had just unexpectedly received such an intimate and powerful account from someone who wasn't even certain he had an epiphany story!

•   •   •

My best friend of ten years, Maeli, was graceful, smart, artistic, and wonderful in every way—the kind of person who is everything you would want to be and everything you could ever want in a friend. A few years ago, we were having lunch in Paris, where we lived and grew up, and we were laughing and having a great time until he said the strangest thing to me—he said, "I am going to die very soon. I am just fed up with this life." I thought he was being overdramatic and was completely kidding, so I just laughed and said, "Come on, Maeli, you can't say things like that," and eventually we moved on to other things, finished our lunch, and went on with our day. Later that week his partner left him, and Maeli called me *very* upset, so as all best friends do, I met up with him to talk about it, console, and distract him.

We hung out that entire day into the night. I tried to make him smile. Though of course he was hurting deeply because of his breakup, by the end of our night he agreed with me that he felt his life was actually going to be better.

One of Maeli's and my greatest dreams since childhood had always been to one day live in New York City together. The day after we had gone out to ease the pain of his breakup, I happened to get a phone call from New York with the incredible news that I had gotten a job I'd applied for there! I left Maeli a message telling him the news and that we were finally going to New York. At this time I was twenty-three and in a miserable relationship that was in its final stages, so I was in a state of complete turmoil. I was so absorbed with my relationship's demise that I didn't pay much attention to the fact that ten days had passed and Maeli still hadn't returned my call.

I will never forget this—it was a Saturday and for some reason I was at work—and Maeli's brother called me. Before he even said anything, I knew. Maeli was dead. He had committed suicide. After I hung up the phone with his brother, I think I went into shock. I went to a bar and got drunk and stayed that way for the next three days. The morning of Maeli's funeral, my boyfriend told me it was over between us and he was leaving me. I felt I just couldn't take it—my boyfriend was leaving me, I wasn't close to my family, and I was burying my best friend. I felt my life was over, and my three-day binge to numb the pain wasn't helping my mind-set. That day when I thought Maeli was kidding around about dying, he had told me he would take twenty-five sleeping pills with alcohol if he was to kill himself. That's exactly what he did.

And that's exactly what I did.

It was funny, but I had no fear. The thought of taking my own life had never even crossed my mind before, but I was in such pain that I had no fear of doing it. It felt like it was the most natural thing. I was feeling such relief at the thought of doing it, and relief was a feeling I hadn't felt for such a long, long, long time. So I did it. After I took the pills, I wrote some letters to my brother and sisters, and then I just fell asleep. A week later I woke up in the hospital.

This is when my epiphany began. When I opened my eyes, for the first five seconds the last memory of when I took the pills came flooding back to me, and my first thought was, "Am I dead?" Then I realized where I was and that obviously I hadn't died (my boyfriend had found me in time), and then I had the thought, "Damn, I'm still here." Then the realization hit me—*I had a second chance.* All of a sudden I wanted desperately to leave the hospital and take my life back. I actually unhooked myself from all of the monitors and things and walked outside to hail a cab still in my hospital gown with my backside exposed for all the world to see! Thankfully, nurses ran out and made me come back in before I could get in a taxi, and I was discharged the next day.

After I got out of the hospital, I did something I had never done before—I went to see a psychiatrist. I can't encourage people enough to do this, especially when they are going through a hard time as I was. One day during therapy, I had another defining moment—I realized that I had been an extremely self-absorbed, very selfish person. Up to this point everything had to go my way, and if it didn't, it was wrong. Nothing was ever my fault but was always someone else's. I always thought that people should love me because I was beautiful and smart and the life of the party. To the outside world, I seemed open and bright, but on the inside

I was very dark—there was no generosity in me. I had very high expectations of everyone around me and of myself, and I felt the world owed me.

But life doesn't work like that. I realized I had to just let go. Nothing is perfect in this world. I had to realize people won't love you less because you're not perfect. Maeli had died. He was my closest friend—closer to me than my family or anyone on the planet—and I couldn't even see how much pain he was in and that he was serious when he told me he wanted to die. Perhaps I could have helped him had I not been so absorbed in my own problems and issues.

During this time I was also grieving Maeli's death. In my grieving process, I cried and cried and cried. After many weeks of this, I don't know how to explain it really, but it was as if I felt Maeli's hand push me as if to say, "It's time. Move forward. Life goes on."

From all of this, I realized I was not alone in this world, and I needed to be at peace with what was around me. I had to open myself up to the world. None of us is perfect, but the point is to try—to always try to be a better person. My life has *completely* opened up and changed. Everything that seemed dark and confusing is now easy and clear, and I am living all my dreams. I'm now in a beautiful relationship, living in New York with fantastic friends and a job that I absolutely love.

It's all really very simple—reach out to people. Reach out. Be generous. Be open and appreciate everything in the world around you. Look, every day is not heaven, it's not always easy—sometimes it's even a fight—but it's nice to go to bed at night and be able to close your eyes and smile because you know you've tried and maybe even helped someone a little. I believe you get back what you give. To be blessed, be generous. And when I say be generous, I mean be generous with your heart. Every opportunity you can give of your heart, do it, and you won't believe the abundance that comes into your life. You'll find that even when things are down, somehow you will be lifted, and like the phoenix, you'll fly again, stronger.

I've achieved more in the past few years than I did in all the years before, and I attribute this to my realizations. When I opened my eyes in that hospital, I began to open my heart.

*Wisdom is the application of knowledge...transforming
the knowing into the doing.*
—GREGORY WILSON

GREGORY WILSON is a professional magician and mentalist
who specializes in pickpocketing, cardsharking, shortchanging,
and psychological deceptions. He has performed his "criminal
act" in forty-three countries and is a consultant for the FBI, CIA,
ATF, Secret Service, and Homeland Security. He's also a two-time
international award winner in the Magic Olympics (held every three
years in Europe) and has released twelve bestselling instructional
videos describing his original deceptions. Wilson also teaches a
course in persuasion for corporations, called "How to Persuade
People Like Magic," and gives "Deception Detection" lectures in
churches. He also exposes the underhanded techniques of politi-
cians in a presentation called "Politricks." He currently resides in
Newport Beach, California. (www.GregoryWilson.tv)

THE INTERVIEW

I met Greg during a visit to the Magic Castle in Hollywood with a
magician friend who was a member. When the conversation rolled
around to my upcoming book, Greg said he'd had an extreme life-
changing epiphany but gets too emotional when he shares it, so we
should reconvene later. The gentleman definitely knows the art of
enticement: I had to find out his story. We didn't connect until
months later but hearing about his crazy, amazing journey was
worth the wait.

*   *   *

I grew up in San Diego with an upper-middle-class background and have had a criminal mind as far back as I can remember. I've got early childhood memories of crazy stunts, like using a red felt-tip pen to draw a small circle with a crude wave and dolphin on the back of my hand to mimic a reentry stamp to get into Sea World for free. I don't know if it was a genetic predisposition, a crazy neurological flaw, or a simple fascination with the forbidden.

When I was seventeen I became a magician, and that seemed to satisfy my need for deception for ten years. But at twenty-seven I became a full-time, full-fledged career criminal. I had the perfect cover: everyone around me thought I was a professional magician. It explained the odd hours, so I could come and go without suspicion. And, frankly, I *was* a magician at the top of my craft— but in a fraudulent way. There's a very short hop from conjuring to con artistry. We learn how to deceive people physically and psychologically, which made it *very* difficult to catch me in the act.

I pulled every con in the book: three-card monte on the streets, pool hustling, card cheating, identity theft, burglary, et cetera. Among cardsharks, I'm what's known as a mechanic, a professional cheat. I took tens of thousands of dollars from casinos and private games and never even came close to getting caught.

I also made hundreds of thousands of dollars shoplifting, using my magic skills to swipe stuff from stores—big things! I had special misdirection and presentational ploys that would even get the employees to help *carry* the stuff out of the store for me. I made over a half million dollars just doing that, obviously tax-free. Ironically, I specialized in taking home security systems. They cost $299.99—with tax, $318. So I would steal them, make my own receipts, and then take them all back. Hundreds of them. It was crazy. Plus, the thousands of credit card slips I "liberated" elsewhere was a whole other cash cow story. I was steeped in deceit 24/7.

All of these crimes were self-taught. They were based on reading, exploring, and inventing new ways to dupe and delude. I thought about this stuff all day, every day, and always committed my crimes alone. I'm forty-eight years old and when I grew up in the seventies there were a succession of cop shows on television like *Police Woman, Kojak, Baretta, Mannix, The Rockford Files*...I noticed one common denominator from every criminal who got caught: they had either snitched or bragged. So I thought when I was a kid—again, criminal mind—"If I ever do this, I'll never tell anybody!"

I later learned that if we suppress feelings or stifle secrets for too long, the result of this concealment or bottling up will be a manifestation of "disease" somewhere in our bodies. Since my unlawful activities were carefully suppressed, the guilt attacked the weakest link in my body—my immune system. I therefore contracted this rare form of arthritis that was ostensibly chronic and degenerative. In other words, it was only supposed to get worse. It was a debilitating disease known as ankylosing spondylitis—it took me a week to learn how to say that.

I couldn't walk for almost six months. I was a bodybuilder at the time, but had lost over fifty pounds in two months. The affliction was so rare that no general practitioner could determine what it was, until finally a rheumatologist diagnosed it—my seventh doctor. It was systemic. My knees were so inflamed that I could only wear shorts. My hands were so swollen they were essentially immobile. I couldn't move unless I took heavy-duty medication and hobbled on crutches. Without my pain pills, I'd scream in agony if I moved one inch. It was horrendous.

I was lying in bed one day in absolute anguish and a friend of mine called. He was a cool Clint Eastwood type who never calls. But he called and then started talking...about God. I said, "Dude, this is not the right time. I'm in miserable pain. The last thing I want to talk about is God." We changed the subject. Thirty minutes later, when he was about to hang up, he brought it up again: "I have a feeling more people are going to come into your life and tell you about God."

So I said, "Oh, great. Jesus junk and Christian crap. I don't want anything to do with it." At this time, I wouldn't even call myself an atheist—atheism is an actual belief system or its own religion. I was more of an "I-don't-care-ist" or an "apatheticist." I'd never really thought about God whatsoever. It just never crossed my mind. It was so weird, because after he said that, three different people, in as many days, came into my life and told me about God. I'm a jaded, skeptical cynic. It's very, very difficult to convince me of something without overwhelming rational or empirical evidence. But I found the coincidence interesting.

So after that happened, as I lay in bed, looking up at the ceiling, I found myself contemplating out loud: "I don't know how to pray; I don't know who You are. I don't know if You're a light source, an energy field, or a personal God, the way these wacko Christians are telling me. But there's only one way to prove it to me. I'm going to pump myself full of pain pills, get on my crutches, and go out and do what I've been doing. If I get caught, I'll *consider* You." So I did. The next day I tested the notion of this God.

And I got caught.

I was shoplifting. And the funny part is, at that one particular place, I didn't even steal anything. They found the stuff I had stashed in the car from other places. Everything that could have gone wrong that day did—to this day I don't even know how.

So I found myself in a jail cell for the first time, admitting that I'd been a career criminal for the past three and a half years. I called a friend who was a lawyer and he promised to bail me out, but it took a while. I was waiting, bored out of my mind, counting the ceiling tiles, chewing off all of my nails. After about five hours, I knocked on the door to the jailer and asked him for something to read. Of course in jail, the only thing they provide is...that's right, a Bible. I was so restless at this point that I fumed, "All right. Give me the G.D. Bible."

So here I was, with Bible in hand. And this sounds very strange and very Hollywood, but I had this warm, glowing feeling, and the urge to recap everything that had gone on. It was even strange to me as it was happening. I ran through it in my mind: "I'm a criminal. I'm suffering from a debilitating disease. I'm laid up in bed. My friend calls out of the blue and talks to me about God. Then three other people in three days talk to me about God. I make an ultimatum with this God. I get caught. I'm in jail. And now I have a Bible in my hand?!"

At this point, I thought, "You know what? How much worse can it be? How much lower can I get? All right. If I open up this Bible and it directly applies to my life—*directly*—I will follow you the rest of my life. You have me hook, line, and sinker. No more running around. You've got my full attention." So I slowly opened the Bible and found myself staring at Psalm 70. Paraphrased, it says, "Save me now, free me from my captors. Get me out of this mess." It could not have been more direct.

When I read that, it hit me so hard between the eyes and in the heart, I wept. I didn't cry. I wept. And I'm not a crier. But I wailed with gratitude, on my knees. It was as if two quarts of fluids just drained from my body. It felt like a white light just whooshed through my body and soul. It was instant; it was profound; it was visceral; and I knew it in my heart of hearts.

You know how they say that your life flashes before your eyes? Well, the images of my past criminal activities flashed before my eyes in a microsecond. I felt instantaneously cleansed, completely forgiven. This weight I hadn't even recognized was lifted. It was the most astonishing experience of my life. From that moment forward, I was radically transformed. In that one heartbeat, I became a Christian. I was raised in a Christian household, but it was meaningless to me. However, in that moment in that jail cell, I finally understood it—God became very real.

Two months later, I had a court date. But my name was not on the register. So I asked the clerk about my status and it turned out that somehow all of the evidence they had on me was gone. The DA was actually furious and confused when he told me, "Get the hell out of here. We don't know what happened. I don't know why I'm letting you go, but get out of my sight." In a previous encounter, he'd told me that he had me for a *minimum* of two years in prison.

I always say now, "God can take your life and free it. He can take your health and restore it."

Right after this happened, since the doctors were still clueless about my arthritis, I decided to explore my own remedy by reading every related book on the subject. The very last book extolled the virtues of cod liver oil. Basically, if you take it on an empty stomach, it bypasses the portal vein of the liver, goes straight into the lymphatic system, which is the sewage center of the body, and self-lubricates the joints. So I tried it. By taking small and regular doses of cod liver oil, in two weeks I was off my pain pills, and in two months I was completely cured. This combination of self-treatment and prayer I call my "God and cod" therapy.

I'm an all-or-nothing kind of guy. There's no dimmer switch in my life. The light switch is either on or off. I was extreme in stealing, conning, and deceiving people. But since my epiphany, I haven't so much as even tasted a grape in a supermarket. I'm the anti-thief now. I'm the cleanest, most upright person you could ever imagine.

For almost twenty years now I've been a full-time mystery entertainer. I also teach a course for corporations called "How to Persuade People Like Magic," and in churches I give lectures called "Deception Detection" to teach people how not to be deceived by first deceiving them—showing how easy it is to be deceived. I've studied and applied the deepest secrets of deception my entire adult life so I know it forward and backward and use it now to give something back.

More than anything, this epiphany has given me a sense of clarity and hope—the hope of future glory and the clarity to know how life works. We clutter life. We complicate it. But it's really quite simple. Wisdom is the application of knowledge . . . the secret of transforming the *knowing* into the *doing*. What Christianity offers me is this transcendent wisdom. I don't pray for money. I don't pray for fame. I pray for wisdom that I can apply to my life and share with others. And the world is now a much safer place—well, at least stores, vaults, card games, poolrooms, and casinos. I can't vouch for everyplace else.

There is a difference between just living and being alive.
We are meant to feel aliveness, to be alive, to restore life
on this earth, and to breathe life into others.

—ESTHER PEREL

ESTHER PEREL, one of the most respected voices on erotic intelligence, is the author of the international bestseller *Mating in Captivity*, now available in twenty-five languages. She is a world-renowned authority on couples therapy, cross-cultural relations, culture, and sexuality. Fluent in nine languages, Perel is a frequent keynote speaker around the world and has been interviewed in leading publications such as the *Washington Post*, the *New Yorker*, and *Vogue*. She was named one of *Elle* magazine's 2007 IntELLEligentia and is the recipient of the 2009 Consumer Book Award from the Society for Sex Therapy and Research. Perel serves on the faculty of the Family Studies Unit, Department of Psychiatry, New York University Medical Center, and the International Trauma Studies Program, and is a member of the American Family Therapy Academy and the Society for Sex Therapy and Research. She resides in downtown New York with her husband and two sons. (www.EstherPerel.com)

View the Interview:
www.epiphanychannel.com/people/esther-perel

THE INTERVIEW
I was referred to Esther by a mutual friend. I didn't know her work, but I trusted my friend, who said she would be a fantastic interview. Also, I loved the title *Mating in Captivity*, and the fact that she was a highly respected sex therapist. Her epiphany was sure to be interesting—and it was, although, as usual, not at all what I

had anticipated. I interviewed her in her loft in New York City, sitting on the very couch where many of the epiphanies we talked about took place.

*   *   *

I would say my greatest epiphany was more of an epiphanous odyssey or succession of epiphanies, if you will, that happened while I was writing my book *Mating in Captivity*, which came out in 2006. I wrote for two years, from 2003 to 2005, and in the process of writing I discovered that there has been one major determinant in my life. It explains to a large degree what I do and who I am and why, throughout my life, seemingly totally irrelevant things keep coming back to this aspect in ways that defy my imagination. In a way, this determinant had absolutely nothing to do with me. It was imposed on me: I am the child of Holocaust survivors.

My book is about eroticism, but at this point I had not really asked myself why I was interested in it. It was when I was talking one day with my husband, who is working in the field of trauma and political violence with torture victims and refugees. Sitting on this couch, I asked him, "How do you know that the people you work with are once again reconnecting with life? How do you know when they cross that line again?" He told me it's when they are once again able to be creative, to take risks, or to be playful—because you can't play if you don't feel safe. Once you begin to feel somewhat safe or grounded in the world, you are able to leap out and experience your exploratory needs, the way a child goes into the world to see what is out there. While we were discussing this, I started to put all the pieces together.

In my community in Belgium where I grew up, we had an enormous number of survivors living there. Among them, there were two kinds of people, those who didn't die and those who came back to life—those who were just living and those who were really alive. The people who were just living were very fearful, didn't take any risks at all, didn't trust that the world was a safe place, and generally could not experience much joy or guilt-free pleasure. Neither could their children. They were *surviving*, but they were not really *alive*. The other group were the ones who knew how to keep themselves alive—they were people who understood the erotic as an antidote to death. Eroticism, sex, when you experience it in its full intensity, is a means of defying death. You feel alive as you do at no other moment. Eroticism implies playfulness, risk, daring, imagination—*aliveness*. The poetry of sex, the vitality, vibrancy, playfulness, renewal, all that stuff—I had seen all these in this subset of Holocaust survivors who really came back to life. Luckily, my parents were part of that group. My parents understood aliveness. I was a symbol of that for them, and I know what being alive really means because of my parents.

Eroticism for me is about the mystical sense of the word *eros*, rather than what modernity has done, which is reduce it to sex. I know now why I'm not writing about sex but rather about that other experience that one can have *through* sex. What I'm capturing is the quest for otherness—you're at the same time completely inside yourself and completely outside yourself, or completely inside yourself and completely inside another. It's a moment where you transcend death, that moment when you basically connect with the Divine.

When I work with couples on sexuality, when I work with desire, it's about how one maintains a sense of aliveness—a connection to one's erotic self. It's really not about frequency, positions, technique, statistics of sex—it's all about that erotic connection. When people come to my office and they complain about listlessness of their sex lives, they sometimes want more sex, but what they really want is *better* sex. And the *better* thing they are looking for is eros, the deeper dimension of sex.

That conversation with my husband, connecting what he'd learned from contemporary victims of traumatic abuse with what I remembered about Holocaust survivors and my family...it made things click for me. In what I call an ongoing series of epiphanic moments, I came to see that I was tracing two parallel narratives: histories of great suffering and death, and histories of eroticism as an expression of aliveness and pushing back against death.

I have moments such as that one all the time in my work, where I make connections between particular aspects of my life and its overarching story of being the child of survivors. Growing up with Holocaust survivors connects you to a larger history. You are not just a daughter of two people or even just a daughter of a tribe. As a descendant, you are a symbol of survival and revival for people, each of whom may have lost two hundred relatives, like my parents. Your life from the first day on is about much more than just you. You carry the name of somebody who's no longer there. You have a mission. The mission is renewal. You are proof that death and dehumanization didn't prevail, that there is life after an atrocity, and that there must be joy in that life lived after the atrocity. It's not just about surviving, but it's about reviving. It's about a spark, of bringing an essence of vitality into the world.

You begin to connect yourself with that larger history, and it makes you feel special—but also very burdened, because you better do *big* things. Nothing in my life could just be okay or good enough. It had to be a lot better than good enough, because (as my parents remembered) if you were *just* good enough, you didn't survive. Only if you were really big, really daring, really cunning, really determined—and lucky—would you survive. Halfway didn't get you there. No problems that you might have could compare to the terrors Mom and Dad had known, so you never could really have a problem or ever really be worried or sad in our family. That has its downside, but it definitely made me somebody who charges at life, who pushes, who goes all out. I dread mediocrity or doing anything halfway; you could see that as either perfectionism or simply ambition. But once I understood what really drives that impulse in me, I saw that it didn't center on being exceptional, but on being *meaningful*. My actions could never be haphazard. My life needed to be meaningful. I make choices based on that. It's never been about work. It's never been about money. It's about meaning.

My moment of very crisp realization about this happened again during the process of writing the book when the fact sank in: "I have signed with a publisher to actually *write a book!*" I'd actually signed on to do something I had never thought I'd do, and I was willing to try even though I wasn't sure I could succeed. I realized that this was the first time I was doing something without feeling sure about the outcome. And you know what? It only could happen after my mother passed away. I no longer needed to feel, "It's got to work, it's a live-or-die situation, if you don't do it perfectly you'll die." And something about that live-or-die, all-or-nothing pressure softened after she passed away. I don't think she imposed any of this on me. But it was only in her absence that I could for the first time do something I wasn't sure about without fearing that I would die if I failed. Nobody knew I had always been holding back. Only I knew.

These epiphanies changed the way I operate. They crystallized what I'm actually working on with my patients. They have focused my thinking because I have a much deeper understanding of myself, of the concept of the erotic, and of how it is connected to much bigger, broader concepts. The way I conduct sex therapy or couples therapy is more a way of thinking than a method, and it's this way of thinking that has attracted more and more people from all over the world to study with me.

What I learned about myself clarified my mission both personally and professionally: it is to be a "connector." I help connect people with their aliveness. I was a symbol to my parents of aliveness—of the capacity to regenerate after the massive death and annihilation my family endured. I connected them with their aliveness, and they showed me what it meant to be truly alive. I am not just a person who is living. I am a person who is meant to restore life on this earth and to breathe life into others. We all are.

God loves us all, no matter what. There is no one in this
world who is a lost cause.

—DESMOND TUTU

DESMOND TUTU was the first black South African Anglican
Archbishop of Cape Town, South Africa, and is currently Archbishop Emeritus. He became known worldwide during the 1980s
as a key opponent of apartheid and was the chair of the Truth and
Reconciliation Commission, promoting restorative and reconcil-
iatory rather than retributive justice for human rights violations
perpetuated during the apartheid era and in the violence following its abolition. In 1984 Tutu became the second South African
awarded the Nobel Peace Prize. He has also been awarded the
Albert Schweitzer Prize for Humanitarianism, the Gandhi Peace
Prize in 2005, and the American Presidential Medal of Freedom
in 2009. Archbishop Tutu and his wife, Leah, are the parents of
four, and in 1998 they co-founded the Desmond Tutu Peace Cen-
tre "to encourage and inspire future generations to commit themselves for world peace." He has also authored several books of his
speeches and sayings, including *The Rainbow People of God: The
Making of a Peaceful Revolution*. He resides in Cape Town and
still tirelessly campaigns for human rights and peace through non-
violence worldwide. (www.Tutu.org)

THE INTERVIEW
It was a dream come true for me to interview a Nobel Peace Prize
winner, but that it was Desmond Tutu was even more special
because of an article I'd read about him that helped change my
life and led to another interview that is in this book. His accomplishments speak for themselves, but when I heard from Linda

Biehl at the Amy Biehl Foundation (see the "New Directions" section) just how kind and wise he is and how much he personally
helped them, I knew he was someone I wanted to include in the
project. Given the Archbishop's schedule, I was extremely lucky
and grateful to secure an interview. He just happened to have a
cancellation, otherwise I would have had to wait at least a year.
Staying up until 3:30 a.m. to speak with him was one of the easiest
things I've ever done; I couldn't wait to hear his greatest epiphany.
I was expecting a remarkable story about a particular moment in
his incredible life. But, as happened so many times in the course
of my interviews, my expectations were surpassed in surprising
ways. His epiphany underlies his center's vision: "A world committed to peace. A world in which everyone lives together as family, and everyone is loved, heard, cared for and unique. A world
in which everyone matters, and the essential good in everyone is
manifested."

*   *   *

I've had quite a few moments in my life that I would consider
an epiphany—an opening, or a revelation that enables you for a
moment to glimpse the glory of God, or the glory that *is* God. My
greatest is the realization that *God loves us all, no matter what.*

I was teaching at Emory University from 1998 to 2000. At the
end of my teaching stint, the students decided they were going
to give me a plaque, and they used a play on words. Instead of
"Nobel" they called it a "Noble" Prize, and on this plaque it read:
"A Noble Prize for preaching (even if it is the same sermon)."

It was funny, and they did this because in my teaching, I was
constantly reminding them that I believe the epiphany that you
really want to have in life is: *God loves you, first up, no matter what.* I would say my epiphany about this has been truly an
extended epiphany. My awareness of the free, gracious love of
God has been cumulative over many years as I've pondered and

deepened my understanding of the magnitude, significance, and truth of this.

I learned and heard about God's love for us, beginning as a child, of course, but several instances and parables in the Bible have struck me more deeply throughout the years to help me grow and reinforce and understand this Divine Love. In the Old Testament, I came to realize that God loves and chooses the Israelites as his Chosen People and takes them out of Egypt. But they had not done anything to deserve being chosen. When He gave them the Ten Commandments, He gives them *after* the Exodus from Egypt. You know? So it's not "Keep my laws *so* that I will love you," but it's "Keep my laws *because* I love you—my law is to enable you to express your gratitude."

And when you look at the New Testament, there are many things, especially Romans 5:8, where Paul says, "Whilst we were sinners, Christ died for us." That is quite something to think about.

Later, I began to understand the parables better, such as the one of the lost sheep where the Good Shepherd leaves ninety-nine perfectly well-behaved sheep to go and look for the lone troublesome one. Often we spoil this lesson in most of our churches because we show Jesus carrying a fluffy little lamb, and fluffy little lambs don't stray from their mommies. It's the obstreperous old ram that strayed, and that's the one that the Good Shepherd invests *all* of those resources in to try to win back.

Again, you see, God loves us no matter what—this kind of Divine Love is incredible. Having this knowledge and understanding of this love is something that just goes through any walls you might have or perceive. You truly know that God has *no enemies*. Even the worst of us in our communities is a beloved of God, and that has taught me to remember that there is *no one* in this world who is a lost cause. There is no one that I can or you can or *anyone* can declare firmly, "You are going to hell."

An epiphany is God seeking to draw us to God. St. Augustine said, "Thou hast made us for Thyself. And our hearts are restless until they find their rest in Thee." If we want true, extraordinary fulfillment, our fulfillment comes only from God, the Infinite. Divine Love is incredible. It's just mind-blowing.

NEW DIRECTIONS

new : different from one of the same category that has existed previously; not existing before; made, introduced, or discovered recently or now for the first time

direction : a channel or direct course of thought or action; a guiding, governing, or motivating purpose

*The goal is to move from just knowledge, which is
information, to understanding, which is awareness.*

—MEHMET OZ

MEHMET OZ, M.D., is a professor and the vice chairman of
surgery at Columbia University, the director of the Cardiovascular
Institute, the founder and director for the Complementary Medicine Program at New York–Presbyterian Hospital, and the health
expert on *The Oprah Winfrey Show*. He is the Emmy Award–winning host of the daily syndicated television show *The Dr. Oz Show*
and contributes regularly to *Time*, *O* magazine, and *Esquire*. He
is the author of more than four hundred original publications,
book chapters, and medical books, including the award-winning
Healing from the Heart and the bestselling book series *YOU: The
Owner's Manual* and its follow-ups. Dr. Oz is also one of the
founding members of the nonprofit organization HealthCorps,
which was created in 2003 in response to his concern about the
increasing need to perform heart surgery on thirty-year-olds
with arteries clogged from poor diets and sedentary lifestyles—
lifestyles that seemed to be reinforced in American schools.
(www.healthcorps.org; www.doctoroz.com)

THE INTERVIEW

I was one of the producers for Dr. Oz's YOU fitness videos. While
I was in New York a couple of months after our first shoot together,
we spoke about his epiphany while he was at the hospital. Later, it
was a bit surreal for me to listen to the recording of our conversation, especially when he said, "Oh, I'm sorry, they need me now in
the OR," and he rushed off the phone. Right after talking to me
about his epiphany, he went into a room and likely saved a life,

and for him, that—along with taping his own talk show—is just a normal day.

*   *   *

I was chief resident of general surgery at New York–Presbyterian Hospital in New York City, still finishing my training. When you are chief resident, you run the care for people who are in emergency situations. A woman came into the ER with a bleeding ulcer and had almost completely bled out, which means she'd almost lost all the blood in her body. She was a Jehovah's Witness and her entire family of about thirty people had come in with her. I told the family that I needed to take her into surgery to save her, and if it was successful, I would need to get their permission to give her blood after the surgery. I understood that the Jehovah's Witness religion has the tenet that a person of their faith cannot receive blood, but I went into surgery thinking that once I got out of the OR they would give permission since the woman would die if we didn't give her the needed blood.

I completed the surgery successfully and went to the family, excited that we had saved this woman's life. I believe the spokesperson for the family was her eldest son, and he proceeded to tell me, "We have decided not to give her blood." I was astounded. I thought maybe they didn't fully understand the situation, so I asked him if he understood that she would die without receiving the blood. He replied, "We understand. She can't have the blood."

You know, I was so angry I couldn't see straight. I felt insulted. And more than that, I felt I had failed as a doctor to convince them of the gravity of the situation. A "disobeying family"—that's how I saw them. They were disobeying me. That's exactly how I felt. How patronizing—but that's how I thought about it. Here I had busted my butt all that time to save this woman, and now they were going to "strip her from me" just as I was going to "grasp her from the jaws of defeat."

But then I began to realize that it wasn't me they were distrusting. It wasn't that they didn't believe that what I was saying was true, and that I was trying to bluff them into giving their mother blood that she didn't want. They actually did believe she would die. They actually took me at face value. They were quite certain that they were signing her death sentence. But they, in their belief system, felt that it was more important for her not to receive the blood and therefore have a better life in the future (somewhere else) than for her to take the blood now to live a little more on this earth.

The epiphany was when I realized *that it was out of their love for this woman that they made this decision*—because, believe me, the easy decision for them would have been to give her the blood, right? That's the easy decision, no one could argue with that. They made the hard decision because of their beliefs—because of their loved one's beliefs. This was a huge epiphany for me because it showed me that it wasn't all about me and my arguments and how much effort I had made and my thoughts and my conviction about what is right. There were reasons this family had that were very rational according to their belief system. These aren't reasons I agree with, but they were very rational in their own minds, and it was their judgment to make.

I began to realize that patients don't always read the same medical textbooks that we doctors read. Too often doctors focus on things that we think are important, not things the patient thinks are important. No longer do I try to talk to patients like they're me. I try to talk to patients like they're them.

The way I talk to people—not just patients, but to all people in general—also began to change. I began to think about the worldview from their perspective rather than my own. When you start doing that, you begin to have very different insights. Once you immerse yourself in someone else's worldview, you can understand their motivations much more effectively. I can really understand your perspective when I try to understand your worldview, which is what healing is all about. The word *doctor* means "teacher" in

Latin. A good teacher gets into the minds of his students and understands what resonates for them, what clicks. The goal is to move from just knowledge, which is information, to understanding, which is awareness.

The other thing I began to realize by beginning to relate to people this way is that people truly are the world experts on their own bodies—we always say that in all of our YOU books. They really are. Patients will always tell you their diagnosis. They actually know what's wrong with them. They may not be able to verbalize it right, they might need your medical insight to appreciate it, but they will tell you exactly what is going on with them. If they are aware or a bit more conscious of what's going on in their body, it makes them that much better of a healer for themselves.

This realization helped guide the way we write the books, which makes the focus not on us teaching you what *we* want you to know, but on us sharing with you what *you* probably *want* to know. It's also led to the Integrative Medicine Center at New York–Presbyterian Hospital, where we use alternative or complementary approaches to help patients because we realized and understood that they wanted it, and it's valid.

By completely trusting and acting on your instincts, the
course of your entire life can change.

—CLIVE DAVIS

CLIVE DAVIS is the legendary music industry executive and record producer who is known as "the man with the golden ears" because of his talent for discovering artists and hit songs throughout his four-decade-plus career. From 1967 to 1973 he was the president of Columbia Records; he was the founder and president of Arista Records from 1974 until 2000, when he launched J Records. Then between 2003 and 2008 Davis was chairman and CEO of the RCA Music Group (which included RCA Records, J Records, and Arista Records). He is currently the chief creative officer of Sony Music Entertainment Worldwide. Davis has won multiple Grammy Awards and is a member of the Rock and Roll Hall of Fame. He is credited with launching the careers of such artists as Janis Joplin; Blood, Sweat and Tears; Santana; Chicago; Bruce Springsteen; Billy Joel; Patti Smith; Whitney Houston; and Alicia Keys, among many others. He currently plays a part in the careers of Leona Lewis, Rod Stewart, Harry Connick Jr., Carlos Santana, Barry Manilow, and Whitney Houston. He is the benefactor of numerous educational scholarships and of the Clive Davis Department of Recorded Music at the Tisch School of the Arts at New York University. He is the father of four and grandfather of six and resides in New York City. (www.CliveDavisdept.tisch.nyu.edu)

THE INTERVIEW

I was introduced to Clive by a close mutual friend several years ago. From the moment I met him, he has been the kind of friend to me that I am grateful for every single day. Over the years I have discovered that many, many other people feel the same way. The kind of superior care and excellence he brings to his work he also brings to all the other areas of his life, and his humor and boundless energy never cease to amaze me. I am constantly inspired by him and his incredible generosity, once again demonstrated when he shared his story with me one spring afternoon in his elegant penthouse office in the Sony building overlooking Manhattan.

*   *   *

It was the summer of 1967, and of all places I was at the Monterey International Pop Festival. I had come out of a corporate law career, never expecting to be involved with music. But life is often shaped by fate, and about a year before an opportunity had come my way, out of the blue, to become head of Columbia Records. The world of creativity and music was totally new to me. So I set out to analyze how the company was operating, where music was heading, and whether the team that I had inherited could move the company forward into the next decade. I didn't know our next step.

By good fortune, Lou Adler had just started Ode Records, and I'd made a label deal with him. Lou is one of the great music producers of all time—he handled artists like Johnny Rivers and The Mamas and The Papas. He and Abe Somer (the top music attorney at the time) were on the board of the Monterey International Pop Festival and they invited me to join them at the festival. All I assumed was that we were going to have fun. I knew that The Mamas and The Papas would be singing, as well as certain other major name artists. So I went there with my wife, expecting at most a weekend that would be entertaining. I had absolutely no idea what was in store for me.

I arrived in Monterey and went to the festival grounds and was literally stunned. It was a culture shock—*everything* was different. People had come from Haight-Ashbury, from other parts of

San Francisco, from all over the West Coast. They were in flowing gowns, with long hair. And here we were in our preppy New York clothes...I remember we just looked so alien amidst this visual outpouring of love and peace—people greeting you with flowers, sometimes putting them in your hair. It was funny and fitting because my first record that I had brought into Columbia, from Lou's Ode Records, was a single and the title of the song was "If You're Going to San Francisco (Be Sure to Wear Flowers in Your Hair)" by an artist named Scott McKenzie. It literally took the country by storm and went straight to number one...and sure enough, at this festival there were more people here with flowers in their hair than not! At first it was a visual—people's faces, the openness, the communal spirit, the hope, the idealism that pervaded them. I experienced a social and cultural shock. And even that paled by the next morning when we got to the festival grounds.

I didn't know that new artists would be appearing at the festival, but when they started performing in the afternoon, it was clear that the music they were playing was completely new, unprecedented. I was sitting in the audience, and this group I'd never heard of came on, just billed as Big Brother and the Holding Company. Then this female dervish came on the stage. She was hypnotic, compelling, electrifying—she shook and sang and conveyed soul like no singer I had ever seen before. Of course, it was Janis Joplin.

I realized that a revolution was in the air, that what I was experiencing while watching Janis Joplin on that stage could change the rest of my life. And it did. My gut told me I had to sign this artist, that I needed to follow my instinct and move from the purely business arena into the creative. I was totally unsure whether I had ears or the talent for picking artists. I had never been trained for it. Before that moment, it had never occurred to me that I would be signing artists. But I just knew I had to move to the forefront and trust this instinct. And that's what I did. I immediately met with Big Brother and the Holding Company and Janis Joplin, and the group known as the Electric Flag, and signed both groups. Over the next thirty-six months I was to sign Blood, Sweat and Tears; Santana; Chicago; Loggins and Messina; and Earth, Wind and Fire.

It was only when subsequently these artists and others I signed came out and succeeded that I got some confirmation of my gift for identifying talent—which I'd never have thought in a million years that I had.

If I had stayed in law and just did tax, corporate work, and estate planning, it would have been a totally, totally different life. But I've now had the opportunity to interface and deal with unique and special talents like the Grateful Dead, Annie Lennox, Aretha Franklin, Patti Smith, Bruce Springsteen—renaissance women and men, people who have affected millions all over the world. It feels good today when people tell me how their lives have been affected by the music of artists that I've either signed, discovered, or developed. I consider it a great honor and gift to do the work I do, and it's financially enabled me to do things like establish scholarships to help others, which is something I always hoped to do, since I was only able to attend college and law school because of the generosity of other people who had established scholarships. Further, I've always felt that the music world has been portrayed inaccurately, usually negatively, regarding the executives coming out of it. The men who historically shaped the world of music—Ahmet and Nesuhi Ertegun, Goddard Lieberson, Jac Holzman, Mo Ostin, Herb Alpert and Jerry Moss, Jerry Wexler, and David Geffen—represented the best in the entire entertainment world; I wanted to help the next generation of music leaders. And so knowing how my career was affected by study, by being immersed in music, I've established this degree-awarding program at Tisch School of the Arts at New York University so those that study music can get a degree to learn and further their profession.

Without question, the most important epiphany of my life happened in the middle of the Monterey Pop Festival. By completely trusting and acting on my instincts, the course of my entire life changed. My life and career have been much more fulfilling and rewarding than I'd ever thought was possible. In truth, I still pinch myself all the time at my good fortune.

Forgiveness is the first step toward true peace and healing.
But it's with reconciliation—*actively restoring peace and har-*
mony—that you can make the biggest difference.

—LINDA BIEHL

LINDA BIEHL is the co-founder and director of the Amy Biehl
Foundation in the United States and the Amy Biehl Foundation
Trust in South Africa, a nonprofit organization promoting justice,
peace, reconciliation, and equal rights for education, employment,
and health. Linda's work is grounded in the life and death of her
daughter Amy, a dynamic twenty-six-year-old Stanford graduate
and esteemed human rights activist who in 1993 was awarded a
Fulbright fellowship to study the role of women and gender rights
during South Africa's transition from the apartheid regime to a
multiracial democracy. Just days before she was due home, Amy
was killed in an act of political violence by a group of young black
South Africans who were fighting to end apartheid and saw all
whites as their oppressors. Four young men were convicted for
Amy's death, and in 1994 they were sentenced to eighteen years
in prison.

   In 1997 the four men applied for amnesty to South Africa's
Truth and Reconciliation Commission (TRC), set up by then
President Nelson Mandela, who appointed Desmond Tutu to be
chairman to help their country heal after the violence and human
rights abuses under apartheid. Linda and her late husband, Peter,
were strongly motivated by Amy's belief in the TRC to achieve
restorative justice rather than retributive justice for those who
confessed to politically motivated crimes; thus they did not oppose
the men's application for amnesty. They testified at the amnesty
hearing of their daughter's killers and offered their support, invit-

ing the young men to join them in continuing Amy's work. Linda embraced restorative justice by building a relationship with two of the youths responsible for the death of her daughter. Today those two young men have become tremendous social activists in their community, working for the Amy Biehl Foundation Trust with Linda and even speaking alongside Linda at public events all over the world. In 2008 Linda was awarded the Order of the Companions of O. R. Tambo, the highest honor given to a non–South African. She was also the first Greeley Scholar for Peace at the University of Massachusetts, Lowell.

Amy's story and the work of her foundation have been covered by numerous media outlets including ABC's *Turning Point*, CBS's *60 Minutes* and *60 Minutes II*, ABC's *The Oprah Winfrey Show*, NBC's *Today*, CNN's *Anderson Cooper 360°*, and many others. A major motion picture based on her story is in the planning stages. (www.AmyBiehl.org)

THE INTERVIEW

I read about Linda Biehl in an interview with Archbishop Desmond Tutu in the July 2007 issue of *Vanity Fair*. In the interview, Tutu discusses the African idea of *ubuntu*, which he calls "the essence of being human…You can't be human in isolation. You are human only in relationships. We are interconnected." He goes on to say, "The greatest good in the concept of *ubuntu* is communal harmony. Anger, revenge are subversive of this great good." As an example, he tells the story of Amy Biehl and her parents and what they have done with the Amy Biehl Foundation. Tutu related how the Biehls learned who had killed their daughter from South Africa's Truth and Reconciliation Commission (TRC), and in response, not only did the Biehls support the TRC's process and the decision of amnesty for the young men, but they invited the men to work with them on behalf of their foundation.

I was absolutely stunned by this story of true forgiveness and reconciliation. It compelled me to ask myself: if we could all follow the Biehls' example, if we could all actually forgive like they have, what kind of world would this be?

Linda was one of the first people I put on my wish list to interview. She was also the first person I cold-called to request an interview, so it was especially thrilling when she agreed. We spoke on the phone almost a year to the day after I read the article about her and she had unknowingly helped me to forgive.

⁎   ⁎   ⁎

My epiphany is more like an accumulation of knowledge. Life is always a learning process—it's about paying attention, gaining knowledge, and then utilizing it to the best of your ability. It's a never-ending quest to constantly learn and grow. I was taught to make decisions and come to my own conclusions and ideas, so that's what I've done my entire life and that's what I've tried to teach my children.

From the moment that Peter, my husband, and I heard about Amy's death, we thought, "How do we honor Amy?" She was involved and cared deeply about peace and freedom in South Africa. The Truth and Reconciliation Commission concept was negotiated prior to the elections in South Africa after apartheid was abolished and was created by an act of Parliament. We were sent the legislation by the Minister of Justice under Mandela, Dullah Omar, whom Amy worked with when they were both at the University of the Western Cape before the elections. Dullah faxed us the legislation right after it was passed, so we thought about that process for several years before the guys applied for amnesty. Archbishop Tutu helped us determine how to participate. We spoke on the phone after the July 1997 date was set for the hearing, and we confirmed that we would come to the hearing and support the process rather than oppose it by bringing lawyers, et cetera. Tutu's advice was simple: "Come, talk about Amy and speak from your heart," which we did, and in the end we decided to honor Amy by carrying on her work in South Africa.

After the trial ended, we started spending time there, supporting the South African process, and advancing peace in the region. People would ask me, "How can you take your family over there? How can you do that?" But for us it was never a question. We thought, "How can we *not* do that?" We reflected on what Amy was about, what she would want, and we worked from there.

We didn't start out with the idea of the foundation. We were eventually asked by South Africans to start it. And it made sense to us. It was the logical culmination, which we came to step by step. The Amy Biehl Foundation—whose aim is reconciliation, violence prevention, and alleviating social and economic despair—came out of an accumulation of experience and, really, intellectual curiosity.

One of the greatest realizations for me has come from dealing with the Truth and Reconciliation Commission. Forgiveness is extremely important, of course, and is the first step toward true peace and healing. But it's with *reconciliation*—actively restoring peace and harmony—that I think you can make the biggest difference. I've realized that what is needed is deeper and more involved than just forgiveness: reconciliation and negotiation are necessary. We need to focus on learning from our mistakes, and we need to work on trust and respect and listening. Nelson Mandela is a great example of this. He is one of our greatest world leaders because he realized that it wouldn't serve his people or country to stay angry or demand revenge. He personifies forgiveness, reconciliation, and negotiation—and is, at the same time, a very strong leader and man.

It's been really gratifying for me to speak about reconciliation and work with kids and people like Nelson Mandela. I'd like to leave something behind to help the world move forward rather than backward. I like this project you're doing because it's about allowing people to tell their stories. We learn from each other this way. We're never really going to have all the answers…and maybe that's what this is all about anyway. Maybe we're always on this journey of learning and growing and striving to understand each other and the world around us. I think that's the exciting thing about being human. You'll find traits that are similar and traits that are novelties that don't fit anywhere. If we can just work together and strive for our best in behavior and thinking, instead of settling for our lowest common denominator, there's hope that things will get better.

*Everyone can make a difference—no matter who
you are, no matter how old you are,
no matter where you are.*

—KATHY AND BILL MAGEE

BILL AND KATHY MAGEE are the founders and CEO and president, respectively, of Operation Smile, a worldwide children's medical charity whose network of global volunteers are dedicated to offering life-changing operations to children born with cleft lips, cleft palates, and other facial deformities. Bill is a leading plastic and craniofacial surgeon with honorary doctorates from six universities and numerous awards including the American Medical Association's Pride in the Profession Award and the Distinguished Service Award from the American Society of Plastic Surgeons. Dr. Magee has trained thousands of doctors worldwide, is a keynote speaker, and has been a guest on many television shows. Kathy is a former nurse and social worker and serves on the board of Operation Smile as a full-time volunteer as well as president. The Magees have been the recipients of numerous awards and honors, including the first $1 million Conrad N. Hilton Humanitarian Prize, the Servants of Peace Award, and USAID's President's Call to Service Award. They are the parents of five and grandparents of thirteen children and reside in Norfolk, Virginia, where Operation Smile is based. (www.OperationSmile.org)

THE INTERVIEW

A friend of mine at a public relations firm suggested that I contact the Magees. I had heard of Operation Smile through the person who edited my first video for *Epiphany*. He explained that for as little as $240, doctors could fix one child's cleft lip. For less than

I might pay for some clothes or a plane ticket, I could change someone's life drastically. So I ended up donating to Operation Smile myself. I spoke with the Magees on the phone while they drove to New York to meet a child from India whom they were helping. Theirs is the only joint epiphany that I have come across. It is amazing to me how much Bill and Kathy have accomplished personally, professionally, and philanthropically over the years. I also am a total romantic, so I loved learning that they have been an item since they were fourteen years old and married for forty-three years. Bill explained how this has been possible: "Our strengths are very, very different. And I think that that's good because she does things I could never do, and I do some things that she *might* not be able to do."

*   *   *

BILL MAGEE: Twenty-eight years ago, I was a young plastic surgeon living in Norfolk, Virginia, and I got invited by a group in Houston, Texas, to take a trip to Naga City in the Philippines to perform surgeries to fix the cleft lips and palates of children. My wife, Kathy, is a pediatric nurse, and we have five children. Our life has been about kids, so it seemed like the perfect thing to do together. We actually brought our thirteen-year-old daughter, our oldest, with us.

Children with cleft palates and cleft lips have a facial deformity that, in many countries, sets them apart and socially ostracizes them—they are basically social outcasts. They also can't eat effectively, so they're very malnourished; they can't speak intelligibly; they don't go to school; they're never going to hold jobs, be productive members of society, or even get married. With surgery, you can change their lives forever. In as little as forty-five minutes, we can take a child from hopelessness to possibility. The child will begin to have a life. That's all these families are asking for.

So we went on that trip not knowing exactly what to expect,

although we thought it would be a good experience. Little did we know it would completely change our lives forever.

We witnessed three hundred families coming in for care, but in the few days we had we could only take care of forty children. That meant we had to turn away 260. I distinctly remember a lady coming up to us with a basket of bananas cradled in her arms, and at her side her eight-year-old daughter, who had a big hole in her lip. The woman said to me, "I'd like to give you this basket of bananas as thanks for trying to take care of my daughter because it's the only thing I have." Tears started coming down her cheeks, and then down our cheeks, because we were leaving and couldn't help her—all we could say was "Maybe next year." But the group we were with wasn't planning on coming back next year.

That was the moment for me. I can remember it viscerally, as if it were yesterday. There was no good reason that these kids couldn't get care. It was just a matter of someone being there to do it. As a plastic surgeon, I was used to seeing people with deformities, and I enjoyed helping them. But I never, ever realized that there were so many children and families who didn't have access to basic care.

KATHY MAGEE: My experience was similar, but what it was for me was the moment we were in the room in the hospital in Naga City, with some 250 kids surrounding us with their families. There were only fifteen of us in the middle. And I could just feel them tugging on my pants and shirtsleeves and saying, "Mom, me. Mom, Mom. Help me." We knew we couldn't treat them all. I just thought, "I've got to do something here, and I'll do anything to make it happen."

BILL: We decided that when we went home we'd ask our friends if they'd help us take care of those 250 kids. When we could solve a problem so easily and help so many lives, it just seemed unreasonable not to. We thought we'd do this once, then the world would be wonderful, we'd be rid of our guilt, and we'd go back to our normal lives. But we never went back to living the way we did before, and we've never wanted to.

Operation Smile started around our dinner table with our five kids, ranging from six to thirteen years old, and it spread very rapidly to our friends, to their friends, and it just continued to grow exponentially. We came back the next year and took care of about maybe 100 or 150 children—and watched another 250 kids get turned away. We went back a third year and watched 300 families get turned away. After that we got invited to go to Liberia, Kenya, and India and raised money to go there. The project has just never stopped growing. We're now in fifty countries with some two hundred employees and four thousand medical volunteers worldwide, and we've treated about 150,000 children now—we'll drive out about 150 medical missions this year.

Since 2002, I am the full-time CEO now and only go in to my private practice a few days a month. Kathy has been a full-time volunteer since we started. She serves as president, working at least eighty hours a week. All five of our kids and our grandkids are involved with Operation Smile in one way or another as well. We all still do volunteer trips too, because it's powerful and moving, and it's fun.

Operation Smile is a global group of people who donate their time, but sustainability is key to the whole operation. Not only do we come into communities and perform surgeries, but we train volunteers in each to continue the work so more children can be helped. Our people throughout the world are from different religions, cultures, nationalities, and geographic origins, but they all share a common commitment to give of their time to help others.

What I've learned since that defining moment in Naga City is that while reason leads you to a conclusion, it's emotion that moves you to action. When people feel passionate about something, they tap into a virtuous cycle—the more they give, the more they get out of it. All of us have our strengths and weaknesses, but in my experience, the great majority of people are basically good. If you give them the opportunity to help by using their talents, they will. But they need some infrastructure to do that. They need to have somebody to help them take the first step. That's all we're doing.

One of the greatest gifts for us was that we were able to share this with our kids. Our involvement has helped us to raise our five children with the values we treasure, and now we see them planted in our grandchildren as well.

KATHY: That trip forever changed who we were because our whole house became involved. Patients stayed in our home. Our kids gave up their beds. We've all learned that by giving, you really receive. Everyone can make a difference—no matter who you are, no matter how old you are, no matter where you are. Elementary school kids go on these medical missions, and all the students of all ages are unbelievable. The volunteer medical teams embrace these young people and bring them along because they know that in the future, they'll make a difference.

BILL: Children really are the only language that all of us have in common around the world. We can repair a child's tortured face and all of sudden it isn't tortured anymore, it's beautiful. Involvement creates change.

If you believe in a child, the child will succeed.
—CAROL LANNING

CAROL LANNING was born in Cedar Rapids, Iowa, received her bachelor of science and her master's degree in education at Southern Methodist University, and subsequently chose Dallas, Texas, as her home. (She still misses the snow.) Carol began her career in the Highland Park Independent School District as a fifth-grade teacher at Bradfield Elementary. After twelve years as a classroom teacher, she began leading accelerated classes for the gifted and talented students at Bradfield. Carol raised two daughters, has been active in the Junior League of Dallas and the SMU Mother's Club, served as a board member for the Campfire Girls of Dallas, and is in the process of publishing a children's book. She has just begun her thirty-fourth year of teaching and has absolutely no plans to retire. (www.br.hpisd.org)

THE INTERVIEW

Carol Lanning was my fifth-grade teacher and is one of the greatest influences on my life. She helped shape me, and every single student of hers whom I know. In fact, she is famous within my childhood community for being a phenomenal teacher. Even my friends who never knew her know *of* her. Recently, when asked by a friend why Lanning had such an impact, I thought about it and wasn't sure exactly. For one thing, she made us feel supersmart, special, and talented, encouraging us to do advanced projects. While the assignments were challenging, her belief in our abilities gave us an immense sense of accomplishment and confidence. But I never could articulate exactly what it was that made her so special until I heard her epiphany. Then it all made sense. We shot

Carol's interview just before the school year began in her classroom at Bradfield Elementary, right down the hall from where she taught me.

View the Interview:
www.epiphanychannel.com/people/carol-lanning

∗ ✦ ⊙

I think there are a series of epiphanies that might happen in your life. But there are some that just…change it. There's really one that changed my life.

My greatest epiphany happened right out of school during my first year of teaching when I was teaching fifth grade. I didn't think I was going to stick with the profession. My classroom was next door to that of another teacher who was very burnt out, unhappy and bitter. I did not want that happening to me, especially when I was interested in other fields such as psychology and medicine. More important, I didn't have a whole lot of confidence in how well I could get information across to my students. I was great at disciplining and entertaining them, but I wasn't sure how well I was actually teaching them.

I had special doubts thanks to one of my students in math. He was very bright, but he just couldn't get division. And that shocked me. He simply could not comprehend the process of division. I couldn't think of anything else to do but just keep going through it with him. This little guy was precious. He stayed in my room after school every day for *three weeks*, and we worked and worked, but he just couldn't get it. By this point, my confidence was shot. I decided that I had to quit teaching—I was no good at it and this was not where I was supposed to be. I even told my principal that I wasn't coming back the next year.

One afternoon I turned to my student and said, "It's not you; it's me. I can't get it across. I'm so sorry." I think he felt sorry for me, because he hastily said, "I'm going to try. I'm going to keep working." So he continued to work with me after school. Then in the middle of a problem one day, he stopped me. I remember him lighting up—you could honestly see sparks come out of the boy's eyes and the lights go on. He interrupted me, "Don't tell me. I think I can do it." And he finished the problem. Then he did two more. We were *so* excited. He got it! I couldn't believe it! I was excited for his sake, and even at his age, he was excited for mine. And—this still moves me—he said, "I'm so glad it's *not you!*" He said he didn't care if he got the math; he was just glad that I could teach! And he was very proud of me that I got it across to him.

That moment is still just as powerful for me now as it was thirty-two years ago. I haven't talked about that experience in a long time, but I remember it so well.

In that instant, I realized that the key to teaching is not all the education and degrees and the latest fancy techniques. It is having the patience and determination, the understanding and the love for the kids, and the perseverance to just keep going. That's all you need. Of course, humor helps too!

If I could get across what I needed to this student, I could convey it to anybody. So I stuck around, and I've been here ever since. When things got tough, I would reach back to that moment. When I've had crazy principals who I thought would drive me off, or hysterical parents, I would always remember: "I can do it. I have patience. I can take students through the steps, and I can get them there." Knowing this has taken me through all these years. And it was that one boy's breakthrough that gave me the confidence. That certainty never left me. In fact, it grew.

If you believe in a child, the child will succeed. I know this now. I always believe in my kids. They know I love 'em. They do. But they don't instantly know I *believe* in them. I have to work at showing them that. That is the challenge. They don't come in assuming everybody thinks they're great. One mistake, and they say, "She thinks I'm dumb." The challenge is to let them know I'm there for them. Always. And in life, that's not automatically the case. Parents aren't always there for them nonstop. Not everyone's there for them. But I am. That's easy for me. It takes a while before they realize that. That is my challenge when they come in—to show them that I know they can do anything, and that we're going to get there together.

I've put this message across since that very first year. That's what builds confidence in students and encourages them to take on challenges and learn. It's key in education. It's not just reading and writing and math. If they know you believe that they can do it, then they can do it. While I'm building up their confidence, I'm also building mine. I'm still working and I plan to keep going for a long time. I'm happy and I think the kids still need me. So I'm still here.

Tapping into one's own unique wellsprings of positivity is a wise and healthy investment in the future.

—BARBARA FREDRICKSON

BARBARA FREDRICKSON, PH.D., is the Kenan Distinguished Professor of Psychology and director of the Positive Emotions and Psychophysiology Lab at the University of North Carolina. She is the author of *Positivity: Groundbreaking Research Reveals How to Embrace the Hidden Strength of Positive Emotions, Overcome Negativity, and Thrive*. Fredrickson is a leading scholar within social psychology, affective science, and positive psychology, and has been the recipient of many honors, including the 2000 American Psychological Association's Templeton Prize in Positive Psychology. She lives in Chapel Hill, North Carolina, with her husband and two sons. (www.PositivityRatio.com)

THE INTERVIEW

I have been studying and reading about positive psychology since 2006, when I accidentally stumbled upon an article in *Psychology Today*. I had never heard about the science behind positivity before, but it completely supported the concepts I was using to develop a series of DVDs, books, and workbooks for children. I've learned much more about positive psychology since that time and it was important to me to interview one of the leaders in this field. When I went to interview Kristin Neff, a psychology professor at the University of Texas at Austin, I told her about this desire, and she immediately said I should try to talk to Barbara. Then she said, "In fact, when Amazon sends me an extra book accidentally, it's always fun for me to see who it is for," and she handed me

Barbara's book, *Positivity*. I arbitrarily opened the book and on the page in front of me was a story about using the principles of positive psychology to have better, more fun, playful sex, which leads to happier, more relaxed lives, higher fertility, easier pregnancies, and many other wonderful health benefits. Sold! She was the one for me, and, luckily, we were able to connect shortly thereafter.

* * *

As a scientist, I have been researching and studying positive emotions for more than twenty years. I started working on positive emotions because emotions research was still pretty new when I started my career, and literally the area of positive emotions was uncharted terrain. Probably 98 percent of the research published about emotions was all on anger, fear, anxiety, sadness, depression, and all our negative emotions. I got interested in positive emotions just out of sheer intellectual curiosity. I noticed that nobody was looking into this side of things, so I wanted to explore it. I had always been attracted to topics that nobody else studied. Sometimes that's a really bad idea. Sometimes it can lead to something good.

We had theories for understanding emotions, but I discovered they didn't really work when they were applied to positive ones. For instance, the main way of understanding emotions was to say that humans evolved to have emotions because they lead to specific action tendencies, like "fight or flight," that saved our ancestors' lives in certain situations. Fear makes you want to run away. Disgust makes you want to spit whatever is disgusting out of your mouth. These emotions promote narrow action tendencies to help our survival. This was the dominant theoretical framework for emotions, but if you apply it to the positive emotions, it didn't really fit. For example, when you ask, "What is the specific action tendency that goes with joy?" people would come up with things like

"It causes free activation" and "Positive emotions make you want to do anything," but these action urges weren't specific like they were for negative emotions. So there were major puzzles that were surrounding positive emotions, and that's what drew me in to the field.

After about ten years of doing work on positive emotions and trying to solve this intellectual brainteaser, I was working with a collaborator where the main piece of news from the work that we were doing was that there was a particular ratio of positive emotions relative to negative emotions that would tip the scales toward flourishing versus just getting by in life. We found data to support the idea that there is an important tipping point positivity ratio of 3:1—meaning that we humans should, over a course of time, strive for an average of at least three positive emotions to every negative one to have a fulfilling life. This basically means that tapping into one's own unique wellsprings of positivity is a wise and healthy investment in the future because this state of mind can enhance your relationships, improve your health, relieve depression, and broaden your mind. I started working on a paper covering our findings about the positivity ratio. This was about seven years ago, and my kids were very young, and I was thinking a lot about how to be a mom, a spouse, and a scientist all at the same time.

One day I was in my living room meditating. I'd had a very informal meditation practice for years; I found it calmed me and really helped me feel less anxious. While I was in the middle of this meditation, the revelation occurred to me, "This is about life and how to live it. This is not just another academic paper I'm writing. This is actually about my life and how I live my life." This notion we were working on, the idea that there was a particular tipping point positivity ratio, was truly offering a prescription for life and how to live it. It was one that I needed to follow, and other people might want to follow it too. It wasn't just an abstract mathematical cool fact or merely an interesting formula I was studying. Before this moment, that's what it was for me. I was not at all looking for a prescription on how to live life. But I realized that I could look to the contents of my own work for a prescription for how to arrange my day, how to raise my kids, how to reshape my marriage, how to interact with colleagues—there were lessons for life in my work for me. That phrase kept coming to mind: "This is about life and how to live it." And I realized that it doesn't just apply to other people; it applies to me. If I want to flourish, then I need to find ways to increase my experience in positive emotions. So this was the moment when my work became extraordinarily practical for me and not just an abstract basic research question. This was a *huge* turning point in my life.

Not only has this epiphany given a deeper meaning to my work, but in practicing it, my life is much more fun and exciting and fulfilling. What's funny is, I actually grew up in a family that was very stoic and unemotional. When I first started studying emotions, it literally took me a while to figure out what they were because they seemed so foreign to me. One of my very dear friends who was also studying emotions but came from a very different kind of family, one that was much more expressive and demonstrative, once said to me, "Barb, you study emotions because you have none." And there was some absolute truth to that. So it was from that backdrop that I was studying emotions. I was intellectually curious, yet it was all very much at arm's length for me. Now I'm always trying to find ways to be more expressive, playful, and lighthearted, and I'm always looking for different ways to focus on beauty and awe and make all of these things priorities in my life with my kids and my husband.

This experience also coincides with me recovering from being a workaholic. It's always a work in progress to balance that out for me, but this was also a turning point. It's gotten me to lighten up and realize the toll the workaholic lifestyle was taking. Even though work is really important, you just can't do it at the exclusion of having balance, health, and good relationships. I enjoy life so much more—it really is like night and day.

The other thing that happened from this is that I was inspired to write my book. I'd had plans to write a book before this moment, but it was a very different book, exclusively about the science of emotions. But I never got going on it. After we discovered the positivity ratio and I realized this had to do with life and how to live it—including my life—I was fired up to try to communicate this more practical information to others because I really felt people would want to know about it. It's been really gratifying to hear how my book is helping others live more fulfilling lives.

My epiphany was completely unexpected. I wasn't at all looking for a prescription for how to live life, but I found it through my work, and it's been an important touchstone for me ever since.

We can actually control our genes and change our bodies and
lives on a cellular level, simply through our actions.
—MICHAEL ROIZEN

MICHAEL ROIZEN, M.D., is co-founder of RealAge and
chairman of the RealAge Scientific Advisory Board. He practices
anesthesiology and internal medicine at the Cleveland Clinic in
Cleveland, Ohio. He has been listed in the *Best Doctors in Amer-*
ica since 1989 and is past chairman of a Food and Drug Administration advisory committee. Dr. Roizen has authored many
books, including the bestsellers *RealAge: Are You as Young as*
You Can Be? and *The RealAge Diet*, and is co-author of the bestselling *YOU* book series written with Dr. Mehmet Oz. Because of
his medical insights, he has lectured all over the world, appearing
on such shows as *The Oprah Winfrey Show, Today*, and *20/20*.
He has been featured in magazines such as *Fortune, Ladies' Home*
Journal, and *Prevention*. His wife, Nancy, is a developmental pedi-
atrician, also listed in the *Best Doctors in America*, and together
they have two children. At the printing of this book, Dr. Roizen
is 64 calendar years of age, but his RealAge is 44.6!
(www.realage.com)

THE INTERVIEW
In August 2007 I was shooting some behind-the-scenes footage at
an It's All About YOU! tour event in New York with Dr. Michael
Roizen, Dr. Mehmet Oz, Joel Harper, and Lisa Oz. I had just
started thinking about *Epiphany* as a real project and while we
were in the greenroom I asked Mike about his greatest epiphany.
We had just met a few minutes before, but without hesitating, he
gave me his answer on camera in an extremely succinct and com-

pelling way. In February 2009 we sat down in another greenroom
in New York, this time on one of our DVD shoots, and he gave me
the detailed story behind the epiphany he talked about in 2007,
along with a bonus epiphany that I hadn't been expecting.

*   *   *

The first part of my epiphany happened in 1986. I am both an
internist and an anesthesiologist, and that year I realized I could
motivate patients who had high blood pressure and were smoking with what I now call the RealAge Paradigm. This means that
certain things, like smoking, can actually age you prematurely and
cut down on the quality and length of your life, but the converse
is also true: if you are not smoking, you can actually feel and look
younger than you are.

I realized that by telling a patient things like "If you smoke,
you're eight years older" or "By controlling your blood pressure,
you get to be twenty-five years younger," they usually changed
their behavior because we weren't talking about the future. We
were talking about what they did *now* that changed their quality
of life *today*, as well as their risk of disability. It was getting them
back to the now, and we were having the great results of getting
them motivated to change their habits immediately to improve
their quality of life.

The reason I was mainly focused on just the issues of smoking
and blood pressure is because the risks of surgery go up by a factor
of three every ten years older you are, so I figured that by controlling smoking and high blood pressure, I could make my patients
much younger and lower their risks of surgery.

So I had been communicating information to patients in this
way since 1986. In 1993—I remember the exact date and time; it
was November 24 at 2:30 p.m., the day before Thanksgiving—I
had a patient in my office with high blood pressure. I imparted
the RealAge information to him about blood pressure, and he

asked me, "How many other things in medicine can you do that for?" I said, "I don't know. Why?" He replied, "Because this is very powerful for me. What docs usually tell me is that I'm going to die a couple of years early if I don't take my blood pressure medication. This doesn't really mean anything to me because that's way off in the future. What *you've* said to me is that if I don't take my medicine, I'll live with the energy of someone who's five years older and live with the risk of someone who's five years older. Now *that* means something to me because it can be applied today." Then he asked again, "How many other things in medicine can you do that for?"

When I replied with an idea of what it might be but that I couldn't be positive, he said, "How much will it cost me to find out?" I roughly ran through what it would take to do the research necessary and estimated that if would require about $25,000. To my surprise, he reached into his pocket, pulled out his checkbook, wrote a check for $25,000, and said, "I want the answer in six weeks."

And that was really the start of it all—our work to get health information out to the public. Our company, RealAge, was born. My patient is the co-founder of RealAge with me. He had an epiphany right there in my office about doing this research because it was so motivating for him that he wanted us to bring it to other areas of medicine if we could.

After we started doing the research and work with the $25,000, the second part of my epiphany began. First, I realized that I didn't know a lot of the data and research that was out there and how good and powerful it was. Here I was, ranked one of the top one thousand doctors in America, and if I didn't know the data, then most other doctors didn't either—most other doctors still don't, although we're getting some penetration now. We set out to collect as much data and research as we could about aging and health, but we also used other criteria for the program, including whether or not four out of five of us were able to change our behavior as a result. For instance, I remember my wife asked me, "You're flossing. Did your dentist finally get to you?" And I said, "No, I just saw how powerful the data was that flossing decreased unnecessary aging, even decreasing wrinkles and impotence, along with decreasing heart attacks and strokes." So flossing was one of those habits I actually changed, and four out of five of us on the board had come back and had adopted the habit, so it became part of our program.

Through our research, we realized that you get to turn on or turn off the genes you were born with. You actually get to change your quality of life through your own actions. All of us (or at least most of us) in the medical profession thought before then that our genes just took us where they wanted us to go. When I learned through our research that, in fact, you *can* control your genes, I had the epiphany that you can really change your life. You can actually change your life on a cellular level.

About five years after RealAge was started (I had been married twenty-six years at that point), our youngest child had just gone off to college. So both of our kids had moved out. I should have realized this a long time before, but all of a sudden I realized just how important the choice of your spouse or life partner is to life. I had always realized it's nice to have a great wife—a wife whom you're attracted to and whom you respect, who does great things, and who brings up kids with you, and so on—and maybe it's part of my background, but I had never realized that it probably outweighs everything else in the quality of life and the quality of your happiness. It wasn't a particular instance that happened, but I just realized how lucky I was and how easy life was because my wife, Nancy, was so wonderful.

I realized that Nancy had made everything work so that I could be successful, and I suddenly realized how relatively unimportant my career is compared to her. It is the major relationship in my life that is the most fulfilling thing and what makes life so wonderful for me.

This epiphany about my wife has, in turn, affected all my relationships because as a scientist and doctor building up a career in science, you work very hard and can get "married" to your work. Sometimes you tend to think of relationships as not being quite as important as the career. But my career could go to heck, and it wouldn't really matter—*it isn't career that's the thing, people are the thing*. Even in terms of my colleagues, like my relationship with Mehmet Oz, our friendship is much more important than a lot of other things. I was fifty-three and had been married twenty-six years before I realized all this, so it took me a while to realize the obvious, right? I'm a slow learner—but better late than never!

Develop your talents and they will make a way for you.
—ELIZABETH AVELLÁN

ELIZABETH AVELLÁN is an American film producer born in Caracas, Venezuela. Her family moved to Texas, where she attended Rice University at the age of sixteen. She is the current co-owner and vice president of Troublemaker Studios, the Austin-based production company that she and her former husband, Robert Rodriguez, founded in 2000, and she is the producer of more than twenty-five films, including *El Mariachi, Desperado, From Dusk Till Dawn, The Faculty, Once Upon a Time in Mexico, The Adventures of Sharkboy and Lavagirl 3-D, Grindhouse, Sin City,* the *Spy Kids* trilogy, *Shorts, Predators,* and *Machete.* Elizabeth is the mother of six children. She serves as a mentor and is on numerous nonprofit boards, such as the University of Texas Film Institute, Capital Area Statues, Texas Book Festival, Rainforest Partnership, UT College of Communication Dean's Council, and Safi Apparel—a clothing company based in Afghanistan that is 95 percent staffed by Afghani women.

THE INTERVIEW
Elizabeth and I were acquaintances before our interview, but I'd never really had the opportunity to sit and talk with her. She is a woman of tiny stature with a great sense of humor, tremendous energy, presence, and grace. As in most cases, I had no idea what her epiphany would be and was mesmerized as we discussed her journey of epiphanies. This account is only a fraction of the conversation we had in her office while her employees, who are like family to her, worked around us and her children quietly played.

* * *

I was one of those kids who was very together, very serious, a bookworm who read a lot and was very spiritually aware. I knew I was different, odd. When I was four, I started asking my parents if I could make my first Communion. My family was Catholic, like 98 percent of the people in Venezuela, where I grew up. The Church usually doesn't let you take your first Communion until you're eight without special permission. I had an older sister, so it was decided that when she took hers, they would give me special permission to take mine. I was excited about the fact that I was going to receive something really deep and special. But three days before the ceremony, I got this fever. It was incredibly high and it came out of nowhere. There was no cold, no illness; it just came over me. Maybe it was the excitement—we never knew. But it was so high, it was dangerous. And as I was lying in bed really sick with this strange fever, I thought, "I'm going to die before I get to do this." Then I said or prayed, "I don't want to die. Let me make my first Communion and You can take me. After that, my life will be fulfilled." I still remember this; it was so powerful. It marked me in a way that few things could. I can remember that day completely. Later that day, the priest came to my house to offer Confession and gave me my first Communion. I got better.

And I wanted more. This moment was the first that set me on the path that my life is about, a quest for spiritual knowledge and an unshakable faith. The faith I'm talking about lets you know, in your heart of hearts, that when a problem comes and you don't know how to solve it, wisdom from above will come and guide you. You will do anything in life because you're never afraid. You know you will always be guided and given the tools for any situation, and that it's all about developing yourself.

I'm always telling young people: develop your talents and they will make a way for you. You're only as good as what you can do with those talents. Only they will make your way—not some networking person that you schmoozed. So if God is moving you into an arena that you know nothing about, but He has given you the talents to be able to do it, you will not be alone. You will never be alone. The guidance is always there. We just have to be willing to listen and see—which has always been the hardest thing for me to do, because I always want to do everything on my own and do what I want to do and what I think is best!

When I was thirty-three years old, I was married to Robert (Rodriguez). His film *El Mariachi* had been a huge success, so we went to film festivals all over the world. I'd met Robert while working at the University of Texas, and before we got married, I had wanted to be a vice president at the university, which is completely unrelated to filmmaking. But what I love and am good at are budgets and people—which is perfect for that position in academia but also, now I know, film production! In fact, right before I met Robert, I saw the movie *Broadcast News*. When I saw Holly Hunter as a news producer juggling all those balls, I thought, "Huh, that's a job I'd be really good at." Robert was a student and my file clerk at the university. Neither of us had any professional experience, but Robert had made about thirty short films. That's the thing that blew me away about him. He'd been developing those talents since he was a little boy. And when you do that, it will take you where you're supposed to go. It just will, even if you're not spiritual in the least. I realized here's one talented man and a very driven woman who understands him, and together we can do something. And we did.

I prepared myself. I took extension courses in production at UCLA and learned as much as I could about production. When *El Mariachi* was this huge success, and we got back from the festival circuit, I realized that if I were to be a producer in this business with these people I wasn't really comfortable with, my life would change drastically. So I did a thirty-day fast. I wanted to focus on the question I was asking God: "What is it You want me to do about this? Do You want me to do this business?" Finally I felt it, about halfway through the fast. I felt it in my heart and I heard it in my head. A voice said, "Yes." It was a very weird thing. And very clear. The truth is, a part of me didn't want it to be yes. I knew it would take me on a very different path. But the voice was so clear that I went ahead with what I heard, even though I couldn't figure out why. I became a producer (for no pay) on Robert's next film, *Desperado*.

There was this guy working on the production who had just been through a horrible experience on another film set. One day we were talking, and he ended up telling me about it. The stories were so bad I honestly wanted to cry for him. Toward the end of our conversation, all of sudden he looked at me intently and said, "What is it about your production—everyone seems so *happy*. Something's really different about you. What is it?" I answered, "You really want to know?" and I began to share my story with him.

And then it overcame me; it was literally like I heard, "That's why I want you in the business. You're to be a light. You are to be a light when many times there is so much darkness." I never really knew why I was supposed to be doing it before that.

Years later, on the movie *Grindhouse*, I experienced some of my very darkest hours. It was the hardest shoot I've ever done. I had to shut down the production for six weeks, and my marriage was unraveling. On that film, I met actor Jeff Fahey, and we became good friends. Jeff is very involved in helping Afghanistan with various charities, and I joined in his efforts to set up a factory to employ 250 Afghani widows. One day I was lamenting about the nightmare I felt I was in. Jeff responded, "Well, you know, you've been through a lot. But if you hadn't shut down that movie, if all this hadn't happened, you wouldn't be helping 250 women in the world right now." And he was so right. That was another defining moment for me. Anything that you go through—anything—there is always someone going through something much worse, and good and light can always come out of the darkness.

I have faith that I will always be guided. I believe that if we develop our talents, we will be led to what we are supposed to be doing. I compare the hard times in life to being in a fog—sometimes a tunnel of fog—where we can only see a few feet in front of us. But if you keep going, a few feet at a time, and take the high road, the fog always lifts, and there is light at the end of every tunnel.

*Go all in. Treat people like you want to be treated;
live and let live; and also give the other person
a break now and then.*
—CRAIG NEWMARK

CRAIG NEWMARK is a customer service representative and
the founder of craigslist.org, based in San Francisco. With years
of experience working with computers for IBM, GM, Charles
Schwab, and Bank of America, he started craigslist in 1995 in his
apartment as a message board about local events and as a simple
email mailing list. Now craigslist is one of the top Internet companies in the world in terms of page views (about twenty billion per
month), serving more than seven hundred cities in fifty-five countries, and its advertisements are still primarily free. Newmark has
been named one of *Time* magazine's 100 Most Influential People in
the World Today and one of the 25 Most Influential People on the
Web by *BusinessWeek*. He started craigconnects.org as a result of
the epiphany he talks about in this interview and works with various organizations such as DonorsChoose.org, the Iraq and Afghanistan Veterans of America, Kiva.org, Consumer Reports, and the
Sunlight Foundation, and he serves on the advisory board of Wikipedia. He is also one of the founders of the craigslist Foundation.
(www.craigconnects.org)

THE INTERVIEW
Craig Newmark has been a hero of mine ever since I started using
craigslist.org around 2004. I noticed that every time I dealt with
craigslist—whether for a sublet, to sell or buy something, or even
just to give away boxes—the experience was extraordinary. And
when I started asking other people about it, they felt the same

way. Every time I heard about people finding an incredible sublet, a superb used car, or an amazing washer and dryer, or how people met (and married!) through craigslist, I grew more and more curious about who the wizard was behind the curtain. I found the craigslist Foundation online and left a message. Several days later, they sent me his direct email, so I wrote him. And he immediately wrote me back. He really does work in customer service at craigslist! He very graciously agreed to do the interview in person and even appear on camera, so right after I signed my contract with Random House for this book, I flew up to San Francisco to meet the guy who revolutionized the way we buy, sell, give away, and find things.

View the Interview:

www.epiphanychannel.com/people/craig-newmark

*   *   *

Quite recently, I had a very strong realization that has caused me to take action in very specific ways. I guess I've done well enough in business that I can think about what is most satisfying for me—which has to do with making a difference, changing things a bit. I have been working with a lot of people lately in public service, thinking about what they do and what I've been doing for craigslist. I reminded myself that customer service, which is how I make a living, *is* a kind of public service.

I work in craigslist customer service half-time, seven days a week. That gives me a lot of other time that I could use. I do need some time for watching TV—I'm a couch potato. But the rest of that time, I realized that there are a lot of people in public service for whom it's more than just a paycheck. It wasn't enough, just doing craigslist customer service. I realized that I needed to take action—I needed to stop just *thinking* about public service and start *taking action*. It was time to go all in.

So I'm in the process of doing that.

I have a foundation that was started several years ago, the craigslist Foundation, and that is a small part of what I do. I'm interested in helping people and groups in public service, supporting them in getting the job done. In some cases I'm just giving advice on social media, trying to help them get the word out. In other cases, I'm getting more seriously involved on a personal ongoing basis.

For instance, I'm working with groups in support of veterans, such as the Iraq and Afghanistan Veterans of America, involving genuine support for the troops rather than just words. I'm also supporting and working with government workers on multiple levels to use the Net for superior public service and with the Sunlight Foundation on government accountability and transparency. I also am involved with large-scale efforts like Wikipedia. People may or may not realize this, but Wikipedia is a really big deal. It is a great example of the balance between professional work and mass collaboration. It is a history of our times that is always being written, and is one of the biggest resources we have reflecting how we think of ourselves and how things happen. It's imperative that bad guys don't go in, put disinformation in there, and screw things up for everyone. A lot of what I will do for Wikipedia will deal with information quality and control, and the ethics of updating content.

How do you deal with groups that practice disinformation on a professional basis? How do you prevent them from hurting everyone? There are people that do that kind of thing for profit. They do a lot of bad stuff everywhere, and we've got to do something about it. Wikipedia needs a little help, a little protection. People of goodwill need to work together to do that, and I'm ready for service. Even a couch potato like me needs to stand up.

People keep asking me questions, which kind of forces me to think, and then think again, about what I'm doing. That's good because the more I think about it, the more I realize, the more I act. The thrust of my work is that I help enable people to help other people—that's what we do as a team at craigslist. Apparently, so far we've impacted tens of millions of people, and as I expand the scope of my personal public service, my target over twenty years is to reach billions.

But I have very informal targets. My goal is that the work I do with craigslist—enabling people to help other people—and what I can do to support the Internet and sites like DonorsChoose. org (an online charity that makes it easy to donate to students and classrooms in need), Kiva.org (an international microfinance organization), and Wikipedia will influence the human species in really good ways.

Most of our lives are based on daily minutiae. We do what we need to do; then we do a little bit more of it; then we do a little bit more of it. And we get through our lives pretty successfully that way. Now and then if we're lucky, we do have some big realization about ourselves—an epiphany that changes things or maybe reinforces what we're about—and if we're smart, we follow it. When I had my epiphany, I know I focused on it pretty quickly, and started thinking about what I should really do. How I should act.

I've just really started. I may not know for ten years, maybe twenty years. But it's setting the direction for my life, and it has helped me understand what I've been doing up till now without consciously realizing it: I've been doing public service through customer service. Realizing this tells me that I need to go all in for all sorts of public service, in the ways I think about that. That feels right to me. It's very individual. Whatever works for a person as an individual, hey, that works for me. The deal is, it's a matter of shared values—treat people like you want to be treated; live and let live; and also give the other person a break now and then.

People have the power to heal themselves—a shift in consciousness can cause a shift in biology.

—DEEPAK CHOPRA

DEEPAK CHOPRA, M.D., is a world-renowned authority in the field of mind-body healing, a bestselling author, the founder of the Chopra Foundation, and the co-founder of the Chopra Center for Wellbeing. Heralded by *Time* magazine as the "poet-prophet of alternative medicine," he is also the host of the popular weekly *Wellness Radio* program on Sirius/XM Stars. Dr. Chopra is the prolific author of more than sixty books, including sixteen bestsellers on mind-body health, spirituality, and peace, and his books have been published in more than eighty-five languages. He is also an international presenter and keynote speaker, as well as a fellow of the American College of Physicians, a member of the American Association of Clinical Endocrinologists, an adjunct professor at Kellogg School of Management, and a senior scientist with the Gallup Organization. Before establishing the Chopra Center, he served as chief of staff at Boston Regional Medical Center. (www.DeepakChopra.com; www.TheVisualMD.com)

THE INTERVIEW

When Deepak and I spoke for the first time, we were on the air live when he interviewed me on his radio show about this book and the Epiphany project. Later we met in person when he worked with my production team in New York on one of his stellar iPhone apps. He kindly squeezed me into his incredibly crammed schedule early one morning for a phone interview. Our conversation was so brief I have to admit I was worried. But when I started reading the transcript, I realized it was totally clear, and he had just

practiced exactly what he teaches by connecting with and expressing the basic, true essence of his experience.

*   *   *

In 1980 I was practicing medicine in Boston, Massachusetts. It is
a habit of mine to take a walk after meditation. One day, at about
ten o'clock in the morning, I was taking my morning walk in the
Fenway Park area, pondering why some of my patients were healing and others weren't.

Suddenly it hit me. *People have the power to heal themselves.* I
had been observing over my years of practice the rare patients who
had done so, who had recovered from their illnesses, and it occurred
to me at this moment that there was a common factor—they moved
from a place of fear to a place of extreme joy and what I would call
the intoxication of love. It hit me that they all had the same kind
of shift in consciousness. You know, it sounds simplistic when I
say it, but actually the shift is very profound and deep. For forty
years people had been studying the effects of stress. But nobody had
actually studied the biology of joy or love. So it occurred to me that
that's where we need to move.

After this initial realization, several epiphanies which I consider part of this overriding epiphany occurred. One part of it
that was very important for me was that there was the return of
the memory of wholeness. The words *whole, health,* and *holy* are
the same word. Health, healing, wholeness, holy.

My entire practice and life focus changed after this realization
that a shift in consciousness can cause a shift in biology. I started
researching it, and I started writing and speaking about it. My
whole life is now about establishing a scientific basis for consciousness influencing biology, and it all goes back to this original
epiphany and this original premise.

Practice self-compassion.
Be your own best, kind, compassionate, caring friend.

—KRISTIN NEFF

KRISTIN NEFF, PH.D., received her doctorate in human development from the University of California at Berkeley in 1997 and is now an associate professor in human development at the University of Texas at Austin. Her research centers on self-concept development, specifically the development of self-compassion. She teaches workshops on self-compassion for clinicians, alongside Chris Germer at Harvard University. She is the author of the book *Self-Compassion: Stop Beating Yourself Up and Leave Insecurity Behind.* Kristin lives in the countryside in Elgin, Texas, with her husband, Rupert Isaacson—an author and a human rights activist—and their young son, Rowan. She and her family were featured in the film and book called *The Horse Boy*, about their journey through Mongolia to search for a cure for their son's autism. She is also the co-founder of the Horse Boy Foundation. (www.Self-Compassion.org; www.HorseBoyFoundation.org)

THE INTERVIEW
Though I had met her husband, Rupert, I finally had the privilege of meeting Kristin and their son, Rowan, in person when she graciously agreed to be interviewed for the book and invited me to dinner. She is beyond lovely, funny, and sharp, and together she and Rupert are a unique and impressive couple. You can go witness that in the beautiful movie and book *The Horse Boy*. I didn't know what Kristin's epiphany would be, but I assumed it probably had something to do with that project. Once again, surprise! It

was not what I was expecting, and her epiphany of self-compassion changed something inside me, right on the spot.

View the Interview:

www.epiphanychannel.com/people/kristin-neff

*   *   *

I started practicing Buddhism when I was in graduate school at Berkeley, and I would go to this weekly evening sitting meditation group. I was learning mindfulness meditation, and it was going pretty well, but I couldn't really get it. It takes a while to figure out what mindfulness is and how you can really use it in your life.

One night at the group a woman started talking about self-compassion—how important it was to have compassion for yourself—and the fact that you couldn't really be fully compassionate with others until you were compassionate to yourself. I remember her talk and that night perfectly. It was like a light bulb went on over my head when she was explaining that this was a way you could relate to yourself. It had never dawned on me before that we actually can take the same care and nurturing stance toward ourselves that we're told to take with the people we care about—and it wouldn't be the same as self-indulgence! It was a radical mind shift for me.

In our culture we don't really talk about having compassion for ourselves. We talk about being compassionate to other people, to be kind, to be giving, to be nurturing to others. But toward yourself, the idea is you're supposed to be self-critical—really hard and tough on yourself—to motivate yourself. I had always been pretty self-critical, and at the time this happened, I was experiencing a lot of changes in my life. I was going through a divorce and had started a relationship with Rupert, who is now my husband. My ex-husband was not at all happy with how I was handling things. I felt a lot of guilt and shame, and it was a very difficult time. But during that talk, I realized for the first time that it was actually possible to have compassion for *myself*. For me, this was an epiphany.

I suddenly understood: "I wouldn't talk to or treat a friend *half* as horribly as I talk to or treat myself. Why am I doing this to myself? Stop it." I could act like a kind, compassionate, caring friend to *myself*. And once I did—once I started being my *own* kind, compassionate, caring friend—everything in my life changed, both personally and professionally.

This was 1998 and my last year at Berkeley. I was finishing up my dissertation and I was doing a two-year postdoctoral period with a woman who is one of the leading self-esteem researchers. I was very interested in self-concept—how people think about themselves. As I started reviewing the self-esteem literature, I realized that psychology was falling out of love with self-esteem. New research was coming out saying there's a lot of downsides to self-esteem, like narcissism. Narcissism and self-esteem go hand in hand. We actually have a narcissism epidemic in this country. We've got higher rates of narcissism than have ever been recorded, partly because kids are raised so much with this unconditional praise, and unfortunately, self-esteem can be confused with thinking you're better than other people. In our culture, being average is not okay—we have to be above average to be okay. The result of that is we're always trying to put other people down to prop ourselves up, and many people are ego-defensive, meaning they can't admit when they've done something wrong because it makes them feel bad about themselves.

So I thought instead of emphasizing self-esteem, what if we were to emphasize self-compassion and start putting the focus on caring about yourself, not because you're special or above average, but because we're humans in the shared human condition? What if we're kind to ourselves just because we're conscious beings who feel pain and want to be happy? With this shift, we can feel good about ourselves, but without having to feel better than other people. I thought maybe we could frame this as an alternative, as a way to help kids and adults to feel good about themselves, by embracing this warm, compassionate, openhearted way of being.

When I started researching it, I discovered it had only been written about in Buddhism; no one in academia had written about it all. So I decided to be brave. When I got to the University of Texas at Austin, one of the first things I did was publish an article defining self-compassion based on my understanding, and then I created a scale to measure it. Then I started doing research which has shown that self-compassion is as powerful a predictor of positive mental health as self-esteem is, but without the problems related to self-esteem, like narcissism. It seems that self-compassion is a very good way to encourage feeling good about yourself without hurting other people. It's really exciting for me as a scientist to be one of the first to explore and research self-compassion and share that work with others. It seems to be impacting people's lives positively. I feel really grateful to be able to be one of the people putting this message forward.

Throughout the years, my practice of self-compassion has absolutely saved my life in many ways. For example, my son, Rowan, was diagnosed with severe autism when he was about two and a half. It was incredibly painful. I already had a very well-established practice of self-compassion by this point, though. What it enabled me to do was, instead of just immediately going into problem-solving mode, which I did later, I really took the time to give myself compassion for how hard it was. I let myself feel my grief; I let myself feel my pain. I gave myself a lot of hugs, nurturing, kindness, and support, and really just helped myself get through it in a very, very compassionate way, as I would with a dear friend or beloved family member.

Practicing self-compassion also helped me have a lot of energy to deal with Rowan. If he was throwing an earsplitting tantrum, or pooped his pants in public and I had to change them, or I had to deal with some other really difficult behavior, I would actually stop and give myself compassion. I would think, "You know, this is really hard right now. I'm going to notice that it's difficult. I'm going to feel compassion, and concern, and caring for the fact this is really hard right now. And as I go through the next steps that I have to do, I'm going to do it held in this space of compassion, care, and nurturing." It makes it a lot easier. There's even some research now that shows if you give yourself compassion, you're actually resetting your chemistry and flooding yourself with oxytocin and natural opiates, so you feel calm, accepted, supported, and able to get through that next moment with a lot more calm and clarity.

Self-compassion has been a wonderful gift for me, and I hope that more people can become aware of it because it really does have a positive effect on how you deal with the difficulties in your life.

HEALINGS

heal : to cause an undesirable condition to be overcome; to mend; to restore to original purity or integrity; to restore a person to spiritual wholeness; to become whole and sound; to return to health

Epiphanies are about transformation. You do it through a leap
of the heart. And the next thing you know, physically, emotion-
ally, or mentally, you're living a different story.

—RUPERT ISAACSON

RUPERT ISAACSON is an author and activist born in London
to a South African mother and a Zimbabwean father. He is the
founding director of the Indigenous Land Rights Fund, a nonprofit organization that helps displaced indigenous tribes obtain
tenure of their ancestral land, and of the Horse Boy Foundation,
which provides the opportunity for children to work with horses
and nature. *The Healing Land*, Isaacson's first book, was a 2004
New York Times Notable Book. His work has appeared in the
*Daily Telegraph, Esquire, National Geographic, Independent on
Sunday, Condé Nast Traveler, Daily Mail*, and *Field*. He lives in
Elgin, Texas, just outside of Austin, with his wife, Kristin, and
their son, Rowan. In the summer of 2007, Rupert and his family
went to Mongolia, where they journeyed on horseback from shaman to shaman searching for a way to heal their son. The story of
this incredible journey is told in Isaacson's bestselling book *The
Horse Boy*, which has also been captured in a documentary film
by the same title. (www.HorseBoyMovie.com)

THE INTERVIEW

A mutual friend of Rupert's and mine asked me to check out a
trailer on YouTube for an independent film. I finally watched it
a few days later and was mesmerized. It was the original *Horse
Boy* movie trailer. Rupert did the voice-over, but you could never
really see his face, only his hair. Several weeks later I was driving down South Congress Avenue during South by Southwest,

Austin's music and film festival, when in my peripheral vision I saw a man on a horse, riding down the avenue. Once I passed him I realized, "Wait, that man had longish blond hair and was on a horse…" I pulled over, turned around, and screamed out my window at him, "Are you the *Horse Boy* guy?!" And that was the beginning of a beautiful friendship. I interviewed him and his wife, Kristin, and had the pleasure of meeting and holding a conversation—several, in fact—with the Horse Boy himself, his son, Rowan, at their enchanting place in Elgin, Texas.

View the Interview:
www.epiphanychannel.com/people/rupert-isaacson

*   *   *

My son was diagnosed with severe autism in 2004. Initially we were told by the best-intentioned experts, therapists, and doctors that there wasn't really anything we could do to help him, which was extremely depressing. I understood why they were saying this: Western medicine didn't really offer any answers. But there was another part of me that said, "No. There is probably something we can do. We just don't know what it is yet."

I am a lifelong horseman. I grew up training horses, and I've always been around them. But I stopped riding when Rowan was diagnosed because I thought he was unsafe around them. He was too inconsistent in his movements. He would spook them, I thought, so I stopped riding and gave up owning horses. That for me meant giving up a major passion of mine, so that spiraled me further down into depression.

However, one day in that same year that he was diagnosed, I noticed that Rowan was calmer—he didn't have such terrible neurologically induced tantrums—when he was out in the woods. We're lucky we live in the country and have lots of trails cut in the woods, so I could spend hours walking them with him.

One day Rowan got away from me and went through my

neighbor's fence into the horse pasture. He threw himself under the feet of a notoriously grumpy old quarter horse mare named Betsy. Betsy is very dominant, very much the boss mare of her herd.

He literally tossed himself on his back right under her, and I thought she was going to trample him. But instead Betsy did something quite extraordinary. She bent her head and began to lick and chew with her mouth and half close her eyes. In horse language, those are gestures of submission, which they do when they recognize someone else higher in the hierarchy. I have never seen a horse spontaneously offer that behavior to a human being before, much less an autistic, babbling two-and-a-half-year-old.

That same year, I was working hard on human rights issues. My funny mixed-up family is from Africa. And to cut a long story short, I work with indigenous groups in Africa helping displaced tribes get their land back. The tribes that I work with all have a very strong tradition of healing through the use of laying on of hands, prayer, and altered states of consciousness. I've seen their healing techniques work time and time again—although these people also use Western medicine when it's around, but it's usually not around them that often.

The same year Rowan met Betsy, I had to bring a delegation of Bushmen from Botswana to the United Nations in New York and to the U.S. State Department. We were staging a protest against the seizure of their land for diamond mines, and associated abuses, including torture. Some of those guys on that delegation were trained healers in their culture. They met Rowan and very casually offered to do a bit of work on him—ritual songs and prayers. I thought, "Why not? The worst thing that can happen is nothing."

For those four days that they were with him, he really did start to lose some of his obsessive behaviors. However, when they went away, he fell back into the worst of his symptoms. He was still going every day to visit Betsy, so one day I decided I should give up the idea that it was too dangerous for him and take him riding.

I spoke to Betsy's owner, my very old-school southern gentleman neighbor, and he said we should have at it.

So I put a saddle on Betsy and said to Rowan, "Do you want to get up?" It was absolutely a rhetorical question. I didn't expect an answer. I'd never had any lucid expressive language from him before. But to my utter shock, he *said* something: "Up." So I climbed up behind him, and asked him something else: "Do you want to go to the woods or the pond?"

Again, I didn't expect an answer. Then he spoke again: "To the pond." I thought, "Well, maybe he's just echoing me." When we got down to the pond, he saw a heron get up and fly. And he said, "Heron." I hadn't known he even understood that word! He was talking to me. *My son was talking to me for the first time.*

Then he started directing me which way and how fast and slow to go! It was literally like the cork had come out of the bottle. When we got back to the barn and I took Rowan off Betsy, I put it all together in my mind. Two things had had this radically positive effect on Rowan: the horse and the shamans. Where is a place in the world that combines these elements? If I could take Rowan to a place that combined shamanic, traditional healing and horses, I knew, just *knew*, that there would be some kind of radical change. Then suddenly it came to me—it's Mongolia. I just had this feeling of the heart: "We have to go to Mongolia. It's the one place on the planet that combines shamanic healing with horses." Mongolia is the home of the horse, where *Equus caballus* was first domesticated six thousand years ago. It's the oldest horse culture on the planet, and there is still a very strong system of shamanism there, even though it was suppressed under Communism. I had this strong gut feeling if we did it, if we went there, there would be some really strong positive change with Rowan. I couldn't say what it would be, but I knew it clear as day. People talk about your gut feelings, but this was literally like a hand pulling on my diaphragm. It was physical, not cerebral at all. I felt as if God were speaking to me. It wasn't a rational decision—it was a compulsion, like I got pulled by my collar. I didn't even have a choice.

So I started doing research and I found out that even the met-aphors and language that shamanic healers use is connected to horses. For example, when they go into their trance they call that "riding the wind horse." And we also have a saying in England, "There's naught so good for the inside of a man as the outside of a horse." We know for some reason, intuitively, that horses make us feel better. Having been around horses my whole life, I've seen what we call in England "riding for the disabled" and in the States "therapeutic riding."

I fielded the idea to Kristin, my wife, who said, "No way." At that point, Rowan was actually too young to withstand the rigors of a trip like that. So I sat on the idea for a couple of years. Throughout that time, we lived in the saddle together, Rowan and I. And his language just kept coming and coming. But his inconti-nence, his tantrums, his inability to make friends, all these prob-lems remained. So now that he was older, Kristin finally agreed that we could go to Mongolia.

When we got there, I thought I had made a big mistake. The first ritual with the shamans was too much—too long, too loud, with too much stimulation—and Rowan hated it. But after about an hour something changed in Rowan. He tuned in to the ritual, started laughing and joking and trying to tickle the shamans and such. Then he turned to this little six-year-old boy who was there, opened his arms, and said, "Mongolian brother." And that was it. I realized, "Oh my God. It's working." We decided to keep at it. The last shaman worked on Rowan for three days.

The shaman told us, "Starting tomorrow, the things that drive you crazy, the incontinence, and the tantrums, you'll see those start to go." I wasn't exactly skeptical because by then I was used to strange things happening. But I didn't want to be disappointed. I was guarding my heart, because it was already breaking.

About twenty-four hours later, Rowan did his first intentional poop by the riverbank, and then two days after that, his first in an actual toilet. He has only had six more tantrums in his life. Speech therapists had told us that they would never get anywhere with

Rowan and had basically given up. He carries on conversations now. The change in him is nothing short of *radical*, and I really can't explain it. I'm not here to sort of be a born-again shamanist or say shamanism cures autism or horses cure autism. Rowan's still autistic. It's just that he's so functional within his autism now that it comes across much more as sort of a quirk. Rowan's dys-functions—the incontinence, the tantrums, the inability to talk, the social isolation—are gone. All I can say is that in his case, it happened through the horses and those healers.

I expect people to be skeptical. Skepticism is very healthy. You don't want people showing up saying, "Give me $10,000, I'm a shaman, and I'm going to cure your kid of autism." Even the price tags on regular therapies, that frequently don't work, are $50,000-$80,000 a year. So people have to be careful.

That said, I'd much rather people thought that I was com-pletely bonkers and have Rowan living the way he does now than satisfy their skepticism and have him living as he did before. The fact is, we got results. Everything changed for us. Everything.

I've written a book, and we made a film about our experience. I am a writer and a journalist, and it's in my blood to write about what I do. But the movie happened because my friend Michael, who's a filmmaker, wanted to do it. Kristin and I agreed, think-ing, "If there is a real change and we've got it on camera, then that adds to the body of knowledge out there. And if nothing happens, at least we've had this amazing adventure together as a family." Thankfully, both the book and film have been received quite well and seem to be touching other lives besides our own.

Since we've had such astounding results using horses and nature with Rowan, I wanted to make that option available to people who normally wouldn't have access. We started a nonprofit to fund a place where we could work with kids on the autism spectrum using horses, called the Horse Boy Foundation. We run it purely on donations, so money doesn't stand in the way for any-one. We're growing every year and we love this work.

Epiphanies are about transformation, leaping from one situation to another situation. How do you do it? How do you get there? How do you leap? You do it through a leap of the heart. And if that leap of the heart happens through a sort of leap in story, you decide to change the story. You decide to go to a new chapter in the story. And you do. Physically, or emotionally, or mentally. And the next thing you know, you're living a different story.

Imagine, believe and move toward your "what-ifs."
—KATE MILLIKEN

KATE MILLIKEN is a film and television producer and the founder of Milligrace Productions, a company specializing in twelve-to-fifteen-minute personal documentaries that are equal parts *This Is Your Life* and *A&E Biography*. Milliken has worked in television for more than fifteen years, beginning as a correspondent for a college cable company focused on reality-based TV, then moving on to cover the world of alternative sports such as snowboarding, mountain biking, and monster trucks for the Outdoor Life Network, Oxygen, Fox Sports Net, TNT, and TNN. She has also been a producer for ABC's *The View* and for VH-1, and is the creator and subject of *Kate's Counterpane*, a Web-based documentary about her journey of being diagnosed with and battling multiple sclerosis and the founder of MyCounterpane.com to connect people with chronic diseases to share information and not feel so alone. She currently resides with her husband and two children in New York. (www.milligrace.com; www.katescounterpane.com; www.mycounterpane.com)

THE INTERVIEW

Three people I know have been diagnosed with multiple sclerosis, two of them dear friends. In an airport I picked up a *Marie Claire* that featured an article on Kate and her journey with the disease. I am a big believer in utilizing both traditional Western medicine and complementary healing modalities. My philosophy is, "Whatever works," which is exactly what Kate seemed to be saying. I clipped the article and emailed links to her website to my friends who have MS. They both called to say that it really helped them. During one of those calls I realized that I should reach out to Kate. We conducted our interview on the phone a few weeks before my book was due. Kate asked me to watch her forty-five-minute film on her site before I wrote about her, and I am so glad I did! The film is innovative, entertaining, informative, moving, and funny—just like her. (But go see it for yourself.) She said she gets at least three calls a week from people who have found the film helpful in thinking about their own journeys with this disease, and her "believe in the what-ifs" exercise has worked wonders in my life.

View the Interview:
www.epiphanychannel.com/people/kate-milliken

*   *   *

In July 2004, I was thirty-two years old and my fiancé broke off our engagement two months before the wedding. One day we were en route to happiness, and the next he walked out the door. I still don't know why. And he didn't have the ability to tell me. I've come to peace with that now, but at the time I was crushed, especially because I am one of those people who wants the answers to things.

Suddenly I was entirely on my own at thirty-two years old. I realized for the first time that I had to take responsibility for myself and start living on my own terms. The broken engagement forced me to do a lot of reflection on what I wanted to do with my life. I'd been an on-camera sports reporter and television producer; I knew I liked television, but it wasn't quite working for me as a career. I decided to start my own business, creating mini-documentaries for private clients. It's what I do now and it has been a total joy: I love what I do.

I had been working incredibly hard to get my business off the ground, and by December 2006 it was finally thriving. My heart was healed, and I felt I could move forward with my life.

Two weeks from that exact moment, two days before Christmas, I was in the hospital. In the course of a single week, I had gone from being incredibly active to finding I couldn't put one leg in front of the other. The doctors found a lesion on my C-4 vertebra, in a spot that could have left me paralyzed. I was stunned when they told me the diagnosis: multiple sclerosis (MS), an autoimmune disease that causes your body to attack itself and eat the myelin that protects your nerves.

MS is terrifying, especially when your body starts acting weird. My present was scary, and my future was even scarier. I lay there wondering why, when everything seemed to be going so well, something like *this* had to happen. My reaction wasn't "Wah, poor me." It was much more cerebral, more like: "This is interesting." And then, on my second day in the hospital, I found myself blurting out, "You know, maybe this will be the best thing that ever happened to me." Needless to say, everyone thought I was crazy and in complete denial. But really, that was the start of my epiphany.

So I began my journey with MS. I suffered the symptoms and began injecting myself with Copaxone, one of the medications in the MS world that can make a positive difference. Copaxone reduces the chance of a relapse by 35 percent, changing the fight against MS from what it used to be fifteen years ago.

But I also knew I had to get control over my stress and my anxiety, since those things trigger MS episodes—which vary from things like a tingling in areas of your body to not being able to walk properly, even going blind. It's such a catch-22 because the disease makes you tired and stressed, which causes you to start feeling really weird, which stresses you out worse because you think you're going into an episode...and that is the worst possible thing because it only exacerbates the MS. The whole goal of dealing with MS is never to inflame your body enough that it starts eating itself. That means staying away from stressful or exhausting situations.

So here I was living in New York City, arguably one of the

most stressful places to live on earth. And, just to add to the drama, I'm thirty-five and single. So thirty-five, single, living in New York, and now I have MS? *This* is really going to help my love life—how can you even *think* you're going to get a boyfriend when you have to tell him that you have a disease that could put you in a wheelchair? I realized I had to find a way to stop, right in the current of the biggest, busiest city in the world, and find a place of calm, and accept my age and situation. I had to figure out a way to get control of myself, and really, really evaluate and find out how this was going to be the best thing that ever happened to me.

One day I dragged myself to a yoga class—one of the things I had been using to help manage my anxiety—and my body started tingling like crazy. I was scared I was going into an episode. I lay on my back on my mat, with tears just streaming down my face because I felt so bad. The teacher came over to me and asked me what was going on. I told him, and he touched my shoulder and said, "It's okay. You're here."

And that was it. That moment changed everything. His words reverberated in my mind: "You're here. You are here." I wasn't dead. I was *here*. I was fighting. In yoga class, you do the warrior poses, so I told myself, "You *are* a warrior!" From that moment on, everything zoomed right in. I was present and I stayed present. Now I knew what that meant and how important it was. Every time I felt myself not being present, I brought myself back with the mantra "I'm here." The future, the unknown, is scary. And I cannot get scared. It causes adrenaline in my body, which feeds the MS. I've got to stay in the known, which is now. That gave me control over my mind when it wanted to jump into the negative zone.

From that point on, my world opened up. I developed other affirmations to help. I would walk down the street, and my mind would start generating thoughts like "I'm so screwed," "I'm never going to make it," or "I'm never going to be able to have children because I'm never going to find somebody." But every time these negative thoughts would come, I would just say, "Out. Out, out, out." Every time I saw someone in a wheelchair, I would say out loud, "Not today. Not today." I'm sure I seemed like a crazy person! But it didn't matter—I was not going to let my mind go to those places, so I'd say these things out loud.

I got turned on to an osteopath, Dr. George Kessler, who really helped me. Not only did he give me nutritional supplements, but he gave me a whole different way of approaching MS. He said, "MS is an inflammation, and what might be inflaming you? I don't use the word *disease*. Your body is going through a really interesting *process*." This radically different perspective was incredibly empowering, and I would even say it helped turn this journey into becoming somewhat exciting.

This is where the third and probably most powerful moment of my epiphany emerged. I started to think, "*What if . . . ?*" *What if* I was able to actually reverse my lesion? *What if* on Christmas Eve I could make a toast to my parents and tell them that I'd done that? *What if* that was possible? I would fantasize about it, and my body would fill with this incredible excitement—it reminded me of those first-date hormones you feel. I took a card and put it on my mirror, with two words: *Reverse it*. And every single moment for five months in the back of my mind I repeated this as a mantra. When I wasn't saying "Out" and "Not today," it was "Reverse it." Reverse it, reverse it, reverse it, *reverse it*. And I never stopped dreaming about how amazing it would be if that happened.

I evaluated my life in terms of stress, diet, and rest. For the rest of that year, I kept up my regimen with the supplements from Dr. Kessler, took my Copaxone shots religiously, practiced breathing, allowed myself to sleep in, stopped thinking I was lazy if I took a nap, and did all the other things I could to support my healing and getting my MS under control. That meant yoga, reiki healing, and of course my mantras. I accepted that this was my new world. I lived in both realms of conventional and complementary medicine and took the best of what both had to offer. I lived in this whole world of possibility that was intoxicating. And I started feeling a lot better.

In December 2007, I went in to check the status of my MS,

which is done by MRI. We got the MRI back—I filmed this, actually—*and the radiologist couldn't find the lesion on the scans!* My doctor was shocked and admitted that he had seen that happen in less than 1 percent of his patients.

There were times during the active phase of my illness that I was so lonely. I would be catching a taxi, or by myself on a Saturday night in my bed, and I would just say out loud, *"Believe." Believe* it's all going to come around, and *what if* it does? *What if* I get the guy that I want? How amazing is it going to feel when I'm standing at the altar? How beautiful will it be when I find the guy?

I was probably going out once a week at this point, and on a blind date I met Tyler. Tyler's mother suffers from ataxia, which is a neurological symptom much like MS that attacks the central nervous system. He had seen the worst of it, and when I told him about my MS, he basically said, "I understand it's a crap shoot, and I'm willing to take the gamble. It doesn't define our relationship."

We dated. We were engaged after five months. We got married after nine months, and right now I am five and a half months pregnant. My life has drastically altered, and I am in a very happy place.

My epiphanies were real, drastic shifts in energy and changes of perspective that came in a moment of clarity. They centered on generating my own sense of hope and allowing an open channel of faith and possibility. I also learned that it's key not to feel so sorry for yourself that it cripples you and keeps you from looking for guidance and clues. Challenges in life can be gifts—lessons in taking risks, taking leaps of faith, conquering obstacles, making things happen, and believing in the what-ifs. This is what makes us grow, and for me, what makes life exciting.

An epiphany is like a key is turned in a lock
inside you, and you're free.
—JENIFER CHILTON

JENIFER CHILTON, is a senior lecturer at the University of Texas at Tyler and co-coordinates the community health program there. She holds a Ph.D. in nursing and her current research focus is on epiphanies and wellness. She received a bachelor's degree in education from the University of Texas at Austin, a bachelor's in nursing from the University of Kansas, and her master's degree in nursing from the University of Texas at Tyler. She resides in Jacksonville, Texas, with her husband and three awesome kids. (www.UTTyler.edu)

THE INTERVIEW
A few days after I launched EpiphanyChannel.com, I received an email from Jeni explaining that she was a nurse researcher completing a study on epiphanies and how they impact wellness. She thought I might be interested in her findings, and of course I was! It is a complete fluke that we are both from Texas, and fortunately it was easy for me to meet with her a few months later in Tyler, Texas. In addition to learning more about her work trying to facilitate epiphanies in the realm of medicine to promote healing, I discovered that it was her own epiphany that prompted her research. I asked her what her epiphany was, and she was hesitant to tell the story at first—she had never told anyone about it before. I feel privileged that she felt comfortable enough to share her experience with me and agreed to let me include it in the book.

*   *   *

When I was about seventeen, I developed an eating disorder. I remember the moment that triggered my bulimia. I was running across the gym, and my dance instructor called out in front of the whole group, "Jeni, have you lost weight?" I said, "Yes, ma'am." She told me, "Keep it up. You look *fantastic*." I wouldn't eat dinner that night.

That's how it all started. I was in dance and was wearing tights all the time. My body was changing. I felt awkward and was *constantly* comparing myself to other people. I had to be perfect.

It might surprise you, but I had a happy, happy family. My mom is great. She's now seventy-eight, but you'd never know it. She has so much energy and is always positive. Growing up, I didn't know how to deal with anything negative—at all. I was changing physically and emotionally, and I was uncomfortable about it. But I couldn't talk to her or anyone else about it. Also, until that point, it had been easy *not* to have sex. Good girls didn't have sex (at least not in Texas, where I was growing up). But when I hit eighteen, I was finally kind of... interested. And I felt guilty about that. I didn't feel I could go talk to her about that either, and I *definitely* wasn't going to talk to my dad. So I buried that shame in an eating disorder.

Fast-forward three years. I was still bulimic, and was teaching dance at a summer camp. One day I was alone walking in the woods and I heard this voice in my head that was very, very clear. It simply said, "Why are you hurting Me? Your body is My temple. I reside in you." And I knew that voice was God's. I went to my knees and prayed, saying, "God, I'm so sorry. Forgive me for hurting You. I don't care anymore. I'll be fat or I'll be whatever I am, but I won't hurt what is Yours." In my mind, I'd accepted I was fat, at all of 134 pounds. It's scary how skewed your sense of self can be. But in that moment, I knew that I would never purposely throw up again. And that was that. The struggle was over. I never did it again. I really was healed.

The amazing thing to me was that after that healing, I *lost weight*! I started eating—eating right—and started running and exercising. The next thing I knew, I looked down at the scale and saw 125 pounds. The difference was that this time I exercised and ate right to be fit and strong—not to be thin. I tried out for the dance team at the University of Texas at Austin and made it. I was finally healthy.

What was strange about the epiphany is that I never felt the need to discuss it with anyone. I moved forward and did not think about it anymore. I went to nursing school, which I loved, and started a family before I graduated. I stayed home for twelve years to raise my children but eventually became a school nurse. My primary interest was working with adolescent females, and I developed a program designed to improve wellness in this population. Now that I think about it, my interest in this group probably had a lot more to do with the struggles I had at that age than I realized.

As a school nurse, I primarily worked with girls on the drill team. What was driving me crazy was that these girls were motivated: they were on the drill team and they had parental support. They should have been the healthy girls, but they weren't. They were overweight, unhappy, getting pregnant, the whole thing. And in working with them, I suddenly remembered that moment in the woods when my bulimia was healed. For the first time, I wondered what had made me forget that experience. I wondered what I should even call it. I've referred to it as an "I know that I know" moment. I've had several such times in my life, when I knew what path to follow, even if on paper it looked goofy. Some things don't make sense to outsiders, but I know they're logical for my life.

Such an experience is like a key is turned in a lock inside you, and you're free. People could be struggling their whole lives trying to fix a problem they can't overcome. Then they have one of these moments, and boom, they start a new journey. I've had doctors say no one's ever really healed from an eating disorder, but I have to say they're wrong.

During this time, I had started a graduate program and was writing a concept analysis paper, and I wanted to write about this experience. So I went to my professor and told her I was searching for the right word to explain this phenomenon. She said, "That's an epiphany." I insisted, "Okay, but what's the medical word?" She shrugged and told me, "There isn't one." So I started researching this kind of experience after I graduated from the program. I wanted to figure it out, "Is this real?" In the course of my study I determined that yes, it absolutely is. I define an epiphany as an internal perspective that encompasses your mind, body, and spirit. It's more than an intellectual process. It's not a cognitive decision. When it happens, you are different, and you can't go back. You can't pretend like it didn't happen.

I had buried my epiphany out of shame about an eating disorder. I'm embarrassed even now that I had any of that. This is the first time I've ever talked about it with anyone, even my husband. But now I have to admit that that's what happened to me—I had an epiphany, and I was free. I became healthy. I changed. I'm now employed as a full-time faculty member at the University of Texas at Tyler and am a clinical instructor in community health. My research is showing that if we can facilitate the induction of epiphanies, it can lead to greater health and well-being. I am getting my doctorate and researching epiphanies because I want to try to help others have epiphany experiences and find ways to healing and freedom.

*Love is all that matters. Love is all that we're here for. When
we lose sight of love, everything goes dark and bleak.*

—LAURIAN SCOTT

LAURIAN SCOTT describes herself as, "first and foremost, wife to
John and mother to five beautiful children, Aslan, Thisbe, Noah,
Ovid and Hattie." Formerly a copywriter, freelance writer, and story
analyst for feature films, today she lectures across the country on
behalf of her family's foundation, the Olive Branch Fund: A Thisbe
and Noah Scott Legacy, including keynote speaking engagements
in health care forums. She also advocates for families affected by
Brown-Vialetto-Van Laere (BVVL) syndrome as the director of
patient outreach and the international spokeswoman for BVVL
International. She is the co-owner of ETS Publishing House and
author of the children's book *Thisbe's Promise*, inspired by her
daughter, and is currently working on a book inspired by her son.
(www.ETSpublishinghouse.com; www.TheOliveBranchFund.org)

THE INTERVIEW

My sister suggested that I contact John, Laurian's husband, about
being interviewed for the project. Skip, as we call him, used to
date my sister and I love him, but we hadn't spoken in forever.
When we got in contact, it was great to reconnect, but very hard
to hear what he and his family have been through. He encouraged
me to speak with his wife, Laurian, about her epiphany. She and
I had never so much as said hello, but she was graciously open,
honest, and vulnerable, and this is still one of the most intense
and emotional interviews I've experienced. I couldn't stop thinking about the Scotts and what they accomplished in the midst of
debilitating grief, driven by a fierce love for their children and

for other families and children in the world. I am also thrilled to
report that about a year after our interview, as a direct result of
their research efforts in genetics, Laurian and John's twins, Ovid
and Hattie (yes, a boy and a girl!) were born and are healthy and
thriving.

*   *   *

The greatest thing that has happened to me, when everything
just seemed to fall into place, was when I met my husband, John.
Before that, giving birth to my daughter from a previous marriage
was the high point, but when I met John, my whole life took a
new, wonderful direction.

We had a very brief courtship and got married. Three months
later I was pregnant with our daughter, Thisbe. She was born
healthy, beautiful, and perfect. I found myself at a point in life
where, instead of asking for anything in prayers, I was always
giving thanks, constantly saying thank You for this, thank You
for that. I grew up Episcopal, not like a devout Christian, but I
believed in God, and I usually prayed whenever I needed something. But here I'd come to a place in life where really I didn't *need*
anything else. In hindsight, I don't know if that's ever where you
want to be, where you have everything to lose.

One day when Thisbe was about sixteen months old, she
started to have a little wheeze, then other puzzling symptoms. We
took her to the doctor, but we weren't really worried; the doctors
thought that a virus had gotten ahold of her and attacked her
vocal chords. At that point, we had no idea that Thisbe might
have anything serious. That same month, I found myself pregnant
with our son, Noah.

Thisbe kept getting worse, and within five months the doctors
gave her a truly horrific diagnosis: a very rare, progressive degenerative motor neuron disease called Brown-Vialetto-Van Laere
syndrome (BVVL). It's like a toddler form of ALS or Lou Geh-

rig's disease: like ALS, it has no cure, and the pain and suffering involved are excruciating. Instead of giving in to despair, I took this diagnosis as a challenge. While all the literature said there was no way I could save her, I was not about to lose my daughter. John and I agreed: we would do whatever it took. So we tried every single holistic, natural, medical, and religious approach that we possibly could to save her.

Thisbe was sick for seventeen months. I've never fought for anything so hard in all of my life: I gave everything of myself, mentally, emotionally, spiritually. But we still lost her. I cannot describe our shock and devastation. It was as if we still didn't expect it, even though she had kept getting worse and we *knew*. We just couldn't believe we had lost her.

About a month after we lost Thisbe, Noah, who was ten months old by now, was in the bathtub, and I noticed that his eyelid was drooping. That had been one of Thisbe's symptoms. Immediately I took him to the doctor, and they put him through a battery of tests. Everything came back okay. His doctors were certain there was no way he too happened to have this rare disease. But two months later, we had him tested again, and this time they confirmed hearing loss, another symptom of Thisbe's disease. Noah also had BVVL. The doctors confirmed it. Just months after losing our daughter, we were faced with losing our son.

By this point, I was barely hanging on. I wasn't the same person who had taken care of Thisbe. I didn't believe in miracles anymore. So I just kind of amassed around me people who did—even strangers, dozens of strangers from a church here in Franklin. I didn't go to church anymore. But they came on. I basically said to them, "I don't believe in anything good. But I need for somebody to, because Noah deserves it."

He died nine months after his symptoms started.

When Noah died, it stole my soul. For me, hope died with Thisbe and Noah. So did my faith. I even felt I'd lost the ability to love. I couldn't feel anything outside the pain, the ache to be with my children again. I didn't know if there was a God. I really hoped for their sakes that there was, and that they were in a better place. I just wanted to be wherever they were. I haven't told anybody this, but I spent that next year longing to "accidentally" leave this world, and sort of trying to.

I didn't want to do anything on purpose, because I wasn't sure if there was a God, and if there was, there might be *rules*. And if there were rules, did that mean that if I decided to end it myself then I would never see my children again? My mind got trapped in this fantasy of going wherever they were—if only I could skip through these rules of the God I wasn't even sure I believed in, and most probably didn't. That became a lot of abusing prescription drugs. I'd go to sleep some nights not knowing if I would wake up, thinking, "I really don't know how many it takes to kill someone, so it won't be my fault if something happens." It was like I was trying to trick God. I know this all sounds crazy because it is. I can't really explain how you are in that state. But I just needed out, and I just didn't want life anymore. I was in a *very* dark place, and no one could reach me.

It finally got to the point where on any given day it wasn't clear if I'd make it through to the next. My husband and family intervened. They were right and I knew it, so I agreed to go away and get some help. They let me choose where I wanted to go.

We live in Tennessee now, but I grew up spending a lot of time in California, and I remembered this monastery at St. Lucia, just south of Big Sur. I didn't even know what type of monastery it was, or what faith they practiced—but that is where I knew I had to go. My family was puzzled by my choice, but they sent me there for a week. It was a Catholic monastery, we found out, and I don't know a thing about the Catholic faith, but I was open to just about anything. My week there was mostly a silent retreat, but it was a conversation with a priest there named Father Bernard that changed my life.

Father Bernard was so compassionate when I told him my story that I just broke down. Then *he* started breaking down. He wept with me as I've never seen a sixty-five-year-old man weep before. I said to him, "I don't feel love for anyone anymore. I don't even *feel*. I know I love my husband, and my daughter, and my dad and my mom and sister. But I don't *feel* love for anyone. I just don't feel it." I was afraid that I was this terrible person, and if I were, that would make me unable to be accepted by God and get into heaven and get to see my children—if there even is a God and a heaven.

And Father Bernard said to me, "If someone was burning at the stake, do you think if there were a person being beaten in her line of vision, that the person being burned could feel or think about that pain of the other person when her skin was being licked by the flames?"

I thought about it a second. "No."

"You're being burned at the stake right now, Laurian, and it's okay that you can't feel outside of the flames. God knows it's okay that you can't feel outside of the flames."

Then I asked, "What if I don't believe in Jesus? What if I don't believe in God?"

"Well, you do believe in God because you already have God."

"But I don't. I hate God. Actually, if God exists, I hate Him."

"No, you don't. Because you love your children. And when you love your children, you have God because God is love."

It was that simple. What he told me brought me peace. It was like a sigh—a long, long sigh. I thought, "Okay, so I'm going to be okay. I don't really have to play by any rules. Maybe I can't take my own life, but I don't have to just believe in Jesus, or just do this or that, or go to this church to get to heaven. Really, all I have to do is just live according to love and I'm going to be okay."

I learned that the only thing I'd never lost is the eternal flame of love I have for my children. That sits right here in my core. In my search for God, the only thing I can say I really believe in right now is love. That is the one thing that I can palpably, tangibly say that I absolutely know. The only part of the Bible I believe in right now is that God is love, and I believe in love. Right now, it's love that guides me. Love is all that matters. Love is all that we're here for. And when we lose sight of love, everything goes dark and bleak.

My husband and I have this urge to give the world the piece of Thisbe and Noah that was here, which was beauty, love, and everything good. As long as we can give that back to the world, then they're still living somehow through us, and we can honor them and their lives. To do this, we've established a foundation called the Olive Branch Fund: A Thisbe and Noah Scott Legacy. We actually started it when Noah was sick, a few months before he died. In our very last-ditch effort to save him, a doctor told us that no one could really help us until the gene is found that causes BVVL. We had no idea how to go about helping science to do that, so we sat down to figure it out. We are still finding our way—and only with the incredible support and help of our friends and family would any of this be possible. We started the Olive Branch Fund to be able to pay a researcher to find the gene. Noah died before we could find the gene and a cure, but just last month we did identify the gene that causes BVVL. We will keep going until we find a cure, and our organization has evolved and is still evolving into an international advocacy organization for all pediatric motor neuron diseases. It's our goal in our lifetime to be able to say if Thisbe and Noah had been born now, they wouldn't have had to die.

The courage and spirit my children displayed inspires us and it's impossible for us to go through life not trying to do what we wish people had done and would do for us. So I guess I do believe another thing in the Bible—the Golden Rule.

If we don't love ourselves, it makes it very
difficult to love someone else.
—NANCY BALLARD

NANCY BALLARD is a registered nurse with a master's degree in nursing and education and has been a clinical instructor in community health at the University of Texas at Tyler's College of Nursing since 2007. Her previous teaching positions included Tarrant County Junior College, Cooke County College in Gainesville, Texas, and Tyler Junior College. She is the mother of three and a grandmother of five and has been married to Herb Ballard for over half her life. She and her family reside in Tyler, Texas. (www.UTTyler.edu)

THE INTERVIEW

Nancy was referred to me by Jenifer Chilton, who is conducting research on epiphanies and wellness. I had never met Nancy or Herb, her husband, before. (Even though we share a last name, we are not related.) It was pouring rain the day I went to their home in Tyler, Texas, and we conducted her interview in their living room. Herb stayed in the room while I conducted Nancy's interview, and when we were finished, I asked him how her epiphany had affected him. He said he was just happy about her change because she seemed to feel so much better now. They had never talked about his point of view of the event before, and both started to tear up. Nancy said, "I sat there listening to what he was saying and realized a new depth of his love for me. And that's thrilling."

View the Interview:
www.epiphanychannel.com/people/nancy-ballard

*   *   *

I lived a life of obesity—of weight gain, weight loss, weight gain, over and over again. Anyone who has battled with obesity understands that. I also have diabetes, which is common with obesity. I understand how they are related because of my nursing background, but in spite of my knowledge and awareness of the great danger to my health, I could not control my weight. I would have periods when I'd lose some weight and be okay, but I never conquered it. It was always a monster waiting for me to weaken. I would lose 50 pounds and then gain 60; lose 100 pounds, then gain 150. I have been on every diet you can imagine, starting in middle school.

In winter 2006 when I went to the doctor, I weighed over three hundred pounds, which was completely shocking and unacceptable to me. I went on a diet and, over several months, I lost a grand total of ten pounds.

One day around this time, I was sitting in the living room, and I just began to pray and tell the Lord that I knew that I had to lose weight, but that I couldn't do it. I said, "You know, I have been trying to do this all of my life and I just simply cannot do it. So if You want it to happen, *You're* going to have to do it."

I said that prayer for a few days, and then I changed my prayer to one for healing, "Just heal me. I don't want to be sick and die, or be chronically ill and unable to be the person I want to be, so just *heal* me." And then a few days later I changed that prayer to a prayer of thanksgiving and said, "Thank you, Lord, for healing me." And that was a prayer of faith, because it hadn't happened. I was not yet healed, but I knew that it was going to happen.

It was June 19, 2006, a few days after this final prayer, and I was sitting in front of the TV. I did a lot of sitting in those days. *Oprah* came on, and the show was on weight management, which caught my attention. I watched that program from beginning to end. Most of the way, all I could do was sit and shake my head. Because I *knew*—I knew it all. I knew that I had to cut down what I ate; that I had to eat the right things; that I had to be active. I knew that my problem was causing high blood pressure, and that it had certainly created a bad case of diabetes. It was a *must* that I lose weight. But I also knew that I couldn't do it.

Then during the last part of the program, the very end, there was a guest on—a lady in her fifties, and I was in my fifties at the time. This woman had lost 160 pounds, and Oprah asked her, "How did you do it?"

She said, "Well, I got up one day, and I tied my shoes. I went outside and walked. I did it for an hour. And I did that every day." And she lost 160 pounds.

I sat up straight in my chair, and I said, "I can do that." That was the first time I'd ever said "I can." I always said, "I want to...I wish I would...I'm going to try...maybe this time...what else can I do?" But never "I can."

One thing I *had* decided was that I would never again lose large amounts of weight until I found a way that would be permanent. I said that after the second time I lost one hundred pounds on Weight Watchers and then just gained it all back. I didn't want to do that again. I didn't want to do any of the well-advertised programs because I knew that their results wouldn't last for me. But this woman's testimony on Oprah's show gave me incredible hope.

As soon as the show was over, I got up, tied my shoes, and walked out my front door. And I kept walking—not an easy thing to do, because I weighed almost three hundred pounds, and it was a typical humid Texas summer day of 105 degrees. I walked for thirty minutes, checked my watch, then turned around and walked the thirty-minute return trip home. When I walked in the front door pouring sweat, I knew that I had changed, and I would never go back to living the lifestyle I'd been living for the past fifty-nine years.

It was dinnertime. I went into the kitchen and found something healthy to eat. I never told anyone about it, but I just simply started living my life differently. Within a year, I had lost 140 pounds. That was three years and three and a half months ago that I started changing my lifestyle, and it has been two years and three and a half months that I've kept off that weight.

I was also on large doses of diabetes medication, including insulin. I had been told that I needed to increase my injections from twice a day to five times a day, including a lot of blood testing and meal planning. All this was more than I could manage with my teaching and my lifestyle, so I faced a choice: get sicker or get well. Gradually, six months after my *Oprah* epiphany, after starting to walk and to eat differently, I was off the insulin. Before the end of the year, I was also off one of the other medications, which was very expensive. And just in the last three months, I've gone off the last medication I'd been on for diabetes. I'll always have diabetes, but now I know how to control it with diet and exercise alone.

My life has changed. I'm healthy and I continue to heal. This journey has been miraculous for me, and the trigger was the *Oprah* show that day. I believe God used that, because I didn't sit down and turn on the TV to watch *Oprah*. I was sitting there and the show came on, and obesity was the topic, so He used that. It was a gift. It was the answer that God was giving me to my prayer, and He continues to answer that prayer as I learn new ways to promote wellness and good health.

I live a life now of excitement and happiness. I can look in the mirror and not be ashamed. I'm more energetic. I'm much more active with my children and grandchildren, and they're very excited about that! I can do more around the home in addition to working full-time.

It also has affected my relationship with my husband in a deep and positive way. Do you know, my husband, Herb, never said one word to me about losing weight during our entire thirty-six-year marriage? I knew deep in my heart that it must be hard for him to have an obese woman next to him. But he never gave me any clue that that was the case. He knew that I did not need to be told. I knew what my problem was. And when I did lose the weight, I didn't lose it for him. I lost it for myself. I have learned to love myself. If you don't love yourself, it makes it very difficult to love someone else. Through this transformation, I came to a much deeper appreciation for Herb and his support and love. We have definitely grown closer, and our love seems to get stronger and more perfect each day.

*If you can tell your story, then you will
heal yourself, and you'll help other people
do the same.*

—ANDREA BUCHANAN

ANDREA BUCHANAN is an award-winning filmmaker and bestselling author. She has produced and directed documentaries all over the world for various television networks. In 2006, in conjunction with Glamour Reel Moments, she wrote and co-directed (with Jennifer Aniston) the film festival favorite *Room 10*, starring Robin Wright-Penn and Kris Kristofferson. Currently a writer/director in television and film as well as an activist, she is the author of *Note to Self: 30 Women on Hardship, Humiliation, Heartbreak and Overcoming It All* and its sequel, *Live and Let Love*. She is a founding board member of the Joyful Heart Foundation. She resides in Los Angeles with her amazing husband, Jason, and their two beautiful children. (www.notetoselfbook.com)

THE INTERVIEW
Cory Booker, who was the mayor of Newark, New Jersey at the time, introduced me to Andrea when he invited me to her book signing in downtown New York. She is gregarious and easy-going and happens to be another fellow Texan who has also now become a dear friend. Several months after meeting, on an abnormally hot Los Angeles day, I went to her charming Craftsman-style home and heard her story.

View the Interview:
www.epiphanychannel.com/people/andrea-buchanan

* * *

Throughout my career, I have primarily been a documentary film-maker and producer. I focused on other people and their stories. I was always afraid to express my creativity in other ways. I didn't realize that I had my own story to tell, that I had something to say. That changed one night over dinner.

There was a group of us and there was a woman at the table I didn't know. The minute I sat down, I had that feeling: "I know her from somewhere." At first I shrugged the feeling off, but it turned out she felt the same way, so eventually we started the whole "I think I know you" routine.

When I told her my name, lightning struck. Her face went pale, she said, "Oh my God. Andrea Buchanan...," and just sat staring at me. I started to panic, thinking, "Oh no, did I do something horrible one night that I need to apologize for?" And she finally said, "I went to high school with you."

"You did?"

"Yeah." What she said next was not what I expected: "My God, you used to be so *beautiful*."

I froze. She rushed to explain: "I mean, not that you aren't now, but you're that girl we all wanted to be. You were so popular and nice. And then you got sick."

I went to high school in a small Texas town. I had been voted most popular, won all these little distinctions that mean so much to a girl at that age. I was primed to be homecoming queen, which is a *huge* deal, especially in Texas. I identified with my appearance, and it defined how people thought of me. I was the "pretty one." I was even primed to go into modeling—a *really* big deal where I grew up.

The summer before my senior year I went away and came back forty pounds heavier, with a goiter in my neck and my eyes bugging out of my head. My entire high school was aghast at my appearance, and so was I. It turned out I had Graves' disease. This illness was an enormous setback. It ruined every plan I'd had for myself.

Eventually I got better, made new plans, and then I took all that pain and *stuffed* it. Literally stuffed it out of sight, and denied all that I'd gone through and what the experience had meant to me—until that night I met my old schoolmate in the restaurant. Suddenly, facing this woman, I felt mortified, so embarrassed, so *ashamed* that I wasn't the beautiful girl she remembered anymore. That was a huge moment for me. In that instant, I realized that I had lost a part of myself when my looks were taken from me. That's how much they had defined me. What happened to me in high school caused me to be a shrinker in life. I was sitting there a shrinker. I didn't own who I was. After all these years, *I still didn't own myself.*

Then she said, "Everybody was talking about your sickness and what had happened to you. It was big news. Then there was a day in homeroom, where you looked at me and you seemed to say, 'I understand you. I get you.' That moment meant a lot to me." She'd been this sort of misfit in our high school. She used to hang out in the "freaks' courtyard" and smoke cigarettes. She just did not fit in at all. Now she sat here explaining to me that my not fitting in twenty years before in a way had given her a kind of permission to feel okay about herself. It was a moment she never forgot.

I'd had no idea about any of it—how people saw me, were talking about me, or how I had affected her life.

So my head was spinning, and we were both weeping at the dinner table. I'll never forget driving home from that dinner. I said aloud, "What just happened?" I was shaking, shaking from the inside out. That moment in the restaurant, meeting the girl from high school, acknowledging my illness and learning how it affected her, changed me. It forced me to acknowledge my experience and heal.

I ended up writing a story about it. I'd never written anything personal in my life, except in my many unfinished journal pages. I was a documentary filmmaker. I was always interviewing people, drawing stories out of them. That's my gift. But when my friend started a writers' group, she said, "You have to write. I want you to write an essay about something personal that's happened to you." I decided to write about this moment in this restaurant. That turned into my first book, *Note to Self.*

In writing about my experience and later my book, I realized that telling your story is the most profound healing that you can do. If you can tell your story, then you will heal yourself, and you'll help other people do the same. I coined a phrase, "Share your shame." In fact, I think it's a disservice not to. I really do. I feel like it's my calling to tell my story and help other people tell theirs.

When you start giving to other people, that's where the true healing happens. Giving of yourself—whether it's helping someone across the street, starting an organization, writing a check, or telling your story—helps you heal.

You are the common denominator in your life, and you have
to take responsibility for that.

—BILLIE MYERS

BILLIE MYERS is an English singer/songwriter who has had
numerous songs on the *Billboard* charts, including the transat-
lantic hit "Kiss the Rain." Her debut album, *Growing Pains*, went
gold in the United States and Canada; her other albums include
Vertigo and *Tea and Sympathy*. She has performed around the
world, including at Lilith Fair and in support slots on tours with
Bob Dylan and Savage Garden. Her music has been featured on
TV soundtracks including *Dawson's Creek*, *Melrose Place*, and
The Real World as well as numerous European programs, and she
has made appearances on television shows such as *The Tonight
Show*, *The Rosie O'Donnell Show*, *Good Morning America*, and
VH1's *Crossroads*. Myers is also one of the spokespeople for the
Jed Foundation, a nonprofit organization committed to reducing
emotional distress and preventing suicide among teens.
(www.BillieMyers.com; www.jedfoundation.org)

View the Interview:
www.epiphanychannel.com/people/billie-myers

THE INTERVIEW

Billie and I met while in Miami with mutual friends, and much to
my delight, we discovered we were neighbors in Los Angeles. She
is engaging, charismatic, and possesses that wonderful British wit.
One day we were discussing our love lives over breakfast when she
told a story about how her life had changed because of a conversation much like the one we were having. Obviously, I pounced, and
got her to agree to an interview. When I went to her house a few

streets away, expecting to hear the epiphany I already knew about, she told not only that one but also another that I found just as thought-provoking.

*   *   *

I had a fairly dysfunctional upbringing. My parents split up and I lived in foster care—all the usual stuff that turns you into a singer/songwriter. With all that came a little anger and a lot of bitterness. It's hard for anybody, especially when you're young, to understand why two adults would fail to take care of their child because they'd rather be doing whatever else they were doing with their lives.

So as I got older I harbored a great deal of resentment, and it affected my relationships. It still does. I'm not known for my commitment enthusiasm. But there comes a certain point in time where you just don't want to be angry with the world anymore, because it begins to take its toll on you. So a friend of mine suggested that I take this therapeutic course. And I have to confess...I'm English. We don't *do* therapy.

But this was a pretty hard time in my life. The contract with my record label had finished; my identity had been so wrapped up in that, I felt completely lost. I'd also just ended a relationship and was hitting emotional rock bottom. So when this friend of mine said, "You should go on this course," I did. At least it took place in the wine country of California.

It was very rustic. They make you turn over your phone and anything else that might connect you with the outside world. Then you're pushed to address what your feelings are—your anger, your fears. You're forced to be honest. The first few days they had people holding plastic baby dolls and *naming* them. I felt that this was rather stupid, and I laughed. Which didn't go down too well: they nearly threw me out.

But I soldiered on. One exercise they had me do was to write a letter as if I were my mother explaining to my inner child—that four-year-old she'd abandoned—who she was, why she left, what her motivations were. At the time it just seemed weird. I'd never looked at the matter from her perspective before. It was always all about me. How could she have done that to me? What kind of terrible person was she?

So this was interesting. I wrote a letter as my mother, my real mother, and explained to the four-year-old me why I was leaving, what was going on in my life at that point that meant I couldn't be there. And then I had to switch and write a similar letter from my father. It gets worse: because I'd also been in foster care, I had to write a letter as if I were my foster parents, explaining how it felt to have this mixed-race child in the house.

So I was writing these letters, and not really thinking about it, when unconsciously I started to get these *amazing* insights. I suddenly remembered that my mother had issues of her own, and what they were. Could she even really cope with having a child? What about the fact that she was white and my dad was black? This was way back in the early 1970s.

Then the course leader said something that made everything just click. She said, "Someone can be guilty, but not to blame."

I'd spent so many years being angry, but at that moment I felt all that drop away. I realized that no parents will ever be perfect. My life may have not been brilliant growing up, but I don't think they deliberately went out of their way to hurt me—that wasn't their intention.

Armed, or perhaps disarmed, by that idea, I marched home and asked my father, "Why on earth would you put me to live with a white family that didn't really like black people? Why would you think that was acceptable? Why would you do that, then go live five streets up the road with somebody else and her children?"

And his answer amazed me. He said that he'd felt putting me with a white family would give me a better start in life.

I can't tell you how huge that was for me. Honestly, it's probably the nicest thing he's ever said to me. I'd had no idea that was his reasoning. He had done what he thought was best for me. This was a completely new way of thinking about my father. Now I know that he valued me, which I'd never felt before. I would never have asked him those questions if not for that one simple phrase: "Someone can be guilty, but not to blame."

Yes, my life was what it was, but it wasn't because somebody went out of his way to harm me. I never asked my mother about her reasoning, because I've only met her once and that was before all of this happened. But I'm sure my mother thought her leaving was for the best too. She probably meant to go off and deal with her own problems rather than get in the way of a child's life. So my big epiphany is—and I carry it with me now, even when I get really angry with people—that for the most part (there are exceptions) *people can be guilty, but they're not necessarily to blame.*

Very seldom do people act with a deliberate evil intent, hoping to have long-term effects that are hurtful. You've got to let go. It doesn't mean you forget. But you let go. That insight helped me. It hasn't changed the past, but I'm not angry about it anymore. It's acceptable, I've learned, to say to somebody, "You were wrong, but I accept that you were wrong, and I understand you didn't do it knowingly. And that's okay, because no one's perfect." Knowing this gives me a sense of calm. I still get upset about different things, but resentment isn't my motivator.

This epiphany led me to another that drastically changed my life in recent years. As a singer/songwriter, I had a relatively successful career, and was signed with a big record label, which treated me very well. But you know, things happen, and I was dropped. And it was really, really difficult. I decided it was everyone else's fault. So once again, I was wallowing in anger and self-pity. This period lasted six years.

One day I was out having brunch with a bunch of girlfriends, so of course we were talking about our love lives—looking for life lessons, wondering why we keep repeating the same behavior. Someone at the table said, "I keep going out with the same kind of guy, I keep suffering this and that." We all looked at her, and there was an immediate consensus: "Yeah, but the one common denominator in these scenarios is you. You don't have to do it. But these are the choices *you* keep making." I kind of laughed it off. Let's be honest—in life, it's much easier to think that everything's somebody else's fault.

But on my way home, it suddenly struck me: "Wait a minute, *I'm* the common denominator in all *my* dramas. I'm the issue. I'm the problem. As hard as that is to confess, I am the one that needs to change." I realized a lot of these scenarios that I found myself in time and time again were of my own making. I had to look at that and take responsibility for it.

Thus endeth my big epiphany, which led me to pull myself together and stop blaming everybody else for my problems and failures. With that realization came the fact that it was time for me to do another album, and for me to enjoy it. So I actually got off my butt and created my long-delayed third album! For better or for worse, I did it. It will either be a success or it won't. But it's no one else's fault. It's not even my fault if it isn't. It just is what it is, you know? So that's the truth. I was the common denominator. Hopefully, I'm the common denominator in another successful project and things and situations in my life that are bit more relaxed and not so temperamental as before. Hopefully. I'm working on it.

MIRACLES

miracle : a surprising, highly improbable, or extraordinary event that appears inexplicable by natural laws and excites admiring awe

*Take the time to stop and reflect on the choices you make and
the speed at which you are traveling in life.*

—JOEL HARPER

JOEL HARPER is a New York–based personal trainer whose
clients include everyone from celebrities and Olympic athletes to
ten-year-old children. He is also a speaker and the creator of the *Fit-
Pack* DVD and *YOU* series DVD workouts. He has been featured
in multiple publications and television shows, including *The Dr. Oz
Show*, ABC News, PBS specials, Fox News, Oprah.com, *Esquire*,
Runner's World, and *O*. (www.JoelHarperFitness.com)

THE INTERVIEW
Joel is one of my closest friends and we have produced many fitness
DVDs together, including his FitPack DVDs and videos for Dr.
Oz. When I started asking people about their greatest epiphanies,
Joel was one of the first people I asked. His epiphany totally took
me by surprise; he had never so much as mentioned this astonishing experience before! He simply doesn't talk about it, he said. His
story made me curious about other people's epiphany stories, and
why people often internalize them so deeply that they don't speak
about them unless asked to. You could say he "fueled the fire" for
this project early on. We conducted his official interview about a
year later one summer evening in his apartment with a spectacular
view of New York City as our backdrop.

View the Interview:
www.epiphanychannel.com/people/joel-harper

◆　　⬧　　◆

I have been a personal trainer in New York City for about eighteen years and I bike everywhere. I have a tendency to book a very tight schedule for myself, and one day I was working downtown in Tribeca and only had fifteen minutes to get to another appointment at my studio in midtown. I was biking as fast as I possibly could on the West Side Highway bike path to make the appointment, and on the way, about sixty feet in front of me, I saw this father and a little girl, maybe three years old, playing on the side of the bike path. I had my iPod on and was cruising along and at the exact moment I reached them, all of a sudden the little girl turned and ran *right* out in front of me.

It happened so abruptly that there was absolutely no way I could stop or even slow down—there just wasn't any time. I realized I was going to hit her. I would say I braced myself, but I don't think I even had time to do that. And then, I don't know how to describe this—but I didn't hit her. My bike and I went through her body. I just sailed right through her body. Or her body went through mine. It was one and the same. It felt like my body was floating. Her body was there and yet just passed right through me. I know it might sound crazy but it's true. Nothing happened to her and nothing happened to me.

It was startling and shocking, but at the same time not. It seemed like, "Oh, I already knew that." In the moment that it happened, I was so peaceful and serene. It was a physical experience, but it seemed spiritual in nature.

I immediately pulled over and looked back. The little girl had gone on to play with some flowers. The dad just stood there in shock, stunned. Neither one of us knew what to do or say. We both knew that if I had actually hit his daughter's physical body, I probably would have killed her. I wish I would have gone up to him, but it felt like there was nothing to say. So I rode on.

When people ask me if it was a miracle, I hesitate. I guess it is miraculous. But labels cheapen the experience. The meaning behind it has much more depth for me. I wish I could send the feelings and my experience of what happened telepathically to others rather than have to explain it in words. It is beyond words.

But the message was simple: what if I had hurt or killed a little girl just because I had overbooked myself and was in a huge hurry? The incident made me realize that I'm not in total control, that my life could be changed in a second. My life would have changed forever if I hit that little girl. Nobody would have been at fault; it just would have been one of those "wrong place at the wrong time" things. But it could have ruined my life and cost her hers.

In that one instant, as I passed through the little girl's body, I realized that I needed to stop and reflect on my choices and the speed at which I was traveling in life. I have a tendency to get so busy and am keeping up such a pace that I will become almost robotic in how I go about my life. It really hit me that I needed to take time and take full responsibility for each and every one of my choices, however small or large they may be. More important, I also realized that a Higher Power, God, or *somebody* was obviously looking out for me and helped me. Because of that, I'm much more aware of others' situations and needs now, and I realized I should never, ever question helping out others. Just rise to the occasion!

*True faith supplies great strength for life and
opens our hearts and minds to greater
possibilities and miracles.*
—CHRISTOPHER LEE

CHRISTOPHER LEE, twenty-five years old when we conducted his interview, is from Northamptonshire, England, and is a deacon in the Anglican Church of England. He worked at the Kiteto Christian College Mission in Kiteto, Tanzania, a tiny town in the rural area of the Manyara region, for three years after he graduated from university. He then studied theology at the University of Cambridge and is always looking forward to the next adventure as an Anglican priest. (www.dioceseofkiteto.org)

THE INTERVIEW

One night while I was traveling and working in Africa, I met two British doctors who had volunteered at the mission Reverend Lee ran. When I told them about *Epiphany*, they suggested I talk to him, but they never told me his name. The night went on, I never met him, and the next morning we were leaving. I remember being upset with myself for not seeking him out and trying to interview him—here I was in Africa and I'd blown an opportunity to get an interesting interview. As we were about to leave, the driver of our van started talking to this man with a backpack who needed a ride. We were headed in the same direction, so I told him we were happy to have him come with us. We introduced ourselves, and I asked Chris what had brought him to Kendwa Rocks. He replied, "I was just vacationing for a bit; I help run a mission in Tanzania." That's right—the missionary priest I was so upset to have missed the night before had just climbed right into my van! On top of that, the doctors had told him about me too, so he'd thought about what his greatest epiphany would be. Kismet? Serendipity? Whatever it was, it was meant to be. We conducted his interview in a speeding van en route to Stone Town, Zanzibar.

View the Interview:
www.epiphanychannel.com/people/christopher-lee

* * *

I was in the church one evening in our mission in Kiteto, Tanzania, where I work. This was in 2005, and we were doing a famine relief project because there was no rain in our area. There was a lot of sickness and death and a lot of children dying because of this drought. We had a worship session going on, and I felt compelled to leave and go outside to pray.

We use gravity to feed water into our housing, so we have a large concrete block with a water tower on top of it, and it's about twenty feet high. Sometimes I would climb and sit on top of it and just relax, meditate, and pray. While I was walking to the tower, I started thinking that maybe I'd just sit at the bottom and not climb it because it's quite tiring just to get up there. But when I got there, there was a ladder leaning against it, which was odd. It had never been there before—I still have no idea where it came from. I thought, "Okay, I guess I *will* climb it," so I went up to the top of it and sat and started to pray.

I was coming to the end of my prayer, and I felt compelled to pray for rain, so I did. All of a sudden, as clear as daylight, this voice outside my left ear said, "Three days." It was an actual voice outside of me, one that I immediately understood wasn't lying. Somehow I knew there had never been a lie spoken from this voice. It was such a clear voice that just listening to it made me feel clean. I don't know, but it felt like it was an angel or God.

All of a sudden I was overcome and realized it really was going to rain in three days, and I climbed down from the water tower.

This was on a Tuesday. Later that day I spoke to the bishop who was going to be driving somewhere on Friday and asked him if he could drive in the rain because it was going to rain on Friday. He sort of looked at me funny and said not to worry, he could drive in the rain fine. I went around and told the people in the area and all our students to take out their buckets because they would need them to catch rainwater on Friday.

Then Friday came. And it was blue sky—I mean, not a cloud in the sky. I was working on an exam for school, and at one point I just stopped in the middle and started to pray. I said, "God, I really thought You spoke to me. I really thought You told me that in three days the rain was going to come. My faith will be really injured if rain doesn't come because, honestly, every part of me believes that it was You." I then finished my exam and went into the building where we have lunch and sat down to eat. All of our buildings have corrugated-iron roofs, and as we were eating, suddenly we started hearing this loud, continuous pinging noise on the roof. We ran outside and there was thunder and these huge black clouds just dumping rain everywhere. The rains had come. It had been three days, just as I had heard. The rains stayed for two to three weeks and supplied us with a lot of water, which we desperately needed to end the drought and suffering.

I remember this story because it's a very loving story. It's like I was taken in loving arms and told, "You know what, Chris? In three days it's going to rain, so don't worry, and go tell people and help them." And I did. It was solely by faith, not by sight. It wasn't about my seeing or knowing anything. But my faith opened me to the message. My epiphany is that faith truly does produce fruit. It's like my faith was a plant, and this experience grew its roots deep and supplied me with a lot more strength for my life. It reminds and helps me to better understand God's love for us as people, and God's love for me as an individual as well—and how each of us can be used to serve others. I remember that story now and again, smile, and think, "Yeah, I've always got that."

> *All you've really got is the moment you're in,*
> *so you better get right with it.*
> —STEPHEN BRUTON

STEPHEN BRUTON was a prolific songwriter, singer, recording artist, and Grammy-nominated record producer who worked and collaborated with Bonnie Raitt, Christine McVie, Kris Kristofferson, Elvis Costello, Carly Simon, Eric Clapton, Alejandro Escovedo, T Bone Burnett, and the Wallflowers, among many others. He was a founding member of the band The Resentments and has several solo albums out with the record label New West. His last projects included collaborating and playing on Kris Kristofferson's album *Starlight and Stone* and the noted collaboration as a music producer and composer with Grammy Award winner T Bone Burnett on the award-winning soundtrack and film *Crazy Heart*. (www.StephenBruton.com)

THE INTERVIEW

Stephen was my first official on-camera interview for *Epiphany*. It was very interesting timing because his epiphany had just happened only a few weeks before. He had been battling tonsillar cancer for about eighteen months when we talked in his backyard in Austin, Texas. He was so present, strong, real, intense, and extremely compelling—quintessential Stephen. He lost his battle with cancer about a year later, on May 9, 2009, just two weeks after he finished his work on the award-winning *Crazy Heart* soundtrack. An outstanding musician and poet, wonderful friend, and example of living every day to the fullest, Stephen stayed in the moment and did what he loved—playing, writing, and producing music—to the very end.

View the Interview:
www.epiphanychannel.com/people/stephen-bruton

＊　　＊　　＊

I had been going through chemo and radiation for tonsillar cancer. My energy level and spirits were low. I was still having a lot of side effects energy-wise and pain-wise with the treatment I was getting, and I was having a lot of problems with my throat. Every day I would take my dogs for a walk because they love it. It gave me some energy, and I felt like maybe it was helping to get rid of some of the poison that was inside me. This particular day was beautiful and the dogs were having a great time, but I wasn't. I remember coming up a little rise and looking off to the side. All of a sudden, I heard a voice in my left ear say, "This might be as good as it gets, so you better get right with it. You better get right with it, right now."

It was just like that. It was a voice in my ear. It was the absolute truth. It was unadorned, and it hit me like a brick because in reality there was a good chance that it *wasn't* going to get any better. When I heard the voice say that, I realized there was no arguing with it. It was like my father talking to me in a certain way. Occasionally he would say something in a way that meant he was going to say it once and that was it. It was coming down, and you better be listening. That's the way this epiphany was for me. It was the truth coming down one time, an absolute truth that I needed to live by.

The epiphany from that afternoon has been working for me every day, all day, ever since. Indeed, this *might* be as good as it gets for me, for the rest of my life, and I need to get at peace with it and enjoy and appreciate the moment I am in.

Most of the time we take everything for granted. Everything.

I always did. I was never infirm in my life. For fifty-eight years I was never sick. I never had anything wrong with me—I broke a few bones, but that's about it. Now, here I've been fighting this, whatever this is, for the last couple of years, and I have to take it on a moment-to-moment level. Not day to day, not hour to hour, but moment to moment.

All you've got is the moment. If you can stay there, you'll be all right. When I stay in the moment, especially battling this disease, anything is doable. If I don't stay in the moment, I start attending my own funeral.

The extraordinary is always possible, no matter what.
—CHLOE WORDSWORTH

CHLOE WORDSWORTH is an author, the creator of the healing modality Resonance Repatterning, and founder of the Resonance Repatterning Institute. She graduated from the University of California at Los Angeles, studied numerous systems of alternative medicine, including acupuncture, and had a private acupuncture practice for eight years. She developed Resonance Repatterning (originally called Holographic Repatterning) in 1990 and has written *Quantum Change Made Easy* in addition to twelve books used in her teaching seminars. She lives in Scottsdale, Arizona, and teaches and gives presentations on Resonance Repatterning and the possibilities it opens for transformation, positive change, and self-healing. (www.ResonanceRepatterning.net)

THE INTERVIEW
I describe Resonance Repatterning as "supersonic therapy." For me, it is Western psychology synthesized with other modalities in a way that helps get to the heart of things much faster than regular psychotherapy sometimes does. It has been an absolute gift in my life. Many people I know have had the same experience, so I decided to make a video about it to help get the word out. When I made the video, I interviewed my practitioner in Austin and a bunch of her clients as testimonials. We sent the video to Chloe to make sure we had her blessing. Not only did we have her blessing, but she wanted to be in it too, and happened to be coming to Austin to teach! I'm happy to say Chloe is now also in the video, which is still in circulation introducing people to the Resonance Repatterning healing modality. A few years after our

shoot, I was able to catch Chloe for a phone interview between her world teaching travels.

*   *   *

I was raised in England and educated at an amazing progressive school my parents founded. In the middle of World War II, they'd managed to borrow $15,000 to buy a dilapidated castle in the middle of 160 acres. There they brought us up free from fear, exams, tests—it was all about learning through play, art, music, theater, dance, and joy. It was a very loving and creative environment.

When I was nineteen or twenty, I took a job as a nanny in Switzerland for a few months over the summer to fund an upcoming trip to the States. My two charges were six and seven. One afternoon, I took the children and a friend of theirs for a walk. We decided to climb up a steep valley slope, at the bottom of which was a stream. Halfway up, I heard a yelp, and when I turned around, one of the children below me was ricocheting down the steep mountainside slope. She landed in the stream at the bottom, and for a second, there was dead silence: just the sound of the stream washing over her. Time stopped, and a voice inside me said, "Get down there *now* or she's gone." And without a moment's doubt, I positively flew down the slope. In seconds I was by the stream, picking the child out of the water and shaking her. And she was fine. No scratches, no bruises, and breathing easily. We chatted away as I took her home for a hot bath.

The image of that experience has always stayed with me—largely because what happened was quite impossible. It was a very steep slope, which took twenty minutes to climb and should have taken me at least ten minutes to descend. Only a bird could get to the bottom of that valley that fast. But something told me, "Do it," and I did it. So something interesting was going on. Time had slowed down and then it sped up. Of course, this is something that many of us have experienced in times of crises or accidents, where a situation is saved because everything goes into slow motion or speeds up. But because I'd grown up the way I did, I took this incident for granted. I expected the extraordinary. I'd had many comparable experiences growing up. I think it was only later on when I analyzed this incident on that mountain that I realized it had been a major epiphany for me.

I've been interested in the healing field since childhood, so after Switzerland, I immigrated to the U.S. and got into the alternative health field. My experience on that slope with the children gave me an enduring sense that there are unlimited possibilities. But I kept seeing in my healing work how we *limit* ourselves rather than accept or expect the extraordinary. I observed that problems like illnesses, marital conflict, and work issues are directly related to life-defeating emotions such as fear, negative beliefs, and unconscious patterns from the past. Our old memory imprints are like a filter through which we see life.

But because of my childhood, I didn't have these same constraints. So I began to examine the extraordinary experiences I'd had in an analytical, left-brain way to understand how they happened. How *did* I make it down that mountainside in one or two seconds instead of ten minutes?

The answer is that I didn't doubt for *one instant* that I could save the girl. I heard that inner voice and just *did* it. I resonated with the *absolute possibility* of it, went into unhesitating action, and experienced the extraordinary. I instantly accepted the situation as it was, free of all resistance, fear, or guilt. There was none of that. Instead of choosing panic and believing that the little girl would die, when I heard my higher consciousness tell me to get down there, I chose to believe I could and in an instant I did.

I call an epiphany "a portal to the Divine." But in new physics, it could be described as tapping into the field or dimension of limitless possibilities, where everything is energy and anything is possible. Ancient healing systems talk about this as well—the Indian system of Ayurveda and the chakra system, Chinese acupuncture—they've all known about it for five thousand years. Finally science is catching up. Everything is really energy. Anything is possible if you access that field of energy. With my knowledge of physics, anatomy, and how the brain works, I've realized that something else goes with self-healing, or extraordinary positive change: there are different levels or dimensions of energy. Most of us are stuck in limitation. We have all these fears and doubts. We don't free ourselves to experience the extraordinary.

For me the question became: what would enable us to experience self-healing and extraordinary change on a practical, everyday basis, rather than just at peak moments like emergencies and epiphanies? I wondered if there was a way to create extraordinary change at any time. I wasn't thinking of this so much in my role as a healer but more as a teacher. I wanted to show people how to do this themselves.

This sort of research and study finally led to the work I am doing now. By 1990 I had created what I call Resonance Repatterning. It is a modality of healing that centers on frequencies. Our body is energy, and all energy has frequencies. When our frequencies are synchronized, we resonate and are in tune with coherence—which generates happiness, joy, love, and so on. When our frequencies are out of sync, we will resonate with the shadow sides of ourselves, yielding tension, upset, anger, fear, depression, and miserable relationships. This is a very short and simplistic explanation, of course, but with Resonance Repatterning we can train ourselves to resonate with our coherent frequencies. We can change our incoherent patterns and instead promote healing and positive change in our lives. And we can do it quickly.

I wanted something that could be quick when developing this work because the epiphany in Switzerland had to do with shifting time. I realized that bringing about extraordinary change in our lives doesn't have to mean years and years of heavy, intense work. I've seen so many cases with Resonance Repatterning where certain ailments or problems deemed incurable or impossible were healed, or where issues that take years of work in traditional therapy are resolved quite rapidly. I've seen people in deep, deep depressions lasting twenty years come out of it within two weeks— or someone's blood pressure problems disappear after just a few sessions. Change has so much to do with our beliefs and how much we are willing to adapt them or let them go and open ourselves to new ones so we can resonate with different, hopefully higher frequencies.

Resonance Repatterning is based on the study of my epiphany, and I teach it all over the world now and there are thousands of practitioners worldwide. The goal is to spark epiphanies and bring healing, positive change to people. I want people to know that the extraordinary is always possible, right now, no matter what.

Celebrate every day.

—WENDI COOPER

WENDI COOPER is the owner and creative director of C Spot Run Productions, an award-winning direct response television production company in the United States. She is the mother of two sons, ages twenty-nine and nineteen, and lives with her beautiful Italian husband in Los Angeles, California. (www.cspotrun.com)

THE INTERVIEW

Wendi is a business colleague of a friend of mine from Austin who was visiting Los Angeles, and we all had lunch. Later, she emailed me saying she'd had an epiphany that helped her get through cancer. It happened that our phone interview took place on her birthday. After we spoke, she was heading to her sister's for a family party, and she told me that her whole family only got together like this for her birthday—it was a reminder that she was still here to celebrate.

*   *   *

To make a long story short, in the past I went through domestic abuse and divorce, and for some time was the single mother of two boys from two different fathers. But for the past thirteen years I've been married to a wonderful man, and I have had a thriving, successful direct response production company since 1994.

Five years ago I thought I had an inguinal hernia and went

in for the operation to fix it. When I woke up from the operation, the doctor stood over me saying that I did not have a hernia but ovarian cancer—stage III-C ovarian cancer, as it turned out, which had oddly enough surrounded a lymph node located in the groin, and to this day no doctor has been able to understand it. They had to give me a complete hysterectomy—I mean complete, I have only a bladder—and I had to undergo major chemotherapy.

They gave me my first chemo treatment of Taxol and carboplatin, which is extremely strong and incredibly toxic. I didn't really know what to expect. Chemo doesn't affect you at first—then several days later you start feeling sick. So the first time you go through the session you're kind of waiting for it to happen. Gradually I started to feel gross, and every day it got a little bit worse, until one night I was lying in bed thinking, praying, "Oh God, I'm not going to be able to do this. I can't do it." I was thinking about my mother, whom I'd been watching battle cancer for years, and now I had cancer. "I can't *do* this." And I meant it with every fiber of my being. I was desperate and terrified.

I was lying there thinking this, praying this, and suddenly I heard this *voice* say to me, "You're going to be okay. Everything will be fine." That's what I heard. It wasn't my inner voice or a voice in my head, but a man's voice outside of me to my left. I can't describe it really, but it was soothing, *very* soothing, and I wasn't scared at all. It was what you would think a Higher Being's voice would sound like. It might sound crazy, but I know I heard it, and I know it was real.

So when I heard it, I sat up and looked around. My husband was still sleeping next to me. I noticed I felt better. I got up and walked into the bathroom. I looked at myself in the mirror, and I felt fine. It was so strange, but I felt perfectly fine, and was not sick the next day. In fact, I never got sick at all from that first chemo treatment after that night.

I believed the voice, and I still believe the voice to this day. It still helps me and carries me. I almost died from chemotherapy eventually—it literally almost killed me—but I always had hope.

Ovarian cancer is not one of those cancers that most people survive. They'd told me I had a 20 percent chance to hang on five years. When I heard that, I freaked out. I started worrying about my kids, that I wasn't going to get to see my son graduate from high school—things like that.

As soon as I heard that voice, I didn't think about such things anymore. I knew that I was going to be okay. People couldn't believe how strong I was, how spirited, how no matter what was happening to me, I always had the strength to work and go on. Hearing that voice gave me the strength, the confidence, the courage to face it all. I knew I was going to get through it. I knew it wasn't going to kill me. Even when it almost did, I knew it wouldn't. And it didn't.

While I was going through my chemo and was suffering all the horrible side effects—like losing *all* your hair from your entire body, the skin coming off the lining in your mouth, bloating, nausea—I watched my mother die. While I was fighting cancer, I was sitting there with her as she died of it. It was a surreal dynamic. But the beautiful thing was, we ended up forging this incredible bond through our struggle to survive.

The last time I saw my mother, I had taken my wig off. She was lying in her bed. She was bald. I was bald. I was in her bathroom. And I looked at her and said, "Okay, Mom. I'm going to try on your wigs." Now, when someone's dying of cancer, at that point, they're totally out of it. They're coming in and out of reality. So I was trying on her wigs, which looked absolutely ridiculous on me, and I remember looking over, my mom looking at me, telling me how beautiful I was, and laughing.

That is my last memory of my mom. She died the next day.

But even as I watched my mother lose her battle, I always knew I was going to survive. I knew it because I found such strength in the memory of that voice that I'd heard.

For me, that voice was God's. He was talking to me. It comforted me, and I feel honored and humbled to have had that experience. It gave me the feeling that He/She/It sees me, and that I have purpose and that I'm recognized by this Higher Being, this Higher Power.

It will be five years in May that I had my diagnosis, and I am still completely cancer-free. My doctor is surprised. He says I haven't just survived but I'm cured, and when he first saw me he told me that there was no cure for my cancer. Now he believes that I'm cured. But I'm not surprised. I don't really worry about my cancer coming back. I know that I will live to be old, because that voice came to me. I know that I'm going to be okay.

That voice shifted my soul and made me realize I have to celebrate every day I'm on this earth. I always tell my sons it's important for us all to try every day to do something great for ourselves and something great for someone else, and it doesn't matter how big or how small—just something great, every day. It's important. We all deserve it.

COMINGS OF AGE

coming of age : the attainment of maturity, respectability, prominence, or recognition; fully stepping into one's adulthood

*Take your place...the future is now...so take your place,
make your mark, be the person you want to be
in your family, in your community, in the world.*

—LAWRENCE WRIGHT

LAWRENCE WRIGHT is the Pulitzer Prize–winning author of numerous books, including *The Looming Tower: Al-Qaeda and the Road to 9/11* and *Going Clear: Scientology, Hollywood, and the Prison of Belief.* He is also a journalist (staff writer for the *New Yorker*), screenwriter (*The Siege* and *Noriega: God's Favorite*), and playwright (*Sonny's Last Shot*). The one-man show he wrote and performs, *My Trip to Al-Qaeda*, was also made into a documentary film, directed by Academy Award winner Alex Gibney. Wright also serves as the keyboard player in the Austin-based blues band Who Do. A husband, a father, and grandfather, he lives in Austin, Texas, where he is also involved in a public sculpture project, Capital Area Statues.
(www.LawrenceWright.com; www.CapitalAreaStatues.com)

THE INTERVIEW
Larry adapted his screenplay about love, marriage, and the craziness of the Texas legislature, *Sonny's Last Shot*, into a sensational play that was a big success in Austin (and at this printing, is being adapted into a television series for HBO) —and I played the lead female role. This role led directly to the epiphany that sparked this project. He was my very first official interview for the book, and continues to be a supportive, inspiring role model and friend to whom I am deeply grateful.

View the Interview:
www.epiphanychannel.com/people/lawrence-wright

In 1990 I was invited to go to the University of Cairo to make a speech. It was the twentieth anniversary of our wedding, so my wife and I decided to have a second honeymoon. We got married in Greece, so after the speech, that's where we went—to the Peloponnese, my favorite region. We were in a little town called Epidaurus, which happens to be an ancient health spa. It also had the finest theater in the ancient world. This theater is still perfectly preserved, and it's just a beautiful, beautiful place. Walking through that classical environment reminded me of all I'd learned about ancient Greece and republican Rome. It struck me afresh what a huge role the citizen played in these cultures, how their common citizens were so empowered. By contrast, so many of us nowadays seem so jaded about the roles we play in society. And what about me? Was I really, fully, living as the person I wanted to be? And then this phrase came to my mind. It wasn't a voice but a very clear thought: "Take your place." Those very words, over and over: "Take your place. It's time to take your place."

"Take your place" means become the person that you want to be. Don't put it off. *Be* that person. Be the person you want to be in your family, your community, your job, your career. It's not something that you evolve into. It's something you decide: "I *am* that person." I had made the mistake of thinking I would grow into that person *eventually*. I must have had a prolonged adolescence, because I didn't really want to assume all the responsibility of being a full-grown adult—a full-fledged citizen, a responsible parent. Those things demand a lot of commitment. What I realized in Greece was that if I am ever going to become what I wish to be, the time is now. I have to take my place—in my family, in my community, in my career. Now is the time. There is no future. Or rather, the future is *now*. With those words, "Take your place," a bell had rung for me, and my life was fundamentally changed. Suddenly I got a lot more focused about everything.

When I got back, I resolved to become a better father and a more central figure in my children's lives. I got more involved with our family life. In my career, I realized that I couldn't go on procrastinating: now was the time. As soon as I got back, I applied for a National Endowment for the Arts grant. I never had the kind of nerve to do that before. To my surprise, I got the grant, and then I got hired by the *New Yorker*! The highest aspiration I'd ever had as a writer was just to write for that magazine, and now suddenly I was working for them. Many of my "ultimate" career goals started becoming achievable.

I also decided I needed to become more active as a citizen, moving my community to reflect the core values that I stand for. Before then, I had never really been extremely civically or philanthropically inclined. None of the causes I'd encountered had deeply engaged me. But something about being in the ancient world, seeing the remnants of that great civilization in Greece, made me think that I needed to contribute something.

I love statues—the way that they organize public space, give dignity and occasion to environments that can otherwise go unnoticed, and call attention to values that a culture wants to enshrine. So one thing I did was start this little nonprofit group called Capital Area Statues. Austin is a wonderful town, but it doesn't have much in the way of public art. So with some friends I started raising money and commissioning artists, and we started putting up statues of local heroes around the city. It has been a lot of fun, and has intensified my consideration of the contribution and importance that art—including my own art, my writing—can carry for people who, like me, are trying to find meaning in life. Some people discover meaning in politics and some people find it in religion, but many of us find it in art. It's a commonality that stretches across all ethnic groups, all generations and genders. One piece of art can reach people in every sector of the community and help them access a way of understanding the world.

I also started approaching life differently. I resolved that I was only going to do things that are really *important* or really *fun*. It's hard to decide what you're going to do with your life. Every opportunity comes with a cost. When you're weighing the alternatives that life presents, on what basis are you making your choice?

Money is usually the main one. I knew I didn't have the time to waste obsessing over that. I wanted to use my life as fully as I could, achieving important goals, but I'm not Mother Teresa, and I didn't want to sacrifice joy and fun. So those are the axes on which I plot my life. Is it important? Is it fun? If it's really important but not fun, I'll do it. I have to say that *The Looming Tower* was probably the most important thing I'll ever do, but it wasn't so much fun as deeply fulfilling. To give everything you have to a goal is pleasurable because you feel like you're being used fully and correctly. But it was a lonely, sometimes dangerous, and very long and complex project. On the other hand, I also play in a band, and that is about as much fun as you can have. It is thrillingly fun. My band and music are not important in any big sense, but boy, is it fun, and so it's right up on the top of my axis of fun.

I'm not mystical. I don't think you can simply adjust reality by changing your attitude. But you have to set your intentions. Things don't just fall into your lap. You have to go out and get them. To do that, you must believe you deserve what you want out of life. And you have to truly believe that you're ready.

True freedom is found within, everything else
is just geography.
—STACEY LANNERT

STACEY LANNERT is a speaker, an author, and the founder of
the nonprofit organization Healing Sisters, for people who have
suffered sexual abuse. She also trains service dogs for the handicapped and teaches aerobics. She is the co-author of the book
Redemption, about her journey of self-discovery and forgiveness.
She lives in Maplewood, Missouri. (www.healingsisters.org)

THE INTERVIEW
I had never heard of Stacey until my editor suggested that I might
be interested in speaking with her. I was fascinated by her story
and had the opportunity to meet her in person in New York after
we spoke on the phone. For all of the upheaval in her life, she
has a particular way about her that is very calming. It's as if she
knows grace "in her cells." Her attitude about life, her strength,
and especially her thoughts on choice and perspective continue
to inspire me.

View the Interview:
www.epiphanychannel.com/people/stacey-lannert

*   *   *

My story is not simple, but here goes.

On July 4, 1990, I was eighteen years old and my father had
been molesting me for over ten years. On this day, he raped my sister for the first time. And I shot him. I shot my father, and he died.

I was in jail for 894 days before I went to trial. I was sentenced to life without parole by the state of Missouri, and was incarcerated. There was a battered women's law at the time, but apparently I didn't qualify. The laws have since changed, so that if I committed the same crime today, my sentencing would be severely reduced—if I served any time at all. We began the appeal process, which lasted about six years, but because of the way the laws were written, the only person who could help me was the governor of Missouri. We basically knew that, but still had to go through the entire appellate process before asking for clemency. Over the course of the next ten years I requested clemency from three different governors. Governor Mel Carnahan had planned to grant me clemency after the elections—and then he died in a plane crash. So we had to wait for the next governor, Bob Holden, who never gave us an answer one way or the other—he just left my file open, which is very unusual. Another four years passed, and I petitioned a third governor, Matt Blunt. Governors usually release their pardons and clemencies on Thanksgiving or Christmas Eve at the end of their terms. On Christmas Eve 2008, I waited and waited—then learned that the governor had commuted five people's sentences, granted them clemency, and I was not one of them.

By this time, I had spent eighteen years in prison because of this horrible mistake I'd made as an eighteen-year-old. Laws are really complicated, and they change a lot over time. I had a sentence of life without parole, but I honestly hoped and believed in my heart for eighteen whole years that my sentence would be commuted and I would be free. But that night when I was not on the list, at thirty-six years old it dawned on me for the first time: "This might be the rest of my life." In my entire existence on this planet, I'd had just eighteen years of freedom—ten of them spent just trying to survive my father.

During my time in prison, I had changed. I found God; I found forgiveness; and I found myself. I was trying to do things to make a difference in the world. I taught aerobics. I worked training service dogs for the disabled. I got involved with that because I realized I was incarcerated because of my own choices. What about the people who are incarcerated by their body and never had a choice? Working with the dogs every day helped me—even though I would come to love them and then lose them—because I knew that I was making a difference in some person's life.

I also worked with the program that helped at-risk young girls. It was similar to Scared Straight, but instead of scaring them, we just gave them a very honest and open account of why we were incarcerated. That's hard to do. It's hard to sit a kid down and say, "I was just like you, and these are the choices that I made, and that is why I'm here." But when you do that, you're changing the future for someone else, and it can fill you with something that nothing else in life can give you. By being honest about my past and the choices I'd made, I was able to open a place inside myself that gave me something back. I don't know how to quite explain it. I know I was the first person three different girls had ever told that they were being molested. Two of the fathers were prosecuted because of what they told me. One of the fathers they couldn't prosecute, but the girl did get out of the house.

So I felt I was making a difference in the prison system, but I wanted to make a difference in the real world, and I honestly felt ready for it. There was so much more that my soul needed to experience. Up to this point I'd always had hope. It's not that I wanted an excuse for my actions. I just hoped that somebody would give me another chance. I had worked very hard on becoming a better person and understanding why everything had happened. I was trying to lead people away from the path that I had taken, and had started being vocal about the wrong choices that I made. I had come to terms with my mistakes.

When I wasn't getting clemency and I realized that prison was going to constitute the rest of my life, it hurt so badly. My soul literally ached. For the first time, I experienced true self-pity, self-righteousness, and deep bitterness. I was absolutely miserable. I was so angry that I had just been left there again without an answer, that nobody cared enough to tell me what would happen to my *life*. Whatever I'd done, I was still a person, and I felt I deserved some kind of answer. I was also bitter that some people wanted me to spend the rest of my life in prison, when I felt I'd never even really got a chance at life. Here I was, boxed in, closed up, where none of my hopes, desires, or dreams would ever come to anything. My pain was excruciating and the minutes just ticked by.

After about a week spent in absolute misery, I woke up one day on my little bunk and suddenly heard myself asking, "Do you *really* want to live like this?" And I realized I couldn't. I couldn't live like this any longer, with every waking moment a piece of hell.

I realized I might not have *many* choices, but I still had some. Little choices, you know, like what color socks to wear; if I wanted to pull my hair back or leave it down; what I wanted to eat for lunch; if I wanted to get up for breakfast. I realized every moment of my life was a choice. And it was that moment, with that realization, that I found true freedom. I realized that true freedom is found *within me*, and everything else is just geography.

No matter what the situation is, we have a choice. Every waking moment is a choice. We choose happiness or sorrow, gain or loss, forgiveness or blame, faith or doubt. We can choose hope. We can choose to help. The choice is ours, and in that choice is freedom.

When this dawned on me, I thought, "You're free. You *are* free," and for the first time ever in my life I experienced peace. It was like a heavy burden was lifted off me. I could breathe. I let go and said to myself, "It might not be the life that I want, but it's the life I've been given, and I can choose to make it positive and make a difference in other people's lives, or I can choose self-pity, bitterness, and anger. Which person would I rather be? What would God want me to be?"

I prayed and asked God to help me come to peace. And again, I felt it. I also finally found true forgiveness for my father and for myself. Some people understand the actions that I took, and the very tragic choice that I made—I felt so trapped. But once I found myself in prison, at times it was easier to forgive my father than it was myself. Until that moment, I never really did forgive myself for the pain that I had caused. In order to truly be free, I had to forgive, and not just him but myself. And I did. I felt that true, pure forgiveness, and it was warm and peaceful and calm.

A couple of days after I experienced this, something miraculous happened. We got an answer from the governor. When we'd applied for clemency, my lawyers asked for the governor just to make me eligible for parole and let the parole board decide on my freedom. He didn't. He changed it from a life sentence without parole to a sentence of twenty years and gave me immediate release. I walked out of prison six days later. Boom. Done. Gone.

I'm now literally free. All of me is free—body, mind, and soul.

It hasn't been completely easy coming home after being incarcerated for eighteen years. There are lots of new experiences: cell phones, Internet, automatic toilets that flush. I wasn't able to keep up with how the world had changed. Or how much I had. At times it's been a bit overwhelming. Prison was safe. I know that sounds completely strange, but there I knew what to expect. I knew what I had to do. Coming out into this new strange world, I knew that I had choices: be a part of it or hide from it, come out and make a difference and join the bigger world or lie back and be happy and content with my little world. I like to think I've joined the bigger world.

Today I feel healed. There are still parts and moments that hurt. Whenever you suffer at another person's hands, there's going to be pain, and it will linger. But there's also a forgiveness, a love that heals the pain. I give lectures to college students to help them open their eyes. Sexual abuse is shrouded in darkness, and as long as we keep it there, the world will be a darker place because of it. We need to show it for what it is. There is a light at the end of the tunnel, but you have to walk through it.

I've started a nonprofit called Healing Sisters. I want to help others find their voice. I want all the pain that I survived to make a difference, not just in my life, but in other people's. Otherwise, what was it for? Healing can be just as painful as the original trauma, and sometimes it's easier to try to just forget everything, and live in denial. That never works. We have to face ugly facts and put them in their place: they're a part of us, but they're behind us. I'm writing a book about my journey to maybe help show that pain and suffering doesn't have to be all there is.

Once I had that realization that true freedom really is within us, it's as if the universe just came together. I'd honestly accepted that I would spend the rest of my life in prison. Then six days later, I walked out. Maybe I needed to figure out what true freedom was before I could have physical freedom. I used to think that if I could just be released then everything could be wonderful. But that wasn't it. It was within me all the time. Freedom really is inside yourself, and it doesn't matter where your body is. But I certainly am thankful that I received clemency and was able to experience all this! *All* this. So it's like the universe just came together for me and, you know, thank God. Thank God.

Nobody is really alone. We're never alone.
Each of us is always connected to Spirit and
through Spirit to each other.

—JUDITH ORLOFF

JUDITH ORLOFF, M.D., is a psychiatrist at the University of California, Los Angeles, a medical intuitive, an internationally known speaker, and the author of several books, including the bestseller *Second Sight: An Intuitive Psychiatrist Tells Her Story and Shows You How to Tap Your Own Inner Wisdom* and *Emotional Freedom: Liberate Yourself from Negative Emotions and Transform Your Life*. Dr. Orloff synthesizes traditional medicine with cutting-edge knowledge of intuition, energy, and spirituality. She has been featured on *The Dr. Oz Show*, *Today*, and NPR, and in O magazine and *USA Today*. (www.DrJudithOrloff.com)

THE INTERVIEW

USA Today calls Judith Orloff a "serene maverick," and that is a perfect description of her. I read this after we had our interview and laughed, because I actually felt more serene after talking with her and told her as much as we were ending our call! Judith's epiphany brings up an important point about our families' stories and secrets. Many times when I asked people whose epiphanies they would want to know about, they said their parents or grandparents, but they weren't around to ask anymore. Her epiphany is a reminder of how valuable and vital it is for us to ask and talk about our stories with one another, especially our family members—because their stories are our stories too.

* * *

I grew up in Beverly Hills, California. My parents were both doctors—my mother a family practitioner and my father a radiologist. I have twenty-five physicians in my family. As a little girl I had premonitions about things. I would predict events like death, or illnesses, or earthquakes. This scared my parents so much that they forbade me to ever mention intuition at home again. So I grew up believing that there was something wrong with me. I got no support for my abilities whatsoever.

I was still very young when I had a near-death experience in a car, which tumbled over a harrowing fifteen-hundred-foot cliff in Malibu Canyon. It went over eight times, and I got catapulted out of the vehicle. My parents got so freaked out after that huge accident that, though I didn't get harmed, they forced me to go see a psychiatrist. That doctor was the first person who helped me to see that in order for me to be whole, I had to incorporate my intuitions and my premonitions into my life. I couldn't keep running from them. He in turn sent me to Dr. Thelma Moss, a parapsychologist at UCLA, who tested my abilities and helped me to develop them early on. While I was working with her, I had a night dream in which I was told to become an M.D., a psychiatrist in fact, so I could gain the credentials to legitimize the kind of intuitions I was having in medicine. I now know it's called "intuitive medicine." So it was on the basis of that dream that I later majored in premed in college and then went to medical school.

While working in the parapsychology lab, I began to open up to my intuition, though my mother was never supportive. She was afraid for me. She was always telling me not to do it. "What will people think? People will say you're weird. Don't do it." My mother loved me and she had her reasons. She was a typical Jewish mother, you know? She had ideas about what it meant to be happy. In her mind it meant being part of the mainstream, which included me marrying a Jewish doctor. But I was never mainstream. I was always on the road less traveled, over in the corner somewhere.

Still, despite Mother's strong views, I wanted to follow my own truth, develop my own voice, so I began to develop my intuition. But when I got into medical school at USC, then did my psychiatric residency at UCLA and started working in hospitals and emergency rooms, I saw that the physicians there equated anything intuitive (or, even worse, psychic) with "psychotic." So I ran from my intuitions again.

After fourteen years of rigorous medical training, I didn't intend to incorporate it into my private practice as a psychiatrist. I have always had a very successful, busy practice—I had inpatients, I had outpatients, I was seeing patients in nursing homes. I was practicing in a very traditional way, offering standard psychotherapy and giving out medication. I didn't want to bring intuition to it because I didn't think it was medically appropriate.

But then, in the first year after I opened my private practice, I had a patient whom I was treating for depression with antidepressants. And after six months of treatment she was getting better. Then I had a premonition that she was going to make a suicide attempt. Because nothing clinically pointed to that—she was seemingly so much better—I didn't even bring it up with her. Within a couple of weeks, she overdosed on the antidepressants that I prescribed for her, and she ended up in a coma for a number of weeks, though she did survive. This was my first big epiphany. It was really the turning point in my medical career, where I realized that, as a responsible physician, I *had* to incorporate intuition in my traditional medicine practice. By not doing so, I had harmed my patient.

I set out to develop my intuition and found people to help me to come to terms with my fears and incorporate intuition into my life and practice. I call them my "human angels." I went full speed ahead, and my practice became much more powerful. I became somewhat well known for my practice and as a medical intuitive. But my mother was never supportive of this.

Several years later, when I was in my early forties, my mother was at Cedars-Sinai Medical Center with lymphoma that had changed cell type to leukemia. She was in hospice, dying. One day as I was sitting next to her on her deathbed, she looked at me and told me that she wanted to "pass the power on to me." To my utter astonishment, she proceeded to tell me that I came from a whole lineage of psychics and intuitive healers. My intuitive abilities came from *her side of the family*. She hadn't wanted to tell me about that until now, but she felt obliged to pass it along before she died. She'd wanted my life to be happy. She hadn't wanted people to think I was strange or weird, particularly as a physician. It was a big admission for her on her deathbed to tell me that my grandmother, my aunts, and other women in my family, on her side of the lineage, had very strong intuitive abilities and had used them. My mother also told me that she also had intuitive abilities that she used with her patients, but she never told anyone. She didn't feel comfortable being labeled as a psychic or a healer. She didn't want to be seen that way, so she'd used her intuition quietly.

This was a huge epiphany for me, a gift that my mother gave me on her deathbed. Basically, she made me realize that I wasn't alone. And that was how I had felt for so many years. I was an only child, receiving these very strong, powerful premonitions, always about scary things, with nobody to support me. That had a huge effect on me as a child. So when my mother told me on her deathbed that there were others in our family like me, and that I really hadn't ever been alone, it meant everything to me. She gave me a missing piece to the puzzle of my life.

I later connected with the other female members of my family who had these abilities whom I didn't even know, and they helped me write the "Female Lineage" chapter in *Second Sight*. Reconnecting with these relatives was *very* important. It was a circle of women coming together, and it completed a circle in my life. This was a huge turning point for me.

The deeper meaning for me is that nobody is really alone. We're never alone. Each of us is always connected to Spirit and through Spirit to each other. It's important to reach out to others with whom you feel a kindred connection. I believe that when you authentically want to connect with people of your own "tribe," and seek them out, you will find them—whether or not they're actually your biological family.

I now have a network and family of friends who totally support me. My whole career and work is based on integrating intuition into traditional medicine. That's what I'm known for, and that's the miraculous journey I'm on. My life feels much more "tuned in" now. I have opportunities open up in beautiful new ways every day. And I listen. I consider myself a student of intuition, and by listening I learn more about it every day. It's just incredible—I'm living my passion. It's a life beyond anything I could ever have dreamt about.

My epiphany with my mother was noteworthy, and I'm grateful for it. My experience with my patient was important, because it allowed me to change at a point in my life when I was very stubborn, and had very fixed ideas. You could say I needed a wake-up call. Now I don't think I need those intense kind of wake-up calls anymore. I believe in little, tiny epiphanies, and listening for very small things because they're meaningful. I think it's a mistake for people to wait for the big "burning bush" or "wake-up call" moments in life, because most of the miracles are in the seamless fabric of the ordinary life. I've learned to revere everything, large and small.

When we support each other, we support ourselves; when we harm each other, we harm ourselves; and when we change ourselves, a little piece of the world is changed.

—EION BAILEY

EION BAILEY is an award-winning actor and the creator and executive producer of *Imagine This!*, a reality series chronicling one-week philanthropic projects for people all around the world. He has starred onstage and in numerous films and television series. His credits include the HBO miniseries *Band of Brothers*, the HBO film *And Starring Pancho Villa as Himself*, the films *Almost Famous*, *Fight Club*, *Center Stage*, and *Mindhunters*, the television series *ER* (NBC), *Covert Affairs* (USA), and Once Upon A Time (ABC) and the television movie *Life of the Party*, for which he won an Emmy Award. (www.ImagineThisTV.com)

THE INTERVIEW
Eion and I met several years ago at a film festival, but I hadn't run into him since. Then just weeks before the book was due, someone sent me a link to a website for his reality show, *Imagine This!* It intrigued me because when I read about the show, it seemed inspired by an epiphany. I contacted his manager, and luckily Eion was in town, so we met and talked about his epiphanies over coffee. He is extremely smart and thoughtful and gave me a copy of the full pilot episode of *Imagine This!* to watch. Featuring Aron Ralson, on whom the award-winning film *127 Days* was based, the show was truly riveting and more informative, uplifting, and entertaining than I ever could have, well, imagined! My hope is that one day much more of this type of programming will make it on the air.

*   *   *

I grew up in the Santa Ynez Valley in California. The area, at
the time, was segregated into the white and the Hispanic communities. When I was a young boy, my older and meaner sister
dared me to shout out "beaners" to three teenage Mexican kids
exiting the high school pool. Having no idea what that meant, I
did, and was immediately introduced to my first Latino fists. That
negative experience stayed with me, and by the time I was in high
school I had an unhealthy perspective on Latino immigrants in
this country. The Mexican kids in our school kept to themselves,
seemed sullen and despondent, and my friends and I were not
very welcoming, to say the least. The crowning achievement of our
idiocy was to skulk around town and light *El Nuevo Tiempo*, the
Spanish-language newspaper, stands on fire: "Down with *Nuevo
Tiempo!*"

At the same time, I was also developing a habit of picking up
every *Lonely Planet* guide written. To this day, I have an entire
library of travel guides covering most countries in the world. At
fifteen, I would rip through a guidebook on Africa as if it were the
most thrilling novel ever written. My father, an airline pilot at the
time, started to give me free passes to fly, called a "write your own
trip pass"—I could go anywhere I wanted if there was room on
the plane. So I started traveling all over the place—Bali first, then
Central America, Europe, Africa, South America, everywhere,
even Mexico.

Then somebody, somewhere along the way, recommended I
read a book called *Coyotes* by Ted Conover. I did. And reading
that book became one of the defining experiences of my life. It
changed me from the inside out. A "coyote" is a smuggler who
helps immigrants illegally get into the U.S. The book is from the
perspective of an American who decides to experience it all for
himself—to go through all the steps an illegal immigrant from
Mexico takes to get here and then live here. In getting to know the

Mexican immigrant experience through this book, my heart just changed. It gave me a deeper understanding of what it is to be an immigrant and an illegal alien in a foreign country. I found myself profoundly saddened by my earlier foolish antics and prejudice.

Reading this book was a great lesson about ignorance or being without knowledge or understanding. It was amazing to see how I could feel one way, and then change my feelings completely. I learned one of our greatest powers as human beings is our ability to change. When we key into something, understand it and believe in it, we have this incredible capacity to grow and change. I hear it said that people can't and don't change. That makes no sense to me. I see it all the time and know it in myself.

So I continued to travel through my twenties, now with my eyes open, and I kept witnessing things that provoked me to wonder why people suffer so needlessly. It seemed that many problems I saw could be resolved with certain straightforward changes. If governments really did care about the welfare of their people, and if communities could come together and work collectively toward solving a communal problem, many of these issues would no longer exist. But something is rarely done, and the problems persisted. That fascinated me.

Then, about four years ago, I was traveling in Peru in the Sacred Valley, alone in a taxi in the middle of nowhere, and saw about a hundred kids walking along this dirt road. I asked the taxi driver where all these kids were going. He pointed up to the mountains and told me they lived up there. I asked where they were coming from. He pointed across the valley. I couldn't believe it. It was this *huge* expanse, and these kids were *young*. It turned out that these kids go from their home up in the mountains down to school in the morning, and at the end of the day, they walk back. They get up at four-thirty in the morning to walk down the mountain, which takes two and a half hours, then, after a day at school, it takes them *five hours* to get back up. They do it unchaperoned, and it's really hard on them, their parents, and their families.

I said, "Let's pull over and pick them up." We stuffed as many kids into this taxi as we could, and drove them up to their village. They were so excited to get the ride and were very playful and polite. But we had to leave the majority of them behind. So I asked the taxi driver, "What if I just pay you for the rest of the afternoon, and we'll just keep going back and forth, getting these kids, and bringing them to the village?" He said with a wry smile, "You're paying. Let's do it." So I spent the rest of the afternoon that way.

When we were driving home, after dropping off the last kid, I turned away from the driver and stared out the window. Tears were streaming down my face. I've never felt such joy in all my life. I'd spent an afternoon and probably a total of $40, but that experience was this invaluable gift—I had given myself a gift. I realized that when you give, what you get in return is so much greater. It just grows, in power and strength.

At that moment, I knew that no longer would I be content as a mere observer. We are here in life so briefly, and as Shakespeare says, "All the world's a stage"—suddenly I knew I didn't want to be in the audience. I wanted to be playing my part. I just didn't know my role quite yet.

When I got home, I started thinking, "I could get those kids a bus. Why can't I get them a bus?" I kept turning it over in my mind. Then I had a moment of revelation. I could combine my experience in entertainment and in travel with my concern for issues I feel can be resolved. I could make a documentary-style reality television show about a team of people who go around the world and undertake projects for communities in need. Suddenly, the seemingly shapeless years of my life fell into a meaningful pattern. I'd never known what drove me to travel, but I'd always felt somehow *directed* to do it. I'd loved acting as a craft and an art, but it was never my end game. I'd always wanted to achieve something else. And this was it. This is what I needed to do. And since then, it has felt like one of the greatest gifts of my life.

Two and a half months later, we were shooting the pilot for

Imagine This! in Peru. Each episode, we take a community facing a problem beyond its control, put together a team of inventors, engineers, environmentalists, artists, and friends, and spend a week working around the clock to solve it. Hopefully, we're successful, and then present it to the community and have a celebration. We also come in with a full-on surprise for the community that's purely for fun.

In Peru, we went back to that village, bought a school bus, converted it to run on vegetable oil, and built the kids a playground as the surprise. That's the pilot episode, and we're in the process of selling it to a network right now. But even if *Imagine This!* doesn't happen to get on television, I have other plans for it and plan to have this kind of work and these kinds of projects in my life from now on. If we switch our perception and see that helping each other is a "hand up" instead of a "handout" things can really change. Giving in that spirit comes back to you exponentially, and life is so much more fulfilling.

What I realize from all these experiences is that I've been learning experientially that we truly are all one. When we support each other, we support ourselves; when we harm each other, we harm ourselves; and when we change ourselves, a little piece of the world is changed.

We access our own power by empowering others.

—ALISON ARMSTRONG

ALISON ARMSTRONG, a nationally known educator and expert on understanding men, is the CEO and co-founder of PAX Programs. She is the designer of the widely acclaimed Celebrating Men, Satisfying Women workshop, as well as other programs, including the Amazing Development of Men and the In Sync with the Opposite Sex CD series. She is also the author of *Making Sense of Men: A Woman's Guide to a Lifetime of Love, Care and Attention from All Men, Keys to the Kingdom*, and the upcoming *The Belated Education of Adam and Eve* and *Transforming the Frog Farmer*. She is the mother of three and resides near Pasadena, California. (www.UnderstandMen.com)

THE INTERVIEW

After I got divorced, I felt like the Rip Van Winkle of dating. I could not believe how different everything was in the dating world and began writing about my experiences. When I received an email about a free seminar from PAX Programs introducing their Celebrating Men, Satisfying Women workshop, I decided to check it out. Alison was the speaker and facilitator, and I was amazed at what I was hearing. I realized that by promoting peace within relationships between men and women—the company is called PAX, after all—peace could spread more widely into society. Ending the war of the sexes might not end all wars, but it's a start. I took a few of the workshops and was fortunate to have Alison as a teacher, so I asked her if she would be interested in sharing her epiphany. We conducted our interview on the phone several months later.

* * *

In February 1991 I realized something important about myself. I figured out that I was a "frog farmer." In other words, my effect on men was apparently to turn princes into frogs. So I began studying men. I was engaged at the time, and tried applying what I was learning to my relationship. Within six months, I broke it off. That's when a mutual friend I shared with my ex-fiancé called me up: "Alison, we've got to talk."

Ellen said, "Men are attracted to you like bees to honey. But when you're done with them, it's as if they've been with a vampire." I was stunned: little ole me? But she'd known my ex-husband. She knew my ex-fiancé. She knew the two boyfriends I'd had before him. She really had my dossier. Going through it, Ellen proceeded to lay out for me all the ways that she had personally seen me "castrate" men. She used that word—*castrate*. She laid out the effects my behavior had had on all these men, the aftermath.

As she was telling me all these things, my reaction was, "Oh yeah, I remember that...Uh-huh...Okay...Yeah, I'm with you so far...All right..." None of it was a surprise. I thought, "Yes, I did that. I'm supposed to do that. What's the problem?" But Ellen wasn't buying it. She said, "I want you to *cut it out*." When she demanded that, I was sitting at my desk in my office, with the sun coming in the window onto the desk. I can remember every detail about this moment. I could draw a picture of it if I had to. When she said that—"I want you to *cut it out*"—I felt as if she wanted me to remove my heart without anesthesia. That's what she was proposing. I. Want. You. To. Cut. It. Out.

I immediately flashed back to being sixteen years old in the back of a Mustang in the alley behind my house, late at night, inebriated, and in a very quiet voice saying, "No, no, no," while this big football player—at whom I had been wiggling my behind for weeks—had his way with me. I remembered being pushed out of the car and standing next to the garage of my house thinking, "This is who men are. They're bigger and they're stronger, and they will hurt me."

All this flashed back to me in an instant. So I said to my

friend, "But then how will I protect myself?" She was silent. Then memories started coming to me fast and furiously, like a montage in a film, boom, boom, boom. I remembered how I felt for the rest of high school; I saw myself in college; I saw how I acted with men all the time, with my husband and my ex-boyfriends. I realized that after that night when I was sixteen, I had used everything I could to emasculate men, to preempt them from hurting me. I had bought into my stepfather's "The best defense is a good offense." I saw that I'd used my sense of humor, my intellect, my looks, even my sexuality to emasculate them—because when a woman is overtly sexual, it throws men off balance. It was always, "Hand them over, and then we'll talk."

At the end of this montage came my epiphany. I saw that every time I had emasculated a man, I'd reinforced my own sense of weakness. My need to disempower men arose from my terror of them. And every single time I did it, it confirmed my belief that I could not handle men head on. They were too powerful, too overwhelming, too scary, and could not be left alone with a full tank of gas, let alone their balls.

It came to me: I had never become a woman. By denying men their power, I'd kept mine out of reach. All those men I'd known hadn't been dating a woman but a girl—one who didn't know squat about who she was, or who men were and how they operate. I also saw that my fears were irrational. In the six months I had been studying men, I had found out so much good about them, how well-meaning most of them are—they just think, speak, and listen differently. I saw that I didn't need to be afraid of them anymore, that if I let them feel their power, that gave me back my own. That's how life works: we're either powerful together or we tear each other down. There's no option where one person's powerful and the other person's weak. It just doesn't work like that. That was my first insight into the paradigm of partnership.

So I said to my friend, "Okay. I'll stop." When I said that to her (I can still feel it), I had this experience of wrapping myself in a cloak—the most luxurious, soft, thick, cushy, powerful one in the world. I knew as I pulled it around my shoulders and crossed it over my chest that *this was a woman's power*. Not a woman trying to be a better man. I felt distinctly feminine, and exquisite, and accepting this feeling changed me forever.

When I went out into the world, I saw men and interacted with them completely differently. It was shocking how attentive they became, how generous and caring and protective. The edges in my face—the bitterness in my lips, the hardness in my eyes—all disappeared. About two weeks later, I was on a break from a class that I was teaching, and this man started looking at me from across the room. I was a woman in bloom—I had just let go of everything, of feeling like I had to force anything. It was classic love at first sight. We have been married for eighteen years.

If men weren't being disempowered all the time, what could they accomplish? When I had my epiphany I was working as the executive director of a nonprofit organization dedicated to the end of hunger and homelessness. I was a huge activist—it was my full-time job. In the process of studying men over the next couple of years, and pursuing my own work, I realized how much children get messed up because their parents don't have their act worked out. Men and women are tearing each other down all the time, and their children are the casualties. As an activist for children, I started thinking about how to address this.

Eventually I decided to conduct workshops for women to help them transform their relationships with men, and we could learn how we could cause that kind of shift to happen, and then I could write a book about it—the "frog farmer book," as I refer to it—and that's how our company, PAX, got started. It wasn't until a year ago, after fourteen years of workshops with hundreds of men and over ten thousand women, that I figured out how to write my book!

By promoting peace between the man and the woman, we're spreading peace from that relationship into the world. It keeps expanding. If women aren't stealing men's power, if men don't feel forced to take it back from other men, if women aren't disregarding their own power and failing to nurture it, and if men stop stealing women's power and instead learn to nurture it, we could get it all done. We could solve our problems. We'd have the energy to get it all done.

*Many important discoveries are made merely by observing and
contemplating what is experienced in everyday life.*

—ROLY GOSLING

ROLY GOSLING, M.D., a microbiologist and malaria epidemiologist from the UK, was the project leader for the Kilimanjaro Intermittent Preventive Therapy for Malaria in Infants Study in Tanga, Tanzania, from 2004 to 2008, funded by the Bill and Melinda Gates Foundation. The study was part of a larger group called the IPTi Consortium, which is a group of universities throughout the world interested in preventing malaria in children under the age of one. He is also an Honorary Lecturer in the Department of Disease Control at the London School of Hygiene and Tropical Medicine. He practiced medicine in London at The Royal Free and University College Medical School from 2008 to 2010 and currently leads the malaria elimination initiative at UCSF's Global Health Group. (www.gatesfoundation.org)

THE INTERVIEW
Roly is in the "Comings of Age" section of the book because he kept saying he wasn't sure if his greatest epiphany was an epiphany or if it was really just called "growing up." For him, it's both. I had the privilege of seeing Roly at work among his staff and with patients in Tanga, Tanzania. He is so obviously a natural leader and caring physician, and he always wears the loudest shirts you've ever seen. We called him "the Mayor," as every single person we came across greeted him and would talk to him about something that was on their minds. We conducted his interview on the back porch of his home in Tanga.

View the Interview:
www.epiphanychannel.com/people/roly-gosling

*   *   *

I have had several realizations while I've been living here in Tanga over the past four years. I realized that when you grow up in the Western world, in a developed world, you have a very busy life, and you're always being stimulated from the outside. You walk down the street and there's color everywhere, people are selling things. You're constantly bombarded by advertising, and I think you have very little time to absorb what you see and take in what is happening around you.

Being involved in research and science, I've seen that the great findings people make usually start with simple observations: Isaac Newton is sitting under a tree, an apple falls on his head, and he has time to think, "How did that happen?" I think that many, many discoveries are made merely by observing what you see in everyday life. In normal life, in the Western scenario, you often just don't have time to think. What I've learned here is, you sit and you just think about what has happened today or what happened yesterday. There isn't a lot of outside entertainment or distractions. You spend lots of time looking at the stars and moon and living and thinking. It is there, in that state of contemplation, that you can really develop understandings or even have epiphanies about things.

One evening after I'd been here a while and working on malaria, I was sitting on my rooftop porch, and I suddenly realized that malaria, in fact, is not a complicated disease. It's a very simple disease. We know so much about it, and in fact we can control it, and we can do something about it, which I think is a shock to people who spent maybe thirty to sixty years studying the disease and think that it's impossible to get rid of. I come from a world of tuberculosis control and research—I've only come into malaria over the last four years—and what I saw with fresh eyes is that things have changed enormously and that malaria is actually quite simple and is now actually declining.

From this realization, I've helped develop a new model of malaria, which is a theory and flow diagram based on our studies and statistics showing how malaria is affecting humans. This model I've helped develop is much simpler than other models. These models allow malaria to be controlled, where previously it was thought to be largely uncontrollable in Africa. Now, there's a small group of us who believe malaria is controllable, and we're trying to tell everyone that for the last ten to twenty years malaria control has been quite effective. Whether it's our work, or climate change, or economic development, we don't know, but malaria is declining and it's declining at quite a rapid rate, especially in the last five years. We feel it's really our chance right now that if we all act together that maybe we can keep it away permanently, despite the fact that in Tanzania, the government's budget for health per person is $4 per year.

Because of my experiences and discoveries, I do believe that having time to think about what's happened in a day helps you and gives you time to observe and discover new things. I honestly don't think I would have these realizations about my research in malaria had I not been living here and learned how to really stop and contemplate.

Sometimes what others might judge as your greatest
weaknesses are really your greatest strengths.
You are only disadvantaged if you think you are.

—ROY WILLIAMS

ROY WILLIAMS is a renowned author and marketing consultant best known for his *Wizard of Ads* book trilogy, each of which has been featured on the *Wall Street Journal* and *New York Times* bestseller lists. He is the founder of the Wizard Academy Institute, a nonprofit 501(c)(3) educational institution located in Austin, Texas. Williams also produces and publishes a weekly column and podcast, "Monday Morning Memo." He is the father of two sons and currently lives in Austin with his wife, Pennie. (www. WizardofAds.com)

THE INTERVIEW

Dachshunds, or "wiener dogs" as we call them in Texas, introduced me to Roy. He owns the marketing company that helped found the annual Wiener Dog Races in Buda, Texas, and I made a documentary about those races called *Lord of the Wiens: A Dachumentary.* Though I did come up with the "dachumentary" part, I borrowed the name of the film from Williams Marketing, which thought up the brilliant theme of the races that year. (*Lord of the Rings* had just won the Academy Award.) I needed help with the artwork as my film took off, and Roy and his team could not have been more helpful and generous. Roy also ended up being my first official writing instructor, as he invited me to take a workshop at his Wizard Academy in the scenic Texas hill country. I interviewed him on the campus two years later on a sweltering August day.

View the Interview:
www.epiphanychannel.com/people/roy-williams

·   ·   ·

My greatest epiphanies came when I realized that I was glad to have come up poor, and glad that I turned out bald. Most people would think I was just plain unlucky. Not true.

I grew up in what would be considered a "disadvantaged" home—on the wrong side of the tracks, with a single mom, on a very low income, the whole tragic mess. But even in my teens I began to realize that you're only really disadvantaged if you *think* you are.

It came to me that I actually had a competitive edge in the real world because things didn't intimidate me. I realized that I just wasn't frightened by things that scare other people. In other words, *I knew how to be poor.* Being poor still doesn't scare me. Going broke doesn't scare me. I'll make it back. You know, being broke is a very temporary condition. So is failure. Most people are terrified when they fail, thinking, "My life is over. My life is ruined." They don't even take chances because they're terrified. Once you realize that everybody's going to fail a thousand times, that you can just get it behind you and move on to your next opportunity, you're less afraid to do the kind of things that bring success.

Teddy Roosevelt said it this way: "Do what you can, with what you have, where you are." You've got what you have, and where you are, and you're limited to what you can do, so don't worry about what you haven't and aren't and can't. Too many people live their life according to what they can't do.

When you grow up poor, those who love you can't hand you advantages, so you have to figure out how to make things happen on your own. People who *do* get handed things often find it hard to escape that expectation—that people who love you are always going to step up and solve your problems. Or it's your boss, or your benefactor, or your rich uncle who's going to hand you something because they love you. Then next thing you know, it's Congress or the president who's going to hand you things because they love you. When you have in the back of your mind that somebody's going to live life for you, there's the danger that you might not get a lot done. Robert Frost said it this way: "Every successful father wishes he knew how to give his sons the hardships that made him rich." I've found that to be very true.

Being "disadvantaged" also kept me out of trouble. I ran around with a bunch of guys from families with a lot more money and influence than mine. They would do things that were just plain stupid that I couldn't join in—because I didn't have anybody to bail me out! I would always peel off from them, and they didn't think any less of me for it because they understood. Anything I got myself into, I'd have to get myself *out* of. And I knew it. When you're that young and you always need a backup plan, you grow up very quickly.

Then there's the whole hair thing. If you go bald when you're a young man, twenty-two, twenty-three years old, and everybody assumes you're thirty-four, thirty-five, they take you much more seriously than they ought to. All kinds of opportunities open up for you. So instead of being upset about losing my hair, I'm glad it happened.

What is interesting is that recently the Ewing Marion Kaufman Foundation did a study on the 549 founders of high-growth companies in the U.S. and found that a huge portion of them came from lower- or lower-middle-class families. So my story isn't unique. It is happening all over America. It's only just now being recognized. But I can say, "Yeah, I knew that. I realized that in my late teens." Sometimes what others might judge as your greatest weaknesses are really your greatest strengths. You are only disadvantaged if you think you are. Do what you can, with what you have, where you are, and see what happens.

Hair Club for Men, my ass.

Life isn't necessarily supposed to be a cakewalk.

—TRACY HAFEN

TRACY HAFEN serves as the director of physical exercise programs for BrainSavers, a company whose mission is to maintain healthy minds throughout aging. She is certified as a personal trainer by the American Council on Exercise and holds a master's degree in exercise science and cardiac rehabilitation from Northeastern Illinois University. Hafen is the co-author, along with the bestselling author Dr. Michael Roizen, of *The RealAge Workout*. She served as the exercise physiologist for Northwestern Memorial Hospital's Center for Partnership Medicine and co-developed its fitness program, and was fitness director for the University of Chicago Hospitals Executive Health Program. Prior to that, Tracy founded and directed Affirmative Fitness LLC in Chicago, serving private personal training clients, and she started the first online national personal training referral service with access to more than eighteen hundred trainers. She is the mother of eight and lives with her family in Centerville, Ohio. (www.BrainSavers.com)

THE INTERVIEW

Tracy and I met when she appeared in the YOU: *Having a Baby* exercise DVD I was producing. I had just finished the original *Epiphany* promotional video and had it with me, so she was one of the first people to ever view it. After watching and giving her feedback, she then mused that she didn't think she'd had a big epiphany yet. But after a couple of days had passed, she told me she'd reconsidered it and realized she did have one. I still marvel at her and her story of unbelievable endurance, determination, and love.

* * *

I was always the kind of kid who had to excel and be the best at everything. I had to break the school record on every fitness test; I had to get straight As every year; I was valedictorian of my high school class. My mom said I was always like this from the time I was tiny, so I think I was just largely born with this perfectionist type A personality. I also believe myself to be a fairly capable person. I think when you have that combination, you do end up largely creating a very good life for yourself that you feel quite in control of. Growing up, I felt a direct cause and effect between what I chose to do and the outcome. I could get the outcomes I wanted by doing what was necessary to get that outcome—for example, studying hard to become valedictorian. That's just the way life works, I assumed.

I was married in my early twenties and living in Chicago with my husband and eighteen-month-old son and was pregnant with our second child. My husband and I were resident heads on the University of Chicago campus while he was getting his Ph.D. In the middle of the night, when I was nineteen weeks pregnant, I felt a sudden a gush of fluid come out of me. The bed was soaking wet. My water had obviously broken and I knew it probably wasn't good, but I just didn't know how serious it was. We went to the emergency room, and the doctors didn't believe my water had broken.

I insisted it wasn't just my bladder, so they finally did an ultrasound to check fluid levels. The fluid levels were on the low side of normal, so there was still some fluid present. They sent me home and told me to stay down and not get up for anything. I called my parents, and they flew out, picked up our baby son, and took

him back to Utah with them so that I didn't have to do anything
but stay still. They said there was nothing they could do in terms
of helping me until I got to twenty-four weeks, when a fetus is
technically viable.

I sat for the next five weeks. I literally sat up on the couch for
five weeks straight, night and day. I never lay down. I never did
anything. I used a bedpan. Every time I lay down, the amniotic
fluid would start gushing out, but as long as I stayed sitting up,
it leaked out a lot slower. By the end of those five weeks, I had
horrible open sores from just having the pressure always in the
same place.

My doctor had me come in once a week to do an ultrasound,
and they saw the fluid levels go down, down, down to where there
was no fluid. When I hit twenty-four weeks, I was hospitalized for
the next four weeks, and literally my feet never touched the floor,
and again, I stayed as still as I could. I did everything in my power
at the time to keep this baby. The whole time that I was lying
there, the doctors thought that we had a 5 percent chance that our
baby would be born and be fine.

Ultrasounds work by bouncing off fluid. By this point, since
the baby wasn't in any fluid, they couldn't get much of a read on
the baby, including the gender, even though I was having ultrasounds every week.

The doctor prepared us for what would most likely happen
when I went into labor or when they decided to induce. The
baby would probably live for a minute or two and die because
it wouldn't be able to breathe. The baby would not have lungs
that could expand and contract. The alveoli, the air sacs in the
lungs, develop from the baby breathing in amniotic fluid. The
baby breathes this fluid in and out throughout the pregnancy. If
the baby has no fluid to take in and out, the air sacs never become
pliable and able to expand and contract. So that's what I was mentally prepared for, although I certainly hoped for a miracle.

They decided to induce labor at twenty-eight weeks. They
took me down to labor and delivery, and it was right off the ICU,

because they knew this baby was going to go right into the neo-
natal intensive care unit. We were pretty much all expecting the
worst, hoping for the best.

When she was born, the doctor just started crying, and then
she said, "It's a girl." And our little baby girl was just screaming
her head off! She was crying and yelling like any healthy baby.
It was very clear that she could breathe just fine and had great
lungs, her color was great, her reflexes were good, she was a good
weight, everything about her was just robust and healthy. And
so, of course, it was a very emotional experience for everybody
because no one had known what to expect. They even kept her off
a ventilator for a few hours because she was breathing normally.
She was fine. Everything just looked great. Basically I had done
everything in my power to keep my baby and it had worked and I
had my miracle.

She had to stay in ICU for a while, though, as all premature
babies do, so we were there pretty much day and night. When she
was eleven days old, I wrote in my journal, "Something is different
with Chaya. Something's wrong. And I don't know what it is. But
something has changed." Something had changed.

Soon thereafter, our doctor told us that she had periventricu-
lar leukomalacia (PVL) and probably would have cerebral palsy. It
meant that she may never walk. It was a 50 percent chance that
she might be close to normal and just walk with a limp, but you
can't tell with babies and you just have to wait and see how the
baby develops.

Chaya never rolled over. She couldn't sit up. She couldn't drink
well without choking. She couldn't grasp toys. So we knew from
fairly early on that she was not developing in any way normally.

She never hit any of the milestones you look for in child development. She's never been able to take a step, she's never talked, she
only was able to eat on her own for a few years and was developing aspiration pneumonia, so she had to be put on a feeding tube
when she was six. Basically none of her muscles work. She has the
understanding now at fourteen of about a four-year-old. Her case

of cerebral palsy is extremely severe. She is one of the most incredible people I know and one of the greatest joys in all of our family members' lives, but she is definitely severely handicapped.

When she was somewhere between ten months old and a year, we were watching a videotape of our family. I had not even remembered my husband filming me while I was in a wheelchair outside the hospital the day after Chaya was born.

My hair is blowing in the wind, and I look so happy. And he said, "So, what do you think?" And I said to the camera, "She's just perfect. She's perfect."

And that's all—that's all I said. I was smiling, saying she's perfect.

It was that moment for me. I just remember staring at the screen with this sinking, amazed feeling. I was so clueless. It wasn't that I was smug, because I wasn't. I did seem grateful. But I definitely had this air of inevitability. As if I was saying, "Of course she is. I did everything I could and it worked, just like it's supposed to. She's perfect. We beat the odds. We got our miracle and that's how it works."

Knowing what was to come, it was shocking to see me the day after she was born saying those words. The reality was, I didn't do it. I didn't save her. I didn't. She's not perfect. Now, I think she's the most perfect person I know, but in terms of her physical condition she's very far from it. The whole time I fought to save my baby, even though I was preparing for the worst, I think the whole time I honestly did expect things would work out like I wanted them to because I was doing everything I could and was willing it to happen.

We don't know to this day why she is the way she is. We found out in going back through the records that on day eleven during the nursing shift change she had pulled out her ventilator tube, and in the records it said she was found dusky and desaturated, meaning bluish. Two weeks later her brain ultrasounds show this problem. It could be that there was a hostile uterine environment that they could never detect. There are things called cytokines, which can cause brain damage in utero that may not show up for a while. So we don't know. It doesn't matter. It is what it is.

It didn't hit me that I had this belief or notion or air of inevitability until I saw that video. I was so naive. I realized in that moment that life is not easy, nor is it fair, and I believe it's not necessarily meant to be. Now I don't expect life to be easy. I don't expect it to be fair. I don't expect things to go the way I want them to just because I do everything right anymore. I hope they will. I still do everything in my power to create my own circumstances and the outcomes that I want. I always have to try to create a good life for myself and for my kids and for the people around me. But I don't expect that it's *always* going to work. And I don't think it's supposed to. I don't think life is necessarily supposed to be a cakewalk. I don't think it's supposed to be fair from the outside—from what we as human mortal beings view as fair.

It does change a life when you come at things from that perspective. It changed mine. Seeing that and realizing it and also then just dealing with and growing with a handicapped child has greatly changed me and my outlook and approach to life.

I see things differently than I used to. Things that would have been big deals to me before just really aren't anymore. I have eight children now, and I am not a parent who tries to overly protect or control my children. I am very much into letting them fail. I do not put the same kinds of pressures on my kids to be like I was, and I think if it were not for this epiphany, I would have expected or tried to demand them to be. I appreciate more other people's way of doing things and what they bring to a situation.

I'm still somewhat of a perfectionist, and I'm far from perfect, but I truly do believe myself to be one of the happiest people that I know, in terms of just finding joy in life and even in finding very difficult and hard things rewarding. I believe it's because I know that, while I can control much of what happens in my life, there are plenty of things that remain outside of my control and ultimately all I can do in any given situation is act to the best of my ability.

Letting go of a dream is hard yet liberating.
Sometimes it's just time to start living a different dream.
—BART KNAGGS

BART KNAGGS is a principal in Capital Sports & Entertainment, an event production company, creative services firm, and sports and music management company, as well as C3 Presents, one of the preeminent independent music promoters in the country. Under his leadership, CSE founded the Austin City Limits Music Festival and reintroduced the Lollapalooza music festivals—both of which have been named Festival of the Year by Pollstar. They manage many other prominent events and clients, including the Discovery Channel Pro Cycling Team. A former Texas state champion road cyclist, Bart participated in the 2003 Tour of Hope, a cross-country bicycle ride to raise awareness for cancer clinical trials, and is a founding board member of the Lance Armstrong Foundation. He lives in Austin, Texas, with his wife, Barbara, and two children. (www.planetcse.com)

THE INTERVIEW
Bart is a very respected and well-known entrepreneur. Though we have friends and colleagues in common, we have never met in person. It was a fun phone interview—he was quite gracious, funny, straightforward, and expressive. He is also one of the people who exemplified a special brand of generosity. Never having met me and with no idea where this project was going (nor did I at this point), he shared his valuable time and story with me the summer I started developing it.

*   *   *

After I graduated from college, I worked for a couple of years and bicycle-raced as a hobby. But when I was twenty-four, I quit my job and decided I was going to try racing professionally. I began leading a kind of waiter/bartender/bike-racer-type life and actually was doing pretty well. I won the state championship of Texas and was competing in the minor leagues of bike racing. It's like the equivalent of minor league baseball—professional, but not the major leagues. I met Lance Armstrong training in Austin. He was five years younger than me, and obviously he was a phenomenon.

My epiphany happened while I was in Altoona, Pennsylvania, competing in a pretty big professional five-day bike race. There was one more day left of the race, and I was staying in a Motel 6 with four other cyclists. Three of the guys were several years younger than me and one guy was older than me and was getting his Ph.D. in chemistry. We'd been there for five days, racing bicycles six hours a day, exhausted, sweaty, doing our laundry in the shower, and were basically stuck hanging out in this tiny hotel room on our off time. So this one afternoon we were sitting there, stuffed on these hotel beds, just channel-surfing, and all of a sudden, we came across *Ben Hur*—the letterbox edition—and it was the chariot race scene.

For me, the chariot race scene in *Ben Hur* is one of the most wonderfully crafted, hugely great cinematic moments of all time. I was excited and said, "It's the chariot race of *Ben Hur*, we've got to watch this!" My older friend agreed with me, but all the young guys weren't interested and argued, "No, no, no—we've got to go back to *The Real World*." And we went back and forth like this for a while, but it was three guys against two, so the channel was changed back to MTV's *The Real World*. I was completely exasperated and went outside with the Ph.D. buddy of mine, and I remember we were walking around the gravel in the Motel 6 parking lot talking. I just thought, "This is crazy. This is ridiculous. How is MTV's *The Real World*, which I consider just the lowest common denominator of entertainment, more important than *Ben Hur*, which to me represents great art or literature?" In my mind, civility and sophistication had just lost out to the lowest form of entertainment, and I wondered how it was that I had been reduced to this situation and what it meant to me.

That was it. It was in that moment that I had my realization. I said to my friend, "You know what? I'm going to quit bike racing." Just right then and there, all of a sudden—I was done. My dream of racing was over. I went back and got on the phone and found a red-eye flight back to Austin the next day after the race. I arrived back in Austin on a Monday morning and was at the admissions office door at the University of Texas when it opened at 8:00 a.m. and told them I wanted to apply to business school. I had taken my GMAT, the test to get into graduate business school, two or three years earlier, and it happened that the deadline for business school was at five o'clock that day! I had to write a paper, get letters of recommendation, and fill out the application form, but somehow I managed to get it all done and turned in that day by 5:00 p.m. I was accepted into business school and began that fall. With that, I started forging a completely new path for my life—a path that has proven to be extremely satisfying and rewarding for me so far.

My epiphany outside that Motel 6 in Altoona was that it was time to grow up and get on with my life. Yes, I had sponsorships as a racer and was making some money, but I was still in the minor leagues—hanging out with other riders all the time, traveling every weekend, training hard, getting by but not making real money—and I was doing it because I didn't really want to grow up. I had been a sort of selfish, playful, kid-jock kind of person. In that moment in the parking lot, I let go of my dream of being a professional racer because I realized that I didn't want to spend any more of my life doing things like living out of a gym bag in some cramped motel room with a bunch of guys arguing over watching *The Real World* versus *Ben Hur* just because I wanted to race.

There had always been this question, this plan B in the back of my mind, of applying to business school. I had always skipped the application deadlines for school every year. But *Ben Hur* versus

MTV's *The Real World* resolved it for me. Even if I hadn't been accepted into business school, it didn't matter—I was through with racing.

I've never regretted my decision to quit racing. I loved racing, and I'm really glad I did it, but I'm also really glad I didn't spend another one to two years spinning my wheels both literally and figuratively.

Letting go of anything you love is hard. Ending a career is hard. Knowing how and when to retire or move on from one dream to another isn't easy, but I knew it was time to start living a different dream. Letting go of a dream can be extremely hard, yes, but it's also liberating.

Your ability to succeed is a direct reflection
of your ability to try.
—SAM DANNIELS

SAM DANNIELS is a rare breed of athlete. Growing up in Toronto, Sam enjoyed nothing more than learning new sports and mastering old ones. In August 2005, at the age of nineteen, Sam broke his back while mountain biking. Though paralyzed from the chest down, he refused to let his damaged body cripple his lifestyle. As a member of the Canadian National Para-Alpine Development Ski Team, he trains year-round, and in 2009 he finished fourth in downhill on his first IPC World Cup and was a recipient of the Canadian Premier's Athletic Award. He competed in the Paralympic Games for the first time at the 2010 Winter Games and won the gold medal in the Mono Ski X event at the 2012 Winter X Games. Always striving to raise awareness of the potential of athletes with disabilities, he serves as an ambassador for the Rick Hansen Foundation and as a volunteer with the Whistler Adaptive Sports Program, and teaches other people with physical challenges to sit-ski. (www.canski.org)

THE INTERVIEW
Sam is a friend of a friend, and when I heard his story, straightaway I asked for his contact information. We have never met in person; we had a conversation about the project on the phone before we conducted the actual interview a couple of days later. He was only twenty-three when we spoke and was preparing to compete in the 2010 Winter Paralympics. Not only was I struck by how incredibly mature and articulate he is, but Sam is probably one of the most confident, resolute people I've ever come across.

View Sam Win Gold:
www.epiphanychannel.com/people/sam-danniels

*   *   *

I grew up with an incredible affinity and love for bicycles. It was my first taste of freedom when I was a little kid. I raced cross-country all through high school. Then I started getting into downhill mountain biking and free-riding—learning how to jump my bike, basically. When I was about eighteen years old, I moved out west from eastern Canada to go to school, but also to pursue a lifestyle—perhaps even a professional career—as a free ride and downhill mountain biker in the summer, and a snowboarder in the winter.

I was one of those teenage guys who is full of piss and vinegar—very rebellious, into punk, hard rock, and those kinds of things. I always had this negative, angry attitude toward life in general. I was just always angry at *something*. One Sunday afternoon in August on just a beautiful, not-a-cloud-in-the-sky, perfect day, I was ripping a bunch of trails with some of my good riding friends. We'd been biking all morning, and there was this jump on the way home that I'd been eyeing all year, a large road gap. It just occurred to me: "Today is the day to do that jump." We did the run a couple times and then I set up to do the jump. I ended up going a little too fast on the takeoff, and I overshot the landing.

The drop was probably eighty feet. My head and shoulders were the first to hit the ground. My back came over my body like a ton of bricks, and I dislocated my spine at the T-4 level.

I have not walked since.

I was nineteen years old and had been rendered a paraplegic from the chest down. Thus began a journey that led to massive changes in my life. I've often described it as dying and being born again.

Doctors had given me a 10 percent chance of surviving. I spent 125 nights in the hospital, and it took them several weeks to stabilize me. After six weeks, I started coming to and realized what had happened to me; no one was in denial about it.

While I was recovering, obviously, I had a lot of time to just lie there and think. I'd met other paraplegics before my injury, and I knew they weren't doomed to a horrible life—not necessarily. So I almost had this eagerness to go out and see what the world had in store for me.

Right before Christmas that year, I went home of my own accord to my parents' place. Then I just decided that I wasn't going to go back to that hospital. It wasn't an environment that was fostering my growth, my development back into being *myself* again. They were treating me exactly the same as they would a sixty-year-old man after a stroke, and it disgusted me. I said, "No. That's not me. My legs don't work. But I am still *me*."

My big realization, which came to me then, was that all of my sports and passions—skiing, cycling, being outside and active— are the ways that I have to find myself as a person. I decided I wasn't going to let anyone or anything change that, ever. I said, "I am still going to go continue to do the things that I love to do, and I'm going to live my life the way I've been planning for all these years." That was my Christmas present to myself that year.

I was nineteen when I left the hospital, a paraplegic college kid with dreams of spending his life somehow doing the sports he loved. Today, at twenty-three, I am back on the West Coast of Canada, a professional skier who happens to use a wheelchair to get around every day. I am a speed specialist with the Canadian National Para-Alpine ski team. Speed specialists race downhill— which is the fastest event in Alpine ski racing, hitting speeds of up to 70 miles an hour. I am completely independent and need absolutely no help with my day-to-day activities.

In the beginning of my journey, other paraplegics, and the nurses and doctors, told me that readjusting to my life was the hardest thing I would ever do. I think now, "Well, if that was the hardest thing I'm ever going to do, then the rest of life should be a cakewalk!" It gives me confidence. It inspires me to know that wherever I go, whatever comes my way, I'm going to be able to handle it. It's extremely empowering to know without a doubt that I have the power to get out and make things happen for myself. I believe we all do. You always have the power of looking deep inside yourself and believing that you have the abilities to change your world, and to change yourself into the person who you want to be.

People always talk about your friends and family as support systems, and of course they're critical, but support also comes *from within yourself*, from your *independence*. If you have a goal, a way that you want to see your life pan out, you can't just sit back and let other people hold you by the hand and push you through it. You need to go out and seek it. Independence is the factor that I think really drives people toward their goals, whatever they may be.

People get reliant on others and are afraid that if they fall, they can't get up alone—to speak in a metaphor, since I'm not just talking about paraplegics. People lose their independence sometimes by not harnessing that light and energy from within them that can drive them to overcome obstacles in their lives. I think we sometimes lose sight that we can get back to ourselves—not the self that we used to be, but an improved self, an even better self.

Before I broke my back, I never really understood that how you approach and see things is going to be a huge factor in how happy and successful you're going to be in your endeavors and in life. I realize now that even if life is really hard, it could all be over at any moment. I always ask myself: "Can you take a step back and take a snapshot of your life at any moment? Are you really not enjoying it? If not, then figure out why and how to change things. Don't get stuck in a routine that makes you unhappy."

I have one quote that I like to pass on: "Your ability to succeed is a direct reflection of your ability to try."

CALLINGS

calling : a strong inner urge toward a particular way of life or career; a vocation, profession, trade, or life's work

Your actions and words are always, always *having an*
impact on another person—especially children.

—BARRY MANILOW

BARRY MANILOW is a world-renowned singer/songwriter,
musician, arranger, producer, conductor, entertainer, and per-
former whose string of *Billboard* hit singles and multiplatinum
albums have resulted in *Radio & Records* ranking him the top
adult contemporary chart artist of all time. A winner of Tony,
Grammy, and Emmy awards, he is also one of Las Vegas's biggest headliners in history. An avid philanthropist, he created the
Manilow Music Project as part of his Manilow Fund for Health
and Hope to help fund music programs in schools. He resides in
Palm Springs, California. (www.ManilowFund.org)

THE INTERVIEW
I am a huge Fanilow and had the good fortune of meeting and
spending a little time with Barry a few years ago. He is beautifully
down-to-earth, and the enthusiasm and joy he exudes is infec-
tious. Of course, I had to inquire about his greatest epiphany, and
I am elated that he was able to contribute this special piece about
the power of love.

*   *   *

So, I looked up what the word *epiphany* meant. The dictionary
defines the word like this: "a sudden intuitive leap of understanding, especially through an ordinary but striking occurrence."
    I've had a few moments like that in my life. But my first thun-

derbolt happened when I was thirteen years old. You would think it might have been my bar mitzvah, but it wasn't.

It was Willie Murphy.

Willie was my mother's second husband, my stepfather. They married when I was thirteen, and we all moved into this tiny apartment in the Williamsburg section of Brooklyn, New York, where I was raised.

I had lived in Williamsburg all my life. Up to that point, I was being brought up by my mother, Edna, and my grandparents, Joe and Esther. My biological father left when I was an infant, and the three adults were raising me along with a neighborhood filled with relatives and yentas.

The three of them knew I was musical but didn't really know what to do with me. The music business was a very faraway land, and besides, there was no money in my family for music lessons.

As I grew up, it became obvious that I had a lot of music in me. So the three adults saved up their money and rented me an instrument that all the Jewish and Italian kids were learning: the accordion. There wasn't much you could do on the accordion, but damn, I was good at it. I picked up reading music very fast, and I actually played the thing so it didn't sound like an old Italian baker outside his store. The only music I was exposed to in my young life was Jewish folk songs and awful pop songs on the radio. That was it.

So when Edna married Willie Murphy, he inherited a very musical kid who didn't know anything about music.

Willie was an uneducated truck driver, but one of the smartest men I've ever met. I'd find him reading James Joyce's *Ulysses* and watching public TV instead of *Leave It to Beaver*. But most of all, it was the music he brought with him that changed my life. He brought with him a record player that sounded fantastic to my ears, since I'd only been exposed to small AM radios. It was what he played on that record player that introduced me to a whole new world.

His record collection was stacked next to this little hi-fi player, and it may as well have been a stack of gold for me. Each album was more glorious than the next—Broadway scores like *Carousel, The King and I, The Most Happy Fella*; great pop singers like Judy Garland at Carnegie Hall, Sinatra and his gorgeous *Only the Lonely* album; musical arrangers like Nelson Riddle, David Rose, Don Costa; big bands like Stan Kenton, Count Basie, and Ted Heath; jazz musicians like Bill Evans, Chet Baker, and Lambert, Hendricks, and Ross; and classical symphonies that, I swear, I thought would blow my head off.

I had never heard music like this. I didn't even know it existed! I tried playing the overtures of the Broadway scores on my accordion, and I did pretty well. But Willie knew that would never do, so he saved his money and bought me a spinet piano. Between Edna and Willie, they pooled their money and sent me off to piano lessons once a week.

Willie Murphy and his stack of gold was my epiphany. I wish that every kid had a Willie in his life. Willie and his music sent me on my way to the life I have now. I'll always be grateful to him. Without him, I'd be playing my accordion outside a bakery in Williamsburg. I just know it.

We're living like we have another planet to go to.

—ANNIE LEONARD

ANNIE LEONARD became the Executive Director of Green-peace USA in 2014. She is the creator of *The Story of Stuff* project, the author of the book of the same name, and the creator and host of the Internet film sensation that has been viewed by more than ten million people around the world, communicating the impact of consumerism and materialism on global economies and international health. She has spent more than twenty years investigating the materials economy, working with the Funders Workgroup for Sustainable Production and Consumption, the Global Anti-Incinerator Alliance (GAIA), Greenpeace International, and other organizations, and was one of *Time* magazine's Heroes of the Environment in 2008. She resides in the San Francisco Bay area with her daughter. (www.StoryofStuff.org)

THE INTERVIEW

Did you know that the 5 percent of the world's population that lives in the United States consumes 30 percent of the world's resources and creates 30 percent of its waste? I didn't. Not until *The Story of Stuff*. I first heard about the website for *The Story of Stuff* in 2008 from a guy in a coffee shop one night as I was working on the proposal for this book. I had no idea what to expect when I finally went to the link. I could *not* believe it. Who *was* this dynamic woman sharing all of this valuable information about production, consumption, and sustainability? I ended up connecting with Annie through my literary agent. (Serendipitously, it just so happened that she was also a client!) Annie is hilarious, passionate, compassionate, and concerned—with very good reason. If you have not seen *The Story of Stuff* film yet, please set aside twenty minutes and go to the website. It will change your life. Or at least the way you see your stuff.

View Story of Stuff:

www.epiphanychannel.com/people/annie-leonard

❀   ❀   ❀

My greatest epiphany is probably not as spiritual or dramatic as a lot of people's. It happened at a dump.

I grew up in the Pacific Northwest in a very environmentally aware family. We had a sense of reverence for nature, especially the trees and forests. I was raised by a single mom with three kids, so money was tight. We never had a sense of deprivation, but we felt a deep appreciation and respect for the things we had. We always did things like mend our own shoes and try to minimize waste. I think my family is where a lot of the passion and drive for my work comes from.

I ended up going to college in New York City on the Upper West Side. My dorm was on 110th Street, and I would walk six blocks every day to class. That's when I'd see these shoulder-high piles of garbage, every morning. I had never seen that kind of waste, *ever*! I was curious about it. I started poking around to see what was in it. And I was just flabbergasted to see that it was almost all paper! I thought back immediately to my beloved forest in the Northwest, and thought, "My God, what is going on here?" Then when I would walk home every day, and seeing that the garbage was gone, I thought, "Where is all that stuff *going*?" That's what piqued my interest in how materials move around the economy.

I became an environmental studies major. I wanted to protect the forests. During my sophomore year for one of my classes we took a field trip to the Fresh Kills landfill on Staten Island—the dump where New York City's garbage went. And this was the defining moment of my life.

I don't even know how to explain it really, this gigantic landfill. There was garbage that went on and on as far as I could see in every single direction—it was just *mammoth*. Many people say it's the highest point on the Eastern Seaboard, and it's one of the only two man-made structures you can see from space. The other one is the Great Wall of China. It is absolute waste and devastation in every direction.

As I stood there looking out at all this stuff, a realization like a bolt of lightning hit me: our entire economy is based on an unsustainable one-way flow of materials to garbage. The *extreme* unsustainability of it, the grossness of trashing all of these incredible resources that the earth provides, was just stunning to me. We're living like we have another planet to go to, but—hello!—we only have one. And the fact that it was so hidden was shocking. I was witnessing this gigantic scene of violence that nobody was talking about.

Right then and there, my whole life changed. From that moment on, I became obsessed with figuring out how this is happening, how it came to be, and why nobody is talking about it. There's this huge dark secret in the way we've organized our society, and if we don't deal with it, it's going be our demise. I realized that we have a major societal blind spot regarding waste. We haul our big bin out to the curb every week and it just disappears, so we never have to think about it. I wanted to run through the streets and tell people.

I started struggling to put together the pieces of what I call the material economy. My whole purpose became understanding how we make, use, and throw away stuff. I needed to know how materials are used and how they relate to the economy so that I could figure out how to change the situation. Everywhere I go, for instance to a new city, the first thing I do is start looking through the garbage cans. I'm constantly surveying my landscape to see what stuff is moving where. What do people value; what's being thrown away; what was designed to be durable; what was designed to be thrown away; who is making these decisions? Imagine being on a giant ship and seeing a hole in the hull. You realize that you're all going to sink if you don't change this. I've had a one-track mind ever since I went to the dump that day; I want to stop us from sinking as a society.

When I left school, I ended up going to Greenpeace International to work on garbage issues, and spent a decade working with a team of twenty people from all over the world. We were trying to get a United Nations convention to ban the export of waste from rich countries to poor countries. I was an international investigator. I visited literally hundreds of factories where our stuff was made, and sites where our stuff is dumped. Whenever some toxic waste went to a different country, I would track it and document the impact, take hair samples from contaminated workers in Haiti or India or wherever the waste went, and organize political resistance. I call myself a "toxic traveler." My travels have shown me the full life cycle of our stuff, the impacts on where it is made and where it's dumped.

I realized that all of our stuff has this hidden life. Now whenever I look at something—a cell phone, a piece of paper, whatever—its whole life cycle flashes through my mind. I know what the forest looks like in the Pacific Northwest, or in Indonesia, where we clear-cut to make this stuff. I know what the factories look like in China or in Mexico because I've been to hundreds of them. I know what those workers are dealing with making this stuff day and night. When you actually know what your stuff is made out of and where it's come from, you have a totally different relationship to it. Some may say it seems like I'm anti-stuff. But I'm not anti-stuff. It's the opposite. I'm pro-stuff. I realize the energy and effort and materials that went into all of our stuff, so it just kills me when people disrespect it!

Because of the time I have spent in developing countries, I realized how extreme international inequity is. We are part of things happening in all these countries that would never be allowed here. Products that we ban are being exported overseas because they're too toxic for us here—but they're okay for people in Bangladesh. We don't want incinerators here because they're so dirty, but we'll take them to other countries. I discovered the environmental double standards we have vis-à-vis other nations. I talk about this in the book, *The Story of Stuff*, and some people feel I'm being kind of extreme. But what we say with our policies is simple: that some people matter more than others. It's not just trees that are wasted but whole communities. All over the world there are millions of people that we're just collectively writing off. The fact that my daughter's okay isn't enough for me. We have to make sure that everybody's daughter is okay.

When I came home from this decade of toxic travel, I was trying to figure out ways to get people to think about the lives of all their goods before and after they use them. While experimenting with a lot of different ways of talking about it, I had another mini-epiphany.

I attended something called the Rockwood Leadership Training, a training program for people who want to make a change in the world. The participants discussed what our purpose is, and how important it is to stay connected to it when we're doing our work. If we do, we will have a wealth of energy, be able to work with more integrity, with more authenticity, et cetera. It's when we get separated from our purpose that we end up using bad judgment and spinning our wheels. We had to give a speech to the group defining our purposes, and my plan was to be the most intellectually impressive that I could muster. So I stood up there in front of this group, and gave this presentation about my goal of bringing about a paradigm shift in our relationship to materials, full of technical terms and jargon. I thought I was being so cutting-edge. And those people had *no* idea what I was talking about! With their feedback, I realized that after twenty years of going to conferences, I couldn't talk like a normal person; I was too deeply immersed in the issue. The other participants reminded me that they hadn't spent two decades at factories and dumps; they said I was starting the conversation twenty years into it, and I needed to start at the beginning.

So I shifted how I communicated. Rather than trying to impress with how much I knew, I started trying to make the connection with ordinary people. That's how I learned to tell *The Story of Stuff*, which later became a film and now is also a book. That narrative had an incredible life of its own—it has reached over ten million people. I get emails from people every single day, from all over the world, saying *The Story of Stuff* literally changed the way they view their stuff, their values, their purpose in the world. When I give public talks, people come up to me—this is somewhat embarrassing—but sometimes they're in tears, saying that it changed their lives. They say that they were caught on the work-watch-spend treadmill. They were not having fun. It hadn't occurred to them that they could stop and say, "Wait a minute. I don't need to work these extra hours to buy this new outfit. I'm perfectly fine the way I am." A lot of people talk about how this information lifted a veil for them, or shined a light. Hundreds of people write every month and say that now they look at the world differently. So this is amazing and great.

Maybe I had this epiphany because I was paying attention, but I think everybody should go to the dump. You get a whole new view of reality. It's almost like having a new pair of glasses that shows you all the secret stuff that's really happening. And then you see it everywhere around you.

Follow your passion. Passion gives you the
ability to truly experience the good times and get
through the tough times because what you're working
toward is so important to you.
—NELL NEWMAN

NELL NEWMAN is the president and co-founder of Newman's Own Organics: The Second Generation food company, which started as a division of Newman's Own in 1993 and has been an independent company since 2001. Since 1982, Paul Newman, the founder of Newman's Own, and the Newman's Own Foundation have donated more than $285 million to thousands of charities. Ms. Newman is also co-author of the book *The Newman's Own Organics Guide to a Good Life: Simple Measures That Benefit You and the Place You Live*. The daughter of actors Paul Newman and Joanne Woodward, she grew up on natural foods at their rural Connecticut home and credits her parents with teaching her by example to be socially responsible, politically involved, and philanthropic. She is an ardent supporter of sustainable agriculture and is a featured speaker and panel member for various organizations and conferences. She currently resides in Santa Cruz, California, with her husband and two chickens. (www.NewmansOwnOrganics.com)

THE INTERVIEW
I have always loved Newman's Own and Newman's Own Organics products and stood in awe of what they have done as a business—basically set up to make money for charity. Before I read an interview with Nell in an issue of *Vogue*, I had no idea that she was the mastermind behind the Organics line; I just thought

she worked with her father. I tore out the article and put her on my wish list of people to interview. My assistant and I did a little victory dance in the office when she accepted my request, and I walked away from our interview even more impressed with the work she does and her commitment to it.

* * *

For me, everything starts with the birds. I was a budding ornithologist when I was very young. It drove me crazy that I couldn't fly! I was especially fascinated by birds of prey, ever since someone gave me an American kestrel or sparrow hawk when I was eight. I would read a tremendous amount, all the time—anything about endangered or vanished species fascinated me. I remember saying to myself, "Gee, the passenger pigeon used to darken the skies for days, and now there aren't any because we *ate* them all." Same story with the Carolina parakeet, the only parakeet native to the United States. Same story with the dodo bird. We *ate* or *shot* them all.

By age eleven, I had become a young practicing falconer. That's when I learned that the peregrine falcon—which is able to dive at 200 miles an hour—was extinct east of the Mississippi and was rapidly disappearing all across the United States due to some weird thing called DDT that we sprayed on food to keep off bugs. I read that DDT was eaten by bugs, then the bugs were eaten by small birds, then the small birds were eaten by peregrine falcons, and at every step of the way it accumulated in each animal's fat tissue. Before anybody knew it, falconers on the East Coast couldn't find any peregrines. They realized that peregrines were rapidly disappearing across the United States because this buildup of DDT was affecting their endocrine systems and their ability to lay a hard-shell egg, so they were breaking their eggs in the nest.

And I had an epiphany! At a very young age, I realized what a tremendous effect mankind has on his environment. We really can change the environment, for the better or for the worse, through our habits and our lifestyles. This deep realization guided the shape and form of my education, and what I do now. It slowly and surely directed me toward getting a degree in human ecology at College of the Atlantic, and then going to work for the Environmental Defense Fund in New York City. I loved working for the EDF but I couldn't stand living in New York. So I came out to California.

I had a friend who was running the Predatory Bird Research Group at the University of Santa Cruz. He called to say that there was a small nonprofit working out of their office that needed an executive director. So, on a whim, I went to Santa Cruz, interviewed for this position, and became the executive director of the Ventana Wilderness Sanctuary, which was working to reestablish the bald eagle in central California. After about two and a half years, I became a fund-raiser for the Predatory Bird Research Group at the University of Santa Cruz, whose primary focus at the time was returning the peregrine falcon in California.

When I moved to Santa Cruz in 1988, I was amazed. There was so much beautiful organic produce in the natural food stores. There was also this incredible local farmers market every Wednesday with twenty to thirty vendors where the produce was just *gorgeous* and it was primarily organic. I had never seen an organic farmers market before. I talked to Pop about what I was learning, and this became part of the catalyst for my next big realization, which came some four or five years later.

In 1992, while I was living in Santa Cruz and fund-raising, I had a very specific realization that instead of constantly having to raise money for the causes I cared about through traditional fund-raising methods, it would be more fulfilling—and probably easier and more efficient—to just *make* money for them, the way Pop was doing with Newman's Own. Pop's model amounted to creating food products, selling them, and then donating the profits to charity. My epiphany was that I needed to take his idea a step further. If I was going to create food products, their impact on the planet had to be gentle. So I wanted to grow things organically. This was a twofold approach to effecting change: I could support Pop's philanthropic ideals, paying royalties to Newman's Own, and also expand the amount of land farmed organically.

This epiphany was really the philosophy behind the beginning of Newman's Own Organics in 1993. I did have to convince Pop on the importance of doing an organic line, though. He didn't really have a good idea about what organic was. He didn't realize that organic was not just a form of hippie food but was a growing practice and carefully thought-out method of agriculture. By being organic, with every product you add to your product line, you fold in more ingredients that have to be grown organically. This expands the acreage of farmland that's treated right, which has a real ripple effect benefiting the farmer, the environment, the wildlife, and the atmosphere. It even sequesters carbon in the soil, so it helps to reduce greenhouse gas. Organic farming really is a multifaceted approach to affecting environmental change, so it's been very gratifying to know that as we grow as a company, a lot of money gets donated to causes and people, and it has a positive impact on the environment.

So it all started with the birds, who taught me how we affect the environment. They led me here, to my organic food company, where I'm still trying to affect our environment! For me, one of the most important things anybody can do is to work in your area of expertise to succeed, so you can then afford to return something to the community. My two epiphanies taught me to follow my passion, and that's what's been the most gratifying for me. Passion gives you the ability to truly experience the good times and get through the tough times because what you're working toward is so important to you.

Believe in your passion. Believe in your power.
Believe in being stubborn.
—DIANE WARREN

DIANE WARREN is considered one of the most prolific and successful contemporary songwriters of our time. She has had over a hundred songs on the Top Ten charts and has written for Aerosmith, Elton John, Tina Turner, Barbra Streisand, Aretha Franklin, Patti LaBelle, Eric Clapton, and Mary J. Blige, among many other domestic and international artists. To date, Warren's songs have been nominated for four Golden Globes, six Academy Awards, and nine Grammys, and she was the recipient of the *Hollywood Reporter* and *Billboard*'s inaugural Film and TV Music Career Achievement Award in 2008. She has been named ASCAP's Songwriter of the Year six times, *Billboard*'s Songwriter of the Year four times, was inducted into the Songwriters' Hall of Fame, and has received a star on the Hollywood Walk of Fame. Her company, Realsongs Music Publishing, established in 1986, is one of the top five music-publishing corporations and is the most successful female-owned and -operated business in the music industry. She also has created the Diane Warren Foundation to support philanthropic causes dedicated to the support of animal rights and protection, and enriching the lives of the elderly and people suffering from life-threatening illnesses, along with music-related charities. (www.realsongs.com)

THE INTERVIEW

When I met Diane at a dinner in Los Angeles, I knew she had written almost every romantic ballad that I'd ever loved, and I had been a fan of hers for ages. I actually had no real idea of the scope of her work, though. I realized this later when I experienced her website, which has a unique sampling of her vast repertoire of songs. The range of the artists that have recorded and are recording her songs is truly mind-boggling. Diane is extremely down to earth, with a funny, dry wit and a million great stories. We finally fit our interview in between her recording sessions in Los Angeles, and her wonderful "outlier" epiphany story is one of the examples I use in my TEDx talk for kids.

Elise's Tedx Talks:

www.epiphanychannel.com/people/tedx-talks

✷ ✷ ✷

I was seven and I loved listening to music. I have older sisters, and would play their records and singles. I remember this one day I was listening to "Up on the Roof" by Carole King and Gerry Goffin, while looking at the album cover. All of a sudden I noticed those names in the parentheses after the songs. At the time I wasn't even quite sure what those names meant, but I *knew* mine was going to be one of them. I thought that day and probably every day after that, "I'm going to be there. Someday my name is going to be there." I knew what I was going to do with my life before I even knew how to do it. Does that make any sense? I realized it before I'd even written a song. Maybe it was a kind of psychic moment. Probably it was a case of knowing the unknowable.

So after that epiphany at seven, I started hounding my dad to buy me a guitar so I could write songs, which he finally did when I was eleven. He brought me an acoustic guitar from Tijuana, and I started making up songs on that. And then I definitely knew: "This is my life." After I finished my first song, I knew there simply wasn't anything else I wanted to do. Somehow I knew I had what it took to be a songwriter.

Then at age fourteen I had another epiphany: I realized that becoming that person in the parentheses took hard work.

I became super-disciplined. Okay, I became *obsessed*. I couldn't do anything but work on music. I couldn't even carry on a decent conversation with anyone, I was so distracted. I had friends, but they couldn't deal with me for very long. I was in high school, and all I cared about was making up songs. I wasn't going out and partying. Well, actually, I did do a bit of that, but I was much more interested in sitting in my room—or in the shed that my dad got me so I wouldn't annoy him—making up songs, writing *all* the time.

Since age fourteen, I have never looked back. There wasn't a plan B. There never has been for me. I knew I'd found where I belonged. Some people never do. I'm lucky I found what I was good at and what I loved.

I never had a doubt that this was what I was going to do. I started seeing music publishers at age fourteen and fifteen with my dad, and everybody turned me down, over and over again. I wasn't ready. It happens when you're ready. But I never wavered. I kept going because I knew I was *going* to be good at this. Faith caused me to take action on what I knew was true for me. It's not that complicated. It's not like I put a lot of thought into it. I just knew: "This is what I am going to do. End of story. Next."

I am a prime, classic example of an "outlier" from Malcolm Gladwell's book *Outliers*. You know, the person who puts in the ten thousand extra hours of practice and work? I'm a textbook case. I had this fundamental realization that it takes belief in your passion and in yourself along with the will and discipline to make it happen. At fourteen, I discovered that I had the discipline that's required. I think epiphanies are important, but it depends on what you do with them. If you have one and you don't take action, you lose.

I wear this necklace that says "Believe in your passion, believe in your power, believe in being stubborn." I live by that. Especially being stubborn—I love that. You've got to believe in your passion; you've just got to keep forging ahead. I put my blinders on, and I just forge ahead. I do the work. I don't sit back or look back. I don't overthink stuff. I don't compare myself to other people. I just do my work. I try to be as great as I can be. I wanted to be great at fourteen, and I want to be great where I am now.

Music makes me happy. It makes me feel something. The fact that I can sit in a room and write a song that might touch someone else too—that it might change them a little or make them feel better, make the pain go away a bit, or make them happy for a minute—for me, that's a very cool and very rewarding thing.

Each and every one of us has a glow, an inner glow,
which we can use to illuminate other people's darkness.
That's what love is, that's what a relationship is, that's what
being a parent is, and that's what being a friend is.
—RABBI SHMULEY BOTEACH

RABBI SHMULEY BOTEACH is the host of the award-winning national TV show *Shalom in the Home* on TLC and the international bestselling author of over twenty books, including *The Kosher Sutra*. He has received numerous awards, including Preacher of the Year from the London *Times*. Named by *Talkers Magazine* as among the one hundred most important radio hosts in America, Rabbi Shmuley hosts the daily *Rabbi Shmuley Show* and has served as Oprah Winfrey's marriage, parenting, and relationships expert on her Oprah and Friends network on Sirius Radio. In 2007 Rabbi Shmuley was labeled "a cultural phenomenon" and "the most famous rabbi in America" by *Newsweek*, and in both 2007 and 2008 was named one of the ten most influential rabbis in America. He resides in New Jersey with his wife and nine children. (www.Shmuley.com)

THE INTERVIEW

I met Rabbi Shmuley one summer in Manhattan at a forum on prejudice in America, where he was a speaker. I asked if I could interview him, and he loved the idea and agreed to do it. I met him weeks later at the studio where he did his XM radio show for Oprah and Friends. This man has remarkable stamina—not only is he the father of nine children, but he'd just taken a red-eye from Los Angeles to New York with basically no sleep, gone on the air, and was on his way to his next gig across town. He

offered to do my interview literally as he traveled to his next desti-
nation...on foot. I remember being moved by his story and how
magical everything felt as he spoke into my little recorder as we
walked across noisy, steamy Central Park, and then at the exact
moment we exited the park, he handed me the recorder—his story
ending perfectly in step with our journey's end.

＊ ＊ ＊

My parents divorced when I was eight, and I think that children
of divorced parents become naturally cynical. The archetypal relationship that's responsible for their very existence dissolves, and
what happens is that they begin to believe that life is made up of
pieces of a puzzle that ultimately don't fit. You begin to question
your place in the world, and if you belong.

That mind-set led me in school, at ages ten, eleven, twelve, to
not really maximize my fullest potential. I was a bit of the class
joker. I would often get sent out of class. I never did homework;
I watched a lot of TV. At around age eleven, I started becoming
close to a Jewish religious educational movement, which is now
the biggest in the world, called Lubavitch. The great rabbi leader
of Lubavitch was the best-known rabbi in the world, a man by the
name of Menachem Schneerson.

When I was twelve, it was arranged for me to have a private
audience with the great Rebbe to receive a blessing before my
upcoming bar mitzvah. This rabbi was the world's leading rabbi
and greatest rabbinical scholar and was quite a saintly man. He
had hundreds of thousands of students, and very few people met
him in a private audience—the waiting list was at least six months
long. But for my bar mitzvah, they gave me these few minutes with
him. It was a few months before my thirteenth birthday, and I
flew up to New York from Miami just to be with him.

The Rebbe would meet people through the night and then
just do a regular day's work the next day. So it's 1:00 a.m., 2:00

a.m., then finally, at about 3:00 a.m. they said to me, "Okay, you're next," and they quickly put this rabbi hat on me and the jacket to be respectful to the Rebbe, and I went in to see him, swimming in this big jacket and this big black hat. I had written him a letter about my parents' divorce, about my life, about how I was very cynical about things, about how I had begun to believe that every sunny day will become engulfed in clouds and every wondrous moment is destined to become ordinary. I wrote all this in this letter, and as I'm standing there alone with him in his office, he pulls out this little pencil and begins circling things in my letter. He was really reading the letter! I knew he only had a few minutes, so it really impressed me; he was taking such an interest.

When he finished reading the letter, he looked right up at me. He had these piercing blue eyes, and I saw in his eyes not the look of authority but an infinite sea of compassion. And he said to me, "You cannot become a cynic, for you will grow to be a great light to your school, to your family, to the Jewish people, and to the entire world. And I bless you today that it will be so."

No one had ever spoken to me in that way. No one had ever spoken to me of discovering my inner light so that I can illuminate the lives of others...to be a blessing to others. Rare is the occasion that anyone will speak to a twelve-year-old in that manner. We treat twelve-year-olds like kids. Here was a man who made me believe that I had some intrinsic gift that it was my duty to share; that I could no longer squander my potential or diminish my gift by believing that I was just so ordinary, that life was profoundly tainted, and that I would never develop my promise. Here was this person making me believe in myself—telling me I was going to be a light to the world! It was unbelievable!

And when I walked out, I had this epiphany. I said to myself, "I bet it can be. If I believe it, it can be." As Theodor Herzl said, "If you will it, it is no dream." And I decided there and then that I was going to try to live up to that beautiful blessing. A year later, I transferred from my Jewish day school in Miami Beach to rabbinical college—right after I turned fourteen—and that started me on my path to what I do today. Instead of feeling fragmented as a result of my parents' divorce, I decided I would try to rescue marriages and salvage relationships, to become a rabbi who is a relationship healer.

It just goes to show you what can happen in an instant, the kind of impact you can make on someone. I'll never forget that in this extremely short three-minute-and-thirty-three-second meeting at three o'clock in the morning (I timed it), this man made me believe in myself again. And I knew when that meeting was over that anytime that I became cynical in life, it would be because I was making a conscious choice to be cynical. Cynicism is not natural to the human condition.

Discovering one's promise and one's potential is the true yearning of our nature. These days when I look around at how America is so celebrity-focused and celebrity-obsessed, I'm reminded of that meeting. What the great Rebbe communicated to me was that to want to be famous is to unwittingly acknowledge that you have no inner light. You must therefore compensate by being in the spotlight, like I did as class clown. But really each and every one of us has a glow, an inner glow, which we can use to illuminate other people's darkness. That's what love is, that's what a relationship is, that's what being a parent is, and that's what being a friend is.

Character is what ultimately rules the day.
People will see the truth of who you are even
when you make mistakes.

—CORY BOOKER

CORY BOOKER served as the mayor of Newark, New Jersey—the largest city in the state—from 2006 to 2013, when he was elected to the United States Senate. Under Booker's leadership, Newark became a leader in the nation among large cities for violent crime reduction and urban development. His political career began in 1998, after he served as staff attorney for the Urban Justice Center in Newark and then as Newark's Central Ward councilman from 1998 to 2002. He has been recognized in numerous publications, including O magazine, *Time*, *Esquire*, *New Jersey Monthly* (which named him as one of New Jersey's Top 40 Under 40), *Black Enterprise* (which placed him on the Hot List, America's Most Powerful Players Under 40), and the *New York Times Magazine*. He is a member of numerous boards and advisory committees including Democrats for Education Reform, Columbia University Teachers' College Board of Trustees, and the Black Alliance for Educational Options. Senator Booker received his B.A. and M.A. from Stanford University, and a B.A. in modern history at Oxford University as a Rhodes scholar. He completed his law degree at Yale University. (www.CoryBooker.com)

THE INTERVIEW

I saw Senator Booker speak with Rabbi Shmuley at the aforementioned forum on prejudice in America in New York while he was still serving as Mayor of Newark, and I was blown away. I don't think I've ever seen a more impressive orator. Needless to say, his schedule is *extremely* tight. Thankfully, he generously consented to a half-hour interview while I was in town. Our interview was conducted in a Starbucks at a Barnes and Noble on the Upper West Side. While riding from the Upper East Side to the Upper West Side in his car with his handlers, I learned that we had something in common: he also had some experience in film. His 2002 turbulent race for mayor of Newark against a four-term incumbent twice his age is chronicled in the Academy Award–nominated PBS documentary *Street Fight* (www.marshallcurryproductions.com). Along with Diane Warren's, Cory's epiphany is used as an example in my TEDx talk for kids.

Elise's Tedx Talks:
www.epiphanychannel.com/people/tedx-talks

*   *   *

I was twelve years old and running for seventh-grade class president. I was running against three other guys, the really cool guys, and I always thought of myself as very awkward. After we'd been campaigning for a few weeks, we had to each make a speech. Then the next day the kids would vote.

The day before I had to give my speech I stayed up really late working on it and rehearsing it. It was going to be the biggest moment of my life, in front of all my peers, the entire grade. I got up to give my speech, was standing at the podium, and . . . I froze. I could not get a word out. I remember shaking violently. The paper was rustling, my hands were shaking so hard. I just couldn't say a thing. I remember that my vice president candidate was standing next to me, bumping me, like, "What's wrong? What's wrong with you?" I just couldn't get anything out. I sort of mumbled through the speech, horrified. The more that it went on, the more horrified I was. It was the singularly most humiliating experience of my long twelve years.

I remember that when it was over, I was devastated. It was one of those things where you could see the pained look on the faces of the other kids. Some kids laughed. I could see that some kids felt awkward too. The teachers seemed to be feeling my awkwardness too. Everybody did. I went home. It was the worst thing that could've happened. I was so embarrassed. It was just horrible.

But two things happened out of that which were great life lessons. First, after that I was just so angry and so upset that I made this oath that I was one day going to be a really good public speaker. That day I swore that I was going to get over this fear. It was kind of weird for a twelve-year-old, but I remember saying this, and interestingly, I changed my behavior after that. Any chance that I had to speak in front of people, whether it was the basketball team or whatever, I would stand up and try to confront this fear. I practiced public speaking and practiced public speaking and practiced public speaking. Now I've given speeches all around the country, to all kinds of groups and in all kinds of situations.

The second thing that helped fuel my confidence to take on this fear of public speaking was that I actually won the election! Winning the election reaffirmed in me that it isn't the flash, it isn't the rhetoric. It's who you are. I think that my classmates knew me—a lot of us had been in school together since kindergarten—and they voted for the person that obviously wasn't the most popular. The other guys really were the popular guys. Even though the only chance that I had to present my ideas and my platform was incredibly ineffective—and basically a complete disaster—people still voted for me. It made me have a lot more faith in people and the electorate and more courage just to be my authentic self. Even on your worst days, one moment doesn't mark the entire man, so to speak.

This epiphany, that people will ultimately see the truth of who you are even when you mess up, has been tested time and time again, and has served me as long as I've been in public office. When I've messed up publicly in a major way, or embarrassed myself and done something stupid, the lesson is always reaffirmed: people are forgiving and loving and they make allowances for inadequacies, as long as you're honest and own up to mistakes—and they know your character to be true. As bad as the day might seem (and I've definitely had days where I felt like curling into a ball, when getting up the next morning takes Herculean energy), this truth about people gets me through.

I think that part of serving in public office is risking public embarrassment or public scorn or ridicule; you definitely take a huge risk. But at the same time, only by putting yourself out there can you really be a part of a movement for change or making a difference. One of my favorite quotes is paraphrased from Teddy Roosevelt, who says, "It's not the critic who counts. It's not the man who points out how the strong man stumbled or how the doer of deeds could've done better. It's the man who's actually in the arena whose face is marred by blood, sweat, and dust, the doer of great deeds." It says at the end of the quote that if, at the very worst, you fail, at least your place is not with those cold and timid folks who never try at all.

Sometimes the dark moment you're in is, in the end, actually a gift; that's also what this epiphany is about for me. That really horrible, most embarrassing moment, at twelve, ended up being a great gift. Not only did it lead me to conquer my fear of public speaking and begin to guide me to this career in speaking and politics, but it helped me see that I love to connect with people in this way. Now when I speak, I feel like I'm not even there anymore, that I'm channeling something larger than myself. And I don't only feel it when I'm giving a speech, but when I'm having a great conversation with somebody or when I'm watching someone sing or perform; it's just something about the ability to connect with something universal in everybody. I went from this ignominious beginning when I was very fearful and terrified to stand in front of my peers and give a speech to now, when I speak, I savor the opportunity to try to share my spirit. I can give speeches to large groups, small groups, about facts or technical stuff, or I could even be teaching kids, but the most important thing, to me, is just communicating your spirit. To communicate and share some of your spirit is a very powerful thing.

We're not here simply to function in society.
We are here to contribute our unique individual gifts, talents,
and skills to the world in a way that only we can
bring them to help society stretch and grow.
—MICHAEL BERNARD BECKWITH

MICHAEL BERNARD BECKWITH is the founder and spiritual director of the Agape International Spiritual Center, a transdenominational spiritual community located in Los Angeles, California, that today counts a membership of thousands locally and hundreds of thousands of worldwide friends, as well as international affiliates. Dr. Beckwith is a sought-after meditation instructor and the originator of the Life Visioning Process. He is the author of the award-winning *Spiritual Liberation: Fulfilling Your Soul's Potential*, *The Answer Is You*, *Inspirations of the Heart*, *Forty Day Mind Fast-Soul Feast*, and *A Manifesto of Peace*. His television appearances include *The Oprah Winfrey Show* and *Larry King Live*, and his own PBS special, *The Answer Is You*. He is also the co-founder of the Association for Global Thought, an organization dedicated to planetary healing and transformation. (www.agapelive.com)

THE INTERVIEW
Almost a year after relocating to Los Angeles for the second time, I was invited to attend Agape Church on a Sunday morning. I had heard of Agape—if you live in L.A., you have probably at least heard of Agape—but I'd never attended. Everyone I'd ever talked to about it said it was incredible, but I didn't get it. Now I get it. And I get why Michael Bernard Beckwith is world-renowned. I met Michael afterward, and he could not have been more gracious and warm. I pulled up to Agape headquarters to interview him a

bit tired and sluggish, and it was pouring rain. After our interview, as I was driving home, I noticed I felt completely energized and inspired, and the sun had come out, along with a perfect rainbow! Michael had referred to his work as "work-play," and I smiled, suddenly realizing I knew exactly what he was talking about.

View the Interview:

www.epiphanychannel.com/people/michael-beckwith

*   *   *

I was a young boy, probably ten. All the students at school had been asked to grow gardens, and I can remember planting the seeds in the soil of my backyard—carrots, radishes, et cetera. One afternoon I went out in the backyard and I pulled a radish out of the soil and bit into it. It was so sweet. In that moment, I felt that the whole universe was contained in this radish. It had begun as a seed, then merged with the soil and air and water until it became the vegetable I was now eating. I thought: "*This* was what they're trying to teach me in church! They're trying to tell me about *this*. This Life. This Presence. This great Life that's in this radish is everywhere! It is this Life Force that they call God. The teachers, and the people like Jesus, and the folks that they were talking about in church, they knew this." Now, in elementary school I didn't have the language that I have now. So I remember as a little boy, I had these kinds of thoughts, and it really opened me up. But I covered up that part of myself throughout the years, trying to fit in and be "normal."

But then in my twenties, I was attending USC, and I began to have a series of inner experiences—dreams, visions, voices. At the time I assumed they were pathological, because I was in the Psychobiology Department studying to be a doctor and this was how they taught us to think. My dreams intensified, with one that predominated: three men were chasing me, and I would wake up just before they caught me. One night they got very close. As I looked behind me I spotted a small tent with a crowd of people trying to enter. When I suddenly realized I knew all the people entering the tent, I figured that my pursuers couldn't hurt me, and I stopped and started screaming for help. But, one by one, everyone entering the tent turned their back on me. Two of my pursuers grabbed me and held me down, while the other one plunged a knife in my heart. The physical and emotional pain was excruciating, and I died on the spot.

When I woke up from this dream, I knew I had been changed forever. The former me had died. I now saw that we are surrounded by a Universal Presence that permeates everything—all that is animate and seemingly inanimate. I called this presence Love-Beauty. The love that I felt in that moment penetrated my soul beyond anything I had ever felt in my life, and the beauty around me exceeded anything I can even describe. My life paradigm shattered, and I knew I could never revert back to it.

My experience led me to explore Eastern and Western mysticism and parapsychology. I became fully dedicated to meditation and affirmative prayer, which became the foundation for what I practice and teach as the spiritual director of Agape International. There's been no stepping out of that energy. I certainly didn't set out to be a minister—I'm still shocked that I am! I thought I was having a private love affair with the Presence, and I didn't want to speak about it to anyone. I was twenty-two years old and had no intention of going public with my inner revelations. But my resistance to the ministry didn't hold out. It's now been twenty-three years since I founded Agape. Everything I teach grew out of that epiphany, from that moment when I literally woke up.

Around six weeks ago, I had another lucid dream. I felt this gigantic being standing next to me—very luminous and very big. It reached down and touched my heart. I felt it dissolving any obstruction that would hinder the flow of life coming through me. At some point in this process, I realized that I was the giant touching Michael. The giant was me, and "Michael" was how I expressed him in this three-dimensional realm in which we live.

I simultaneously knew that there is a giant in *everyone*. Everyone has this giant, luminous being that is their true self. The human incarnation is the instrument through which the Eternal breaks through into time.

Everyone is a sleeping giant, so to speak, waiting to hear the call, waiting to surrender to it, waiting to act on it. We've gotten caught up in thinking we are what we look like, the physical, the exterior. We think we're the lamp *shade*. We've forgotten that we are the *light*—the electricity and the luminosity that lights up every man, woman, and child. The light is who we truly are.

This more recent dream has shifted me once again and has built upon my earlier epiphanies because I knew this, I taught this, and I felt this, but in this dream, I had a direct encounter with it—with the intense power and gigantic presence that is within all of us. I realized that we're not here simply to function in society. We are eternal beings. We are here to contribute our unique individual gifts, talents, and skills to the world in a way that only we can bring them to help society stretch and grow. We are here to become a beneficiary presence on the planet.

You can manifest your destiny when you stop
waiting and start creating.
—ORIAN WILLIAMS

ORIAN WILLIAMS is an award-winning film producer whose
credits include the Academy Award–nominated film *Shadow of a
Vampire* and the BAFTA-winning and critically acclaimed film
Control, as well as the comedy *Tennis Anyone?* and the documentary *One Fast Move or I'm Gone: Kerouac's Big Sur.* Among his
many accolades, the versatile producer was chosen by *Variety* as
one of 2007's Top Ten Producers. Prior to his film career, he was a
commercial producer and also dabbled in journalism, public relations, acting, and the music business. He resides in Los Angeles,
California.

THE INTERVIEW

I have known Orian for several years but had not realized that
he was one of the producers of the film *Control,* a film that mas-
sively impacted me. The minute I found out, I knew he'd be an
excellent candidate for *Epiphany.* And I was right. He has so
many entertaining stories and a passion for storytelling; I could
listen to him forever and wish I had room to include more of his
many epiphanous accounts. What became apparent to me during
the interview is that Orian has serendipitous things constantly
happening to him, and he always notices and follows the opportunities they present. He never ignores them or takes them for
granted, and this serves him well. I always use him as a prime
example of being excited about, acting upon and expecting serendipity in life. You'll understand what I'm talking about when you
read his account. We conducted our interview on a hot summer
afternoon in Los Angeles in his home office—the same house that

he pulled up in front of over ten years before, where his epiphanies and adventures began.

∗   ∗   ∗

I look back on it and didn't realize my epiphanies were epiphanies until later on. It wasn't like an immediate sort of "Oh my God, this is the secret—the golden chalice!" or whatever you want to call it. But there were two moments in my life when I started looking forward in my life in a different way than I had just moments previously. It was like something changed or shifted and I was off on different path with another approach to life. One of these moments was the moment that I decided that I could and would be a movie producer.

I lived in Los Angeles for five years, then went back and forth to Texas, then New York, then back to Texas. Finally, I stopped in Jackson, Mississippi, where I grew up, for about a year, and my thinking was, "Okay, time to find a wife, have kids...I'm going to just stay here. This is it." And that was it. I started producing commercials there. I met a girl...and then she met another guy. So that wasn't it.

Something had always been in the back of my mind drawing me back toward L.A., but I wasn't quite sure what that was. I had come back to visit some friends and there was this director I was working with, but I wasn't really sure what it was I was going to be doing—didn't know what my calling was, though I had passions for photography, literature, dialogue, meeting people, art, traveling, all these things. I thought, "How can I combine them into one job?" And so I thought I'd come back to L.A. to explore.

So it's January 1997. I pack up my car, but before I go, I pull off to a bookstore. I want to find an audiobook that will keep me focused on something other than just music. So I find Robert Evans's book *The Kid Stays in the Picture* and I listen to it twice on the way to Los Angeles.

I am amazed and moved by this guy's voice, his rhetoric, and his ideas about producing and what it means. His vision is more about life's experiences and a theory behind producing rather than just a formula for how to become a producer. There's something about his style and his connection with the whole industry and how he was only thirty-four when he was running Paramount Studios that really inspires me. Finally I pull up outside my friend's place where I'd be staying for the next couple of weeks just as the final minutes of the tape are finishing and rolling out in my car. Robert Evans says his final words...something like, "Just do it. Screw whatever anyone else says." I turn off the car, and I think, "Wow. I think I know what I want to do with my life now"—though I was actually still unsure. I make my way up the stairway, knock on the door, and my friend Adam greets me. When I walk in there's a beautiful, tall girl sitting on the couch.

"Who is this?" I think.

Suddenly Adam gets called out of the room and I'm left there, still holding my bag, talking to this girl. I'm still buzzing from the drive across the country listening to Evans. The girl tells me she wants to use Adam's phone.

I say, "Go ahead. I don't know. Sure. Of course."

So she picks up the phone, dials the number, and says in a dull yet edgy voice, "Yeah, hey, it's me. So what do you need?...Wine? All right...Yeah. Okay...Okay, I'll get that...Fine, right. I'm coming...Yeah. Whatever...Okay. I'm hurrying. All right, Evans. I'll talk to you later." She hangs up the phone.

And I say, "Wow, you were really mean to that person."

She replies, "Oh, Evans. He's just obnoxious."

"Evans? Who's Evans?"

"Oh, he's a producer. You know that guy Robert Evans?"

And I am stunned. Could this be the same Robert Evans? "Uh, yeah. Wait, did I just tell you that I...? Are you kidding? Is this a joke?"

"No. That's Robert Evans."

"No, it's not."

"Yeah." She is looking at me at this point as if she's a little annoyed and like I'm more than a little strange.

"Listen, I just drove across the country, and I listened to his book on tape *twice*! I just finished it! It just ended right...just out there...And you're telling me *that* was the guy?!"

"Yeah." But she seems a little more amused than annoyed now.

"Okay. This is weird."

"No, hold on." She grabs the phone again. She calls him. "Hey, Evans, this is Jo...Yeah. Listen, I'm going to bring a friend over for dinner. Is that okay?...Yeah, he's cool. He loves your book, by the way...Yeah. He just listened to it...Okay. All right. We're on our way." She then turns to me and says, "Listen, why don't you shower? I'm going to go get the stuff and meet you at the house." I'm still standing there holding my bag in an utter state of amazement.

Within an hour, Adam and I are driving up the hill to Robert Evans's home and I'm actually sitting in his foyer waiting for him! He walks out. He's got the voice. "Which one's the kid? Which one's the kid?"

Adam points to me, and I speak up. "I'm the kid."

He says, "Come here." And we walk down this hallway and go up to this picture—it's one of the eight-by-tens he had described in detail in his book on tape. I mean, the whole house, I knew the floor plan—everything—from that book!

He says, "Who's that?"

I say, "That's the Pope."

"You're damn straight it's the Pope. And I'm going to make a movie about the Pope, because you know what? The Pope ain't the Pope. The Pope's the Pope."

And I said, "Okay." It didn't make sense, but it was great.

He looked at me and said, "Let's go to dinner."

And in this span, this "moment" of two hours, I just decided: "Producing. That's what I want to do." My whole life changed. I started operating from a different point of view. I started looking inside to find out who I was and where I was going rather than looking to the outside. It's not concrete. It's abstract. I started looking at the things that aren't right in front of me or that I could touch—I looked into my heart and found things I was passionate about. For me it's about the things I grew up loving. I looked back into my life, and the things that motivated me to be who I was, and I started looking back on my inspirations—music, bands I love, books, films, photography, travel—and knew that producing was a way for me to live a passionate life. Buying that book on tape and then meeting Robert Evans embodied the whole experience for me. *The Kid Stays in the Picture*—it's literature... it's movies... I'm traveling. It was everything wrapped up into one. And now that's what producing is for me.

Evans never became a mentor to me, but he is a hero because of this experience. Meeting him and talking to him made me realize, "Of course I can produce. This is it." The bits of advice he gave me along the way also reinforce my epiphany. He said it's always, *always* about the material, and be passionate about what you're doing or else it won't matter a hill of beans.

I use this epiphany to guide me in all my decisions regarding my career. You go into your heart, find the things that keep you alive, the things that keep you motivated and those are the things you're passionate about—those are the things I should be making movies about. This was affirmed by another epiphany.

It happened just as my first movie was about to come out. I'm sitting here in my office right about that time, and I just look up at my bookshelf and this book of Anton Corbijn's photography was facing me. I go right up to it and think, "He should be directing movies. Anton Corbijn should direct movies." I turn to my computer, google Anton, and get his email address. Within five minutes I send him an email that says something like, "You don't know me. I'm a fan of your work. I think you should be directing movies. If you have any interest in receiving material from me, let me know." The next morning I get an email from Anton Corbijn saying, "That's unbelievable that you contacted me this day, in this week, because I've been thinking about making movies, changing my focus from photography to film, and thinking about a feature for the first time. So good on you. However, if you send me a script or a book that has anything to do with the music industry, I'm going to send it back. So don't do that."

Of course, I end up wanting him to do a film about the band Joy Division. He turned down the film twice. And so it goes...until we met in person one day, and after that conversation, he agreed, and the rest is history. We did *Control* together, and it won awards at Cannes and BAFTA and all kinds of great things happened.

The moment I read the first response from Anton I went from waiting to creating. Before that moment I'm not sure I ever really grasped the concept that I can come up with an idea and make it happen. Now I realize I really can manifest my own destiny.

We are all just so much more powerful and resilient and
intuitive than we've ever been told.
When we let go of the way we think life "should" unfold
and be, we allow true miracles to happen.

—ARIANE DE BONVOISIN

ARIANE DE BONVOISIN is a speaker, author of numerous books, and the founder of First30Days.com, a website that helps people transition through dozens of changes, whether the change involves a health diagnosis, losing a job, moving to a new city, or getting married. She has a degree in economics and international relations from the London School of Economics and an MBA from Stanford University. She worked at the Boston Consulting Group and with media giants BMG, Sony, and Time Warner before pursuing her dream to make a difference in people's lives. (www.first30days.com)

THE INTERVIEW

Ariane and I were introduced by a friend who thought she'd love the concept of *Epiphany* and maybe could help as I developed it, so we met up in New York. We clicked immediately, and she was instrumental in encouraging and helping me move this book forward and later attended and covered the Nobel Prizes with me for EpiphanyChannel. When she officially shared her stories, we were both moved when she described her "epiphany of surrender." Her epiphanies were moving and valuable to me when I heard them because of what was going on in my life at the time, and I still turn to them from time to time as I do with so many of the accounts I've collected.

View the Interview:
www.epiphanychannel.com/people/ariane-de-bonvoisin

*   *   *

By the age of twenty-nine, I had worked at three very big media companies; Bertelsmann, Sony, and Time Warner, in very senior positions and was the managing director of a $500 million fund. Life was bringing me a lot of stuff that I thought I wanted and would make me happy. Not only did I have the "perfect" job and the "perfect" boyfriend but I had the "perfect" New York City lifestyle. I traveled and went to all the best parties and restaurants. To the world, I had it all.

And I was miserable. By the time I hit thirty-one, I started getting pretty unhealthy and put on a lot of weight. I was thirty pounds heavier than I am now and disturbing things started happening. I was getting rashes all over my body and no doctors could tell me what was wrong. It got so bad that I had to check myself into the hospital. They put two needles in me and started dripping everything from steroids to antihistamines. I remember being on this hospital bed thinking, "This is *crazy!* I mean, I'm a girl that runs marathons and climbs Kilimanjaro and crazy stuff like that, and here I am in a hospital bed with drips in me." And there it dawned on me: "I am allergic to my life! I'm allergic to the guy I'm dating, I'm allergic to my body, I'm allergic to the job that I'm going to every morning…"

When I finally got home, I started journaling. I got really honest on paper. I started writing all my fears, what I regretted, what I really didn't like in my environment that I was in. What I realized was that this dream career, this job, was simply toxic for me. I had climbed a very high ladder and it was either the wrong ladder or it was leaning against the wrong wall. And so began the journey to unravel it all and admit the truth to people—that this seemingly perfect, happy, fabulous life of Ariane was really off course, that I was actually quite unhappy. I hit a lot of resistance not only from my family, friends, and colleagues but also from within myself. For the first time in my life, I had no idea what would come next. But I finally had the courage to leave that job and take what I thought would be two, three, maybe four months to get healthy and decide what I needed to do.

It turned into two and a half years. During those years, I walked around the planet, read books, did nonprofit work, met a lot of people, and started listening to my own intuition, to the voice I heard sitting on that bed in the hospital that night. Basically what I've realized is that every single time something has not been right for me, personally or professionally, I have always *known*. I've always, always known. There is a part of me that guides me, tells me if I'm on my soul's path—toward what I want to contribute to the world, if I am with the man that is right for me, et cetera. Every mistake I've made has been when I've ignored that voice. It's connected to something bigger than my mind or my ego or the person who wants to fit in with what's accepted.

I came to the point where I always asked myself this question: "How does this *feel*—to my heart, my body?" Not what do my friends think is right, not what my parents tell me, but how do *I* feel about it? That's become the question more than anything: "How does it feel?" Always trust it.

That decision brings the amazing peace and calm that comes with knowing that you are on the right path, that you are consistently listening, showing the courage to do something that might not be accepted because it's a bit "different." I feel grounded and lighter, like I've found something *inside* of me that is my own guidance, something bigger than my limited scared mind.

And now I've been able to create a company to help people make those changes they've always wanted—difficult changes that they know deep inside themselves are right for them. People start with a really strong intuition about what they need, but they're not sure how to start, what's on the other side of that change, or how it's going to be perceived. It's great to help people get back in touch with who they really are and what they really want. What I learned from all this is that we are all just so much more powerful and resilient and intuitive than we've ever been told. We just need to hand the microphone to that inner voice, that intuition, that is always there, on 24/7, and not switch it off. That's what I'd always done before, in my prior "perfect life." It took lying in a hospital bed, covered in rashes, with an IV dripping in me, but I finally learned to *listen*.

The next thing I had to learn was how to *surrender*. As I said, I'd had this idea to build a company that would help people initiate change, or face changes that were forced on them—anything from a death or a divorce to a job loss. I named the company the First 30 Days as a metaphor. For about two years, I interviewed people all over the world who were going through change. I made a lot of phone calls, I interviewed people formally and informally to try to understand change and why people have such a hard time going through it, why we are so resistant to it. I hired people. I put about $100,000 of my own money into the business, which I ran out of my little apartment space here in SoHo. After two years of this—of no salary, of no good news, of no one giving me a break, of no one doing any press, no one wanting to give us funding, and really nothing good happening—I really started questioning what I was doing with my life. If you do something for two years and you're not getting any kind of green light, you really start questioning: "Am I being stubborn? Is this the wrong idea? Should I be doing this? Am I completely crazy?"

I remember sitting on the couch, it was about midnight, and I just started sobbing. The tears came from feeling like I just could *not* do it. It was a big idea, I was alone, and maybe I wasn't the right person. So I started to have a little bit of a conversation with God, or "my friends upstairs," as I say, and I was *embarrassed*. I told God, "I'm really sorry, I can't do it. I've tried for two years, it's too much. You need to give this dream to someone else. It's a big, beautiful idea, but someone else has got to execute it. You picked the wrong person for this."

I just let the whole thing go—gave the idea back to the Force that created it. I said, "If by chance you still want me to do this, you're going to have to do the work because I've tried my way and it's not working. So you're going to have to open some doors, make some phone calls for me, bring some people into my life— because I've done as much as I know." I gave up the idea that I could control *how* the journey was going to happen, or even *when* and *where* it was going to happen. I let God or the Universe take over. I completely released it.

Within a month of this night, this night of surrendering the dream, the editor of O magazine called, I found some investors, I hired a business partner...within a month! And I had just let it go sobbing on the couch. Surrender means letting go of the way life "should" be, of the way it's going to unfold, whom it's going to unfold with, and when and where it's going to unfold. Since I learned to let go and surrender, miracles have happened. True miracles.

If you have a passion for something and do it
with excellence, you will prosper.
Money and career will follow.
—JOHN LEHMAN

JOHN LEHMAN is the chairman and founding partner of the investment banking firm J. F. Lehman and Company. He served as Secretary of the Navy in the Reagan administration from 1981 to 1987 and is the author of the book *Command of the Seas.* In 2003–4 he was a member of the 9/11 Commission, and he serves as a member of the Foreign Policy Research Institute. He also served as an advisor to Senator John McCain in his 2008 presidential race. Dr. Lehman serves several nonprofits, including Partnership for a Secure America, and he is the chairman of the Princess Grace Foundation–USA, a public charity established after Princess Grace of Monaco's death to support emerging artists in film, dance, and theater. He and his family live in Bucks County, Pennsylvania. (www.pgfusa.com)

THE INTERVIEW

John is the uncle of one of my best friends and onetime roommate, so I've been around him over the years. But to me he was always just Amy's fun and genial uncle. I had no idea that he served on the 9/11 Commission or that he was instrumental in helping end the Cold War. He and his family are lovely, and he is completely unassuming. When Amy asked him if he would be interested in doing my interview, he readily agreed.

*   *   *

It was 1962, I was nineteen years old and a sophomore at St. Joseph's University in Philadelphia. I was very engaged in what was going on in the world, so I did a lot of reading and studying of what was going on. I had been taking classes in international relations with some very good professors who got me very interested in national security. The more I learned, the more frustrated I got by how stupidly our foreign and national security policy were being run. At the time, the Cold War was going on, and the government orthodoxy was that we had to accommodate the Soviet Union. The thinking was that their system wasn't really so bad and there were a lot of things wrong with our own, so our policy was to work out a compromise. And I thought that was ridiculous.

I felt that what we should be aiming to do is to *win* the Cold War—not by fighting with weapons, but with *ideas*. The more I learned, the more strongly I felt that this could be done and that our strategy at the time was simply inept, crafted in ignorance of history. By this point, I was particularly interested in defense and national security policy.

I remember the exact moment when it all came together for me. I was in the backyard at a picnic talking with my father. He asked me what I was going to major in. I said I was pretty much decided on international relations. And he asked the classic fatherly question, "How are you going to make a living at that?" It was this moment, right then, that I found clarity on what it was I wanted to do. I told him I wanted to help make policy. My dad went on, "Well, that's great. You should follow what you are interested in, but also think about how you're going to make a living. Are you going to be a career civil servant?" I said, "Absolutely not. I want to change the government. You can't do that from inside the bureaucracy." So I wasn't sure how, but I knew that's what I wanted to do. I never wavered. I never had any doubts.

When I got back to school, I declared my major and continued reading as much as I could, filling the gaps in my understanding. I wanted to get more graduate study, master the tools of the trade, and learn more about the dynamics of world affairs and military affairs. I started taking more economics and history courses. I also wanted to get some military experience, and I had always wanted to be a naval aviator.

I finished my degree in international relations at St. Joe's, then I went to Gonville and Caius College at Cambridge and completed a bachelor's and master's in international law. I came back and finished my doctorate in international relations and economics at the University of Pennsylvania. I also joined the Navy Reserves. As soon as I was able, I got into flight school and got my wings. For twenty-five years I flew in the Navy Reserves.

In life, you tend to meet people who think as you do. During this time, Henry Kissinger was a fellow at the University of Pennsylvania, and I met him through a professor of mine. While at Cambridge, I'd gotten to know Dick Allen, who would become Kissinger's deputy in the Nixon administration. So when it came time to put together their team, Henry and Dick asked me to join them.

I worked for Henry Kissinger in the White House for eight years. Then I started a company in London and Washington and did that for four years, after which President-elect Reagan asked me to be Secretary of the Navy. I accepted and ran the Navy for six years during his administration, from 1981 to 1987.

The administration knew we had to have a strong military to deter the Soviets. Also, we needed to restore our confidence in ourselves. Free institutions are a hell of a lot more effective, and much more in conformity with human nature, than the totalitarianism of the Soviet Union. We didn't need to accommodate the Soviet Union. They were wrong. We knew they would end up in the dustbin of history, so there was no need to accommodate them. All we had to do was to keep calm and keep the pressure on them, and we knew they would crumble because their system was so wrong, economically ridiculous and inept. There was never any doubt in my mind. Nor, more important, in Reagan's mind. And that's what happened. Reagan wanted to boost the Navy to put the pressure on the Soviets. I led the effort to build the six-hundred-ship Navy, which ended up being a definite contributor to the final collapse of the Soviet Union.

It was a great honor and satisfaction to be a part of that team. It was wonderful to have the opportunity to work with people like Kissinger and Reagan and Dick Allen and other people who saw the world the same way as I did, and to carry our vision out. My epiphany and the trajectory it set me on let me play a role when President Reagan was making a huge change in the world by winning the Cold War. It was great to fulfill my ambitions and realize my convictions by being a part of that.

From all these experiences, I learned that it's extremely important to follow our instincts—assuming we've thought about it and learned enough to understand what we're deciding about. If you know in your heart that's what you want to do, you should do it. Whatever your passion is, even if you don't know how you're going to make a living at it, you should still pursue it. If you have a passion for something and do it with excellence, you will prosper. Money and career will follow. If you have an insight that you are going to be happy doing something, and you don't do that because you think people will think less of you because of it or won't approve, then you're making a mistake. Happiness doesn't come from what other people think, but what you have a passion for, from what's in your heart that you know to be true for you. As Shakespeare wrote, "This above all, to thine own self be true."

We have the power to challenge and redefine beauty every day
through our words and actions.

—BEN BARRY

BEN BARRY is the founder of the Ben Barry Agency in Canada, the first modeling agency in the world to represent models of all ages, sizes, backgrounds, and abilities. He is also author of *Fashioning Reality: A New Generation of Entrepreneurship*, and a popular speaker on body image and entrepreneurship. His profile has been featured on MTV, Fashion Television, and *The Oprah Winfrey Show*. Barry received his Ph.D. at Judge Business School at Cambridge University that examines perceptions of beauty around the world. He is chair of the board of directors of the Toronto Fashion Incubator and a member of the board of the Canadian Foundation for Women's Health. He has been honored with the Queen's Golden Jubilee Medal and is the first male recipient of the Governor General's Awards in Commemoration of the Persons Case. (www.BenBarry.com)

THE INTERVIEW

I was referred to Ben by his uncle when he learned of my project. He gave me a brief overview of Ben's prodigious background, and I definitely was interested in talking to him. At the ripe old age of twenty-seven, he was incredibly accomplished and is definitely someone to always watch. For one reason or another, it took more than a year for us to schedule an interview. I ran into his uncle at an event a few months before the book was completed and exclaimed that I needed to try to get in touch with Ben again, and he said, "Well, that should be easy—he's staying with us for the next two weeks." And just like that, I got to have my interview in person with the very affable and driven Ben Barry on a balmy California afternoon at his aunt and uncle's fabulous pad in Marina del Rey.

* * *

Thirteen years ago, I was a freshman in high school in Ottawa, Canada. I was like any other normal teenage boy in Canada—going to school, playing hockey, and hanging out with my friends. One night I was at my friend's house, and she had taken a modeling course and was showing me photos of herself. She wanted to model, but the agency she was with said she had to lose weight. She was a size eight, and they wanted her to shrink herself down to a two. Neither she nor her mom thought that was possible. Going over the photos, I thought I could see them being used in a magazine or on a billboard. So I said, "Well, if your agency's not helping, I think you would be great. Why don't I take your pictures and send them off, and see if I can help get you a job?"

Of course she laughed. "Ben, what do you know about this business? If the professional agency said I can't do this, I don't think you know any better."

"It can't hurt. At least let me try." So she gave me her photos.

In Ottawa, I found the name of a local magazine, and sent the fashion editor these images of her with a note saying, "Dear Editor, I think this model would be terrific in your magazine. Please call me." I signed my name and put down my parents' phone number. I sent it off and that was that. I didn't honestly think very much of it.

A few weeks later I was having dinner at the kitchen table and the phone rang. It was the editor from that magazine, and she wanted to book my friend for a back-to-school shoot! Then she said something like, "I'm not sure who you are, but I'm assuming you're her agent." I didn't really know what I was, but I agreed, and then the editor wanted to fax me the contract and asked me what the name of my agency was. Well, my name was the first name that kind of popped into my mind, so I told her it was called the Ben Barry Agency. And that's how my company, the Ben Barry Agency, started—when I was fourteen years old and I honestly knew nothing about fashion, beauty, or modeling. Or so I thought.

My friend became a working model and sent her friends to me. Pretty soon I was operating out of my parents' basement. I would do it after school. I would pick up messages on the phone at lunch, and during my breaks I'd return calls. A year into it, I had about thirty-five models. Most were my friends, all girls.

When I hit fifteen, I started to think I really should learn more about the industry. It's not like there was some book you could read on how to be a modeling agent. My family was planning a trip to Toronto for spring break, so I decided to try to meet with modeling agencies to learn more, introduce myself, and show my portfolio of models. Everyone pretty much blew me off once they met me and realized I was fifteen. Many of them told me to call them when I graduated and they'd give me an internship. But the last agency I met with was called Elite Model Management—one of the largest agencies in the world.

I met with their vice president, and he wasn't fazed by my age at all. He looked at all of my models. He showed me the photos of all the models he represented. One of the things I noticed was that all his models looked identical. They were all primarily five-nine or five-ten. They were all between the ages of about fifteen and twenty-one, size zero to a size two, and they were all primarily white. He said he'd be happy to mentor me. All this was so exciting. I went back to my basement office in Ottawa and started to think about what he had taught me.

When I went back home, I decided I didn't want to give everyone I was representing false hope. I didn't want to tell them they could make it as models if the industry just wanted this one particular look, which they didn't have. I let 95 percent of the people

I was representing go. I felt terrible doing this, but I didn't want to play with their dreams.

I then spent about another year recruiting the type of model that was this "fashion beauty ideal." With my Elite mentor's help, my models started working in Toronto, New York, and Europe, and then something *huge* happened—one of my models booked an eight-page spread in *Seventeen* magazine.

Now, this was super-exciting because it was a magazine all my friends read, and this meant I really, *really* had made it. When the magazine came out, I was with my friends having lunch in our high school cafeteria, and as we were eating, one of my friends pulled the *Seventeen* issue out from her bag and passed it to me. I probably had a smile that was a mile and a half wide. I quickly flipped open to the pages of my model and showed it to everyone. And all my friends were very supportive and excited for me and commented on how beautiful the pictures were. But very quickly their comments started to change. They started saying things like, "That's a really great skirt, but it would never look right on my legs. It would make my thighs look huge." Or "She has like no fat on her. I could never wear that top." "It's a great shade of foundation, but it wouldn't work with my complexion." And so on.

I started realizing that although they knew nothing about her, a lot of my friends were turning this woman into a role model, comparing themselves to her and then putting themselves down. That was ridiculous for many reasons: this model had other people dress her and make sure her clothes looked perfect during the shoot; she had hours of hair and makeup, had studio lighting and was airbrushed . . . not to mention the fact they had no idea who she was as a person. But it didn't matter. It didn't matter that they had different bodies, different priorities, and different complexions. All that mattered at that moment was that they didn't look like her.

I was sitting at the cafeteria table observing my friends, realizing this, and something rumbled in my stomach. In my gut, I could feel that something wasn't right. My excitement began to sour.

It took me about a month. I showed the magazine around and got the same reaction. Most of the people were comparing themselves and then making really harsh comments about their own bodies, faces, and everything about themselves because they didn't resemble that model in the picture. After I'd talked to maybe 150 people, I had the confidence I needed to change what I was doing. I knew I didn't want to continue to hurt my friends' self-esteem. Besides, they were the people buying the products the models were advertising! It didn't make sense that they felt excluded and inferior instead of inspired and empowered.

So that moment at the cafeteria table, when I first showed off the magazine, changed everything. I realized I was caught between two worlds. On one hand, I was in the fashion industry, part of creating the images that wallpaper our visual world. On the other hand, I was still in high school and could watch my friends react to those images. The impact they had was not what I'd intended or desired, and it was not the impact that I wanted to continue to make in the world. So I decided to change things.

I went back to everyone whom I had let go the year before from my agency and asked them to sign again. I told them that I wanted to change the way the industry works, and I'd like them to help me do that. Once again, I had a group of models that reflected all different sizes, ages, backgrounds, and abilities, as well as traditional-looking models. The idea was that beauty is about variety—a variety of ethnicities, sizes, heights, ages—and also spirit, character, energy, spark, excitement about life, expression, and emotion.

When I started sending out all the new pictures, everyone rejected my models, saying they were "too real." I responded, saying that having everyone look at this traditional fashion beauty ideal was hurting people's self-esteem. The overall response from designers and advertisers was, "We're sorry. We don't want to hurt anyone, but that's not our problem. What we're doing works. What we're doing is making money."

I saw my mistake. I had been using the language of social responsibility, trying to explain what had happened when my friends saw *Seventeen* magazine and how that impacted their body images and self-esteem. Now I realized that I had to use the language of business. So I started asking my clients about their customers. I asked them to think about what would happen if the consumers saw a model wearing an outfit, and the model was their size, their age and background, and they liked what they saw and could actually *identify*, because they could imagine what that outfit or what that makeup shade would look like on *them*. Finally some clients started to pay attention, and people started to hire my diverse models.

At this point, I graduated from high school and went to college in Toronto—and, of course, my agency went with me. We've steadily grown and are one of the only agencies out there that focuses on having a diverse group of models. I've started to talk about how the industry can change, and also what consumers can do to help make that change.

Some major corporations have caught on to this movement of diversity of beauty—for instance, Dove, *Glamour* magazine, and designer Mark Fast. But when you look at *Vogue*, *Harper's Bazaar*, *Elle*, or big designers like Versace, Ralph Lauren, or Dior, they still use the same models in their shows. The ads still primarily look the same. It wasn't enough to have case studies. Dove wasn't enough. A small emerging designer wasn't enough. I realized we need hard-core empirical evidence to convince the executives that there is a change in the mind-set of consumers, that people do crave authenticity. To convince these huge national brands, I've decided I need to provide research.

So right now I'm working on my Ph.D. at Cambridge and conducting research in eight different countries to see if women will increase their purchasing intentions if they see someone who reflects their age, size, and background, as opposed to a traditional

Western beauty ideal. The evidence is very clear that women do want to see people in advertising images reflecting the reality of who they are. My research will, I hope, help change the way the industry considers beauty, and also make advertising more exciting, instead of dispiriting, to the consumer.

Fashion is fun. It's about play, experimentation, and expressing different facets of who you are. It should not be seen as a critique of your body or yourself. Nor should it make you feel bad when you look in a mirror. It should make you look in a mirror and feel empowered, self-confident, and playful.

We have the power to challenge and redefine beauty every day through our words and actions. I love my work. I love it because I believe in it. I believe beauty belongs to all of us, and I will never stop pushing to expand the ideal of beauty until it is an authentic and empowering reflection of all of us.

If you don't believe in yourself, nobody else is going to.
So go for it. Find what makes you happy and do it.
—DAVID HUDGINS

DAVID HUDGINS is a television writer, executive producer, husband and father. His credits include co-producer on the WB's hit television series *Everwood* (2003–2006) and co–executive producer on NBC's critically acclaimed and award-winning series *Friday Night Lights* and *Parenthood*. He was also the creator and executive producer of the Fox television series *Past Life*, and has been nominated for numerous Writers Guild Awards. He is the founder of The Catherine H. Tuck Foundation in honor of his sister, Dr. Catherine Hudgins Tuck, to help women who are fighting cancer with their everyday costs so they can focus on healing. He resides in Los Angeles, California, with his wife, Meghan, and their four boys. (www.catherinefund.org)

THE INTERVIEW

As I've said, I've realized that our epiphanies contain some of our greatest wisdom, so I like to reach out to people who are doing things in the world that I admire because they usually have great stories and insights to share. David was a writer and producer on *Friday Night Lights*, one of my all-time favorite television shows, so I wanted to interview him. Though David and I are both from Dallas, we had never met. When we got in touch, he was still writing for *Friday Night Lights* and was in production on his own series that was about to launch on Fox—that is the definition of "crazy busy"—but he still made time for this interview with me amid the madness in his office. Since our interview, David has realized his dream of starting a foundation in his sister's honor to help women who are in cancer treatment to stay financially afloat. I always cite David's story as very clear example of an epiphany's "Ripple Effect." All epiphanies ripple out and many times they take twists and turns and will have completely different timing than you ever expected. And like David's, they just keep going and going and going...

View the Interview:
www.epiphanychannel.com/people/david-hudgins

＊　＊　＊

I grew up in Dallas, Texas, and in the mid-nineties, I was living there, married with two kids, practicing law. Over time I recognized that while I didn't *hate* law, I didn't love it either. I observed the older partners in the firm—very nice people—and saw myself in thirty years. "That will be my life. I'll practice law at this firm. At sixty years old I'll be going to the country club and to bar association dinners, after raising three-point-five kids inside a white picket fence." All that was fine, but it wasn't enough for me. I didn't want "fine." I wanted great.

I started reflecting on what really makes us happy. After a lot of soul searching, I decided that it's about *doing*—acting on our deepest aspirations and doing what we really want to do in life, whatever that is. For me, I had to finally admit that meant making movies. I'd done theater in high school and had always been creative. I'd always loved to write and loved films. But how would I ever make them? How did you get into that business? I had no idea.

But then something happened. Some childhood friends of mine in Dallas, Luke and Owen Wilson, made a movie called *Bottle Rocket*. These guys had *no clue* what they were doing. They had just had a funny idea, got some money, and shot this movie. Nobody knew whether it would get shown anywhere, and it wasn't a big hit—but it made their careers. I remember going to the movie theater to see that movie and thinking, "If they can do it, *anybody* can." I'm kidding, but seriously, the Wilson brothers inspired me and got me really thinking about what I could do. But I was just doing that—thinking about it—when we got news that changed our lives.

My older sister, Catherine, got diagnosed with breast cancer. About two years into it, I was visiting Catherine in New York. She was undergoing chemo at the time, and we were in her room talking. I had been a lawyer for about seven years at this point, and I started complaining about it. Finally she stopped me and said, "What do you *want* to do?" I paused and said, "Well, I want to make movies. I want to write and make movies."

"Well, what are you *waiting* for? Look at me. Use me as an example. You have got to grab life while you can, David. Do you want to be sixty-five years old, looking back saying, 'I wish I had done this, I wish I had done that'?"

That was the moment it clicked for me. Catherine was right. When I left her that day, my life took a whole new direction.

Fortunately, I have a very cool wife who is completely supportive, and she was on board with what I felt I needed to do. I quit my job, and we sold our house and moved the family to the hills of Tennessee, where my parents had a cabin, so we could stay rent-free while I wrote.

As with almost anything that's valuable and worthwhile, there was a lot of risk involved. Everybody thought I was crazy—including me at times. Late at night, I'd lie awake in bed. "Am I really doing this? Am I really going to quit this job, take my wife and two little boys and move to the hills of Tennessee?" But I kept moving forward, no matter how scared I got.

We thought we'd only be at the cabin for six months. Uh, yeah. We ended up living there over *two years*. Finally I had a screenplay optioned. It was not a lot of money, but that didn't matter. Somebody thought I could write. Somebody was willing to pay me for my work. It was time to pack up and move to L.A.

So once again, we uprooted our family (now with three boys), and moved to Los Angeles.

This was all in 2001, right after 9/11. I had no job and was sitting around wondering what to do. Then, surprise! Megan got pregnant with our fourth boy. Love him to death, but he was not planned. We came to a very dark moment. I said to myself, "It's a good thing I kept my license current, because I may have to go back to the practice of law. I may have to give up. I may not get to do this."

So my first year in L.A. was really tough, especially when I was watching my boys go to school and my bank account get smaller and smaller. But I stuck with it. And thank God I did.

At a birthday party, I met a guy named David Kissinger. I was excited just because he was Henry Kissinger's son, but my sister-in-law who works in the entertainment business said, "No, dummy, he's the head of NBC Universal Television. You need to give him your scripts." I didn't want to be *that* guy—the one who says, "Hey, I met you at a party. Here, read my script." But she told me that was how L.A. works, and I had to do it. So I gave him my script. He liked it. He got me a meeting with an agent. The agent signed me. A week later I had my first job. And it's been a hell of a ride ever since.

Acting on my sister's advice changed everything for me. I can't tell you how satisfying it is to do something you love. It's made me incredibly happy. I get to work with actors and really smart writers. I see the world. I'm creating something. And I knew that I was never going to be fulfilled unless I tried to do that. I tell my boys all the time, "You can do anything. Don't let anybody tell you that you can't. And don't tell yourself that. If you don't believe in yourself, nobody else is going to. So go for it. Find what makes you happy and do it."

I have tremendous gratitude for Catherine and how instrumental she was in changing my life. When she died in May 2001, at only thirty-nine, I had just gotten my first job. It's nice that before she died she knew I might be on my way.

What brings true happiness is true connection
with each other.

—FRANK DESIDERIO

FRANK DESIDERIO, C.S.P., is First Consultor of the Paulist Fathers and former director of the Paulist Center in Boston, Massachusetts. Prior to that, he served as president of Paulist Productions in Los Angeles, and his executive producer credits include both movies of the week and documentary projects such as ABC's *Judas*, the series *The Jesus Experience*, A&E's *Healing and Prayer: Power or Placebo*, the History Channel's *Visions of Mary*, *Joseph: The Silent Saint*, *St. Peter: The Rock*, and *Judas: Traitor or Friend?* Fr. Desiderio also served as president of the Human Family Educational and Cultural Institute, which awards the prestigious Humanitas Prize to film and television writers. He has served as the rector at St. Paul's College and as the director of campus ministry at the University Catholic Center at the University of California, Los Angeles, and produced two weekly religion and public affairs programs for Paulist Communications. He is also a poet whose verse has appeared in the *National Catholic Reporter*, *Prairie Messenger*, *Bread of Life*, and *Spring Hill Review*. His latest project as a producer is the award-winning documentary *The Big Question: A Film About Forgiveness*, which launched him into his current ministry of forgiveness and reconciliation. (www.ForgivenessRetreats.org)

THE INTERVIEW

I decided to put Father Frank's story last because you probably would not be holding this book in your hands if it weren't for him. Fondly referred to as the "Hollywood Priest," he has been a colleague and friend of mine for years. Because of his continuing belief, encouragement, and early active role in pushing this project forward from the second he heard this "random idea" I had, *Epiphany* now exists and has inspired, encouraged, and transformed me in many ways. My hope is that in some way, it has enriched your life too.

✦   ❋   ❊

Like a lot of people, I found being a teenager very tough. I would never want to go back to being a sophomore in high school. You're trying to figure out how to be in the world, who you are, where you want to go, who you want to be with—all those big questions—but mostly it comes down to, "Do people think I'm cool or not?"

I was living with a lot of fear about what people thought of me, trying to control my image, comparing myself to other people and not feeling like I measured up, competing to prove I was better, smarter, or whatever. It was just exhausting and self-defeating, and I started closing more and more into myself. In my junior year, I was invited to go on this weekend religious retreat that my school was sponsoring. I went to a Catholic high school, but not everyone at the retreat was Catholic. Some of my friends thought it would be fun and talked me into going too. It was called ECHO—Encountering Christ in Others. I wasn't really expecting anything out of it and didn't really want to go, but I went because they were.

Over a Friday night, Saturday, and Sunday morning, there was a series of talks, and I remember one of the talks on the retreat that happened on Saturday. It was about the masks we create that give us a false sense of self, and how we can let those masks down and get more in touch with our authentic selves. Along with the other guys that were going through it with me, we just all kind of broke down. We realized that we had been posturing and putting on a show for each other's benefit, and had been judging each other—harshly. We saw that we could all just let it go and stop doing that. On a very basic level we were all the same: we all cared about the same things, we all wanted the same things, and we were the same kind of people. After that, on Saturday night and Sunday there were talks that were more about creating the connections and recognizing the common bond that we had as children of God—and the fact that we were all created by God, and on that level we were all equal.

This breakthrough got me out of the self-absorption that was torturing me. I realized that life was about bringing my authentic self, without the masks, to God. I started to get my self-worth out of my relationship with God—out of the knowledge that I was always loved by God, that I was validated by Him and no one else. The epiphany was that I was lovable as I am, I could love other people as they are, and that really we all live in this kind of connection and community. That's how we're built—to be supportive and loving toward each other. Our judgments and posturing are all just part of a false self. Ultimately you can't get to happiness if you keep hidden because you don't really connect with other people. What brings you happiness is true connection.

This experience formed a real bond and a real brotherhood among all of us at the retreat, and I'm still close friends with a lot of those guys. We see each other at least once a year, if not more often—they see each other all the time because they live in the same area. I live on another coast, so I don't see them as much. But a bond was created.

A huge change came in the culture of our high school after that. We all became much more caring and cooperative. There wasn't as much competition, and we formed real, long-term bonds of friendship based on a real sense of compassion for one another. I think that's the key to it. When you see other people's pain and fears and realize that theirs are a lot like yours, you start to connect on the level of compassion. You start suffering with them, knowing how they hurt and how you hurt the same way, so you have more of a real heart connection.

This self-realization had a major impact on my life. Having learned about being lovable and connecting to people on a very basic level, and witnessed how it drastically changed my life and so many of my friends' lives for the better, I wanted to help other people come to that same awareness.

This retreat was only for guys, but I continued to participate in lots of retreats like it throughout the rest of high school and college, and a number of them were coed—as a matter of fact, I met my college girlfriend on one of those retreats. I probably over the years participated in fourteen or fifteen of them and began to lead them in college. I'd gone to Catholic schools, where priesthood is held out as a model, something to aspire to. I'd put that idea on the back burner in college, but as I continued to participate in those retreats, work on retreat teams, then lead them in college, it seemed to me that priesthood was a way to help people, full-time, to share that transformative experience. I could pay it forward. That's what I try to do with my preaching. It's so much a part of my spiritual DNA now—it comes out in whatever I'm doing. After I was ordained, I worked as a chaplain on those retreats for college kids at American University. The first one I went to in high school was one of the first of its kind, but now we have these kinds of retreats all over.

What I gained at those retreats was a life-transforming realization. I began moving from being a child into being an adult and to answer what I refer to as "the call." There was a strong sense of call for me regarding the priesthood that I realize began then. When I contemplated the decision to pursue priesthood, there was a real sense of peace around it. There was a sense of calling for me, and in answering the call, I found fulfillment.

EXERCISES

1. It's important to honor your epiphanies and make them a tool that you're fully utilizing in your life. Maybe you already are, but this is still a great exercise for anyone to do. It's important to be very specific about your own greatest epiphany or epiphanies. Please answer the questions I ask everyone for my project—and write it out—pen to paper is best, but you can type it too.

   • What is the story of your greatest epiphany in life? What led up to it? What happened in that moment? What happened afterward? Did your life change? If so, how?

   • If you can, please summarize your epiphany in one or two sentences. What was the wisdom gained or the lesson learned? (This is your quote and title of the piece, as in the book.) What would you want to pass on to others? How do you utilize or cultivate sparks of epiphany?

   When you write your story out, really put yourself there sensorily. Try to really see, smell, feel, hear what was happening when you had your epiphany and write down every detail. (No one has to see these!) If you want to share them, that's great, but for now, don't worry about that, just get it out and down on paper. You may realize while working and thinking about this that you actually have had more than one major epiphany in your life. Write them all out. Telling your story has a different kind of power and is really important, but this exercise of writing them down is amazing. You will discover things you hadn't thought of or noticed before, and you will remember things you never have before, and it will probably have different meaning for you now than it did then. Just let it pour out—**do not edit until it's all down on paper!**

If you think you haven't had an epiphany, just think about some kind of realization you've had—it can be anything—the more profound and powerful for you, the better, even something as simple as figuring out math or how fun it was to kiss for the first time. Just write out the story of a moment of great revelation without any judgment on it.

2. Write out an epiphany you'd **like** to have.

3. Think about how you can be developing the **four elements** present in every life-changing epiphany—all are listed below with some questions and exercises.

LISTENING. Whether they were calmly contemplating the sky, meditating or praying, clinging to hope in a crisis, desperate to heal, or searching for an answer, people were listening and paying attention to signs and what was going on around them when they had a life-changing epiphany.

Listening and sound experts, such as Julian Treasure, explain that we are losing our listening skills in our louder and louder world. Not only is it noisier, but we're impatient and want everything in sound-bites. **One easy thing you can do to counter this and develop your listening capacities is to make sure you are in silence or at least quiet for a minimum of three minutes a day.**

- How are you listening/paying attention in life? Do you have a practice/ways of listening to yourself? To others? To the world around you? Write down everything you could do be more present to yourself and your inner voice, to others, and to the world around you. Practice at least one thing daily on that list.

BELIEF. When people had an epiphany, they never doubted for one instant that whatever happened was real for them. They had absolute faith and trust in their experience and themselves, knowing the action they were taking because of their epiphany was right for them, regardless of what anyone else thought.

- We can strengthen belief in ourselves and the way life works for us. Become aware of the meanings/perceptions you are attributing to things. Are you slanted positively or negatively in interpreting happenings in life?

- Is there anything you would you like to have an epiphany about? Study/research/immerse yourself in those subjects—which might even be yourself. (Take some time for introspection.)

Self-belief is learnable. We can all develop and bolster our self-belief in numerous ways. Here are a few:

- Deal with the inner negative voice. Remember, that negative voice and talk wasn't yours originally. Develop a practice of **self-compassion**. Act like your own best friend. (See Kristen Neff's epiphany.) Do you catch yourself talking to yourself in ways that you would never speak to another person? What are some of the negative mantras you might be telling yourself?

- Reflect on your strengths and accomplishments. Also think about what your friends would consider to be your strengths. Write them down.

- Educate and immerse yourself in what you love and are drawn to. Seek out tools to help you develop your gifts and talents as well as help remove negative beliefs and blocks. These tools include books, classes, retreats, workshops, life coaches, therapists, religious and spiritual leaders/teachers, and groups you can join to develop your interests and receive support.

ACTION. Every single person whose epiphany positively changed his or her life took action. Each of them took the first step toward whatever the epiphany compelled him or her to do, even with no idea what would happen after that. **You must take action for an epiphany to change your life. Period.**

- When we talk about taking action, it can be the smallest baby steps. Practice taking action in any area of your life. Stretch yourself. Make yourself uncomfortable. For example, go a different route to work. Speak to different people than you have before. Do something that you've never done before that is challenging—run a marathon or commit to climbing a mountain or get a life coach.

- How are you taking action in your life? Make a list of things you can do to acheive one goal or fulfill an epiphany you've had. It may entail things as simple as researching classes on-line or buying a book or making a phone call. Do one thing on your list each day and add to the list as ideas come to you. One day you'll realize you're doing multiple things on that list or that your goal has been reached. You will not believe how you will gain momentum toward your goals with such a simple exercise.

SERENDIPITY. After people began to take action on their epiphanies, circumstances seemed to fall into place so that they could take the next step. It is as if the world conspires to support your decisions and actions, to confirm that you are on the right track.

The definition of serendipity is "the occurrence and development of events by chance in a happy or beneficial way." It's so beneficial that companies like Yahoo and Google are orchestrating serendipity in the workplace because it leads to some of the most creative and innovative breakthroughs and ideas, and psychologists are studying it to figure out how we can foster more of it in order to lead happier, more fulfilling lives.

We all have serendipity and synchronistic occurrences in our lives. According to research, the "luckiest" people in the world notice it, love it, expect it, act on it and are grateful for it. It's so important to choose to notice it. Be excited about it. Be grateful for it and **act on it**. (Epiphany stories to look at: Orian Williams and Stacey Lannert.)

- Do you notice and get excited about serendipity/synchronicity in your life? Are you grateful for it? Write down a few of your serendipitous stories and get in touch with the wonder of serendipity and feel gratitude for it. The more you are noticing, expecting, acting, and are excited about serendipity, the more it will occur for you.

4. By fostering these four elements of listening, belief, action, and serendipity in our lives, we will cultivate an environment for epiphanies and develop a continuous cycle of having them and living a life based on them. **Examine your epiphany you wrote about earlier. Can you see the pattern of listening, belief, action, and serendipity in your story?**

5. Think about ways you have "rippled out" in the world. Preferably this will come from an epiphany that you acted upon, but it doesn't have to be the case. Really think about specific examples of lives you've touched and helped just by your actions, sometimes almost accidentally. Try to follow the ripple out as far as you can. This is a great exercise. We so rarely think about this in an in-depth way and truly take in how we have affected a person or people in positive or even negative ways. To stop and take stock of this is very powerful. We all are having an effect in the world on a daily basis with our thoughts and actions. We are all much more significant than most of us realize. We all are rippling out in the world, whether we want to or mean to or not. What do you want your ripples to be? It's important to bring it into our awareness and focus on it every now and then, and it's quite empowering, encouraging and humbling to do so.

6. Ask your parents or other loved ones in your life about their greatest epiphany. See what they say. See if it opens up dialog. See if you don't learn something about them that you never knew before and if it doesn't develop a new kind of intimacy or even healing of some kind. Maybe if you are a parent, your written epiphany can be shared with your children or you will find a way to ask them about theirs and tell them about yours. This is also a great exercise to start opening up about family histories and passing down oral histories. (Epiphany stories to look at: Judith Orloff, M.D. and Billie Myers.)

READERS' GUIDE DISCUSSION QUESTIONS

Whether discovering purpose in life, awakening to new possibilities, or finding a new direction after a catastrophic setback, each person's epiphany is a gift, providing new insights for life and a window into the universal truths that connect us all.

1. An epiphany is "a moment of sudden or great revelation that usually changes your life in some way." Several other definitions are shared in the book, including Maya Angelou's that an epiphany is "when the mind, body, and soul come together and see an old thing in a new way." How would you define an epiphany?

2. Have you ever had an epiphany? Did it change your life?

3. Do you feel a person needs faith in God, the Divine, or a Higher Power to have an epiphany?

4. Did reading this book help you remember or realize your own epiphanies? Did it spark any new epiphanies for you?

5. According to Elise, every epiphany involved listening, belief, action, and serendipity. If you've had an epiphany, were these elements present in the experience?

6. Which stories in the book resonated the most with you? Surprised you? Shocked you? Disappointed you? Inspired you? Why?

7. The book is divided into six categories. Do you find one of the categories more interesting or compelling than the others?

8. How would you categorize your epiphany? Could your epiphany fit into more than one?

9. Do you agree that it is very important to ask your loved ones and those closest to you about their epiphanies? In your inner circles, whose epiphany would you most like to know? Could you open the subject with him or her?

10. If you could ask anyone about his or her epiphany, who would it be? Why?

ACKNOWLEDGMENTS

acknowledgment : thanks, appreciation, recognition, gratitude, obligation

The journey is the reward.
—CHINESE PROVERB

Once upon a time, I embarked on a journey called *Epiphany*. Fortunately, the age-old maxim "Ignorance is bliss" applied in this case instead of my trusty "Knowledge and understanding eliminate fear," because had I actually known and understood what this journey would involve, I probably would have chickened out and missed out on one of the most extraordinary, life-affirming experiences I've ever had. This book represents the ending of a life chapter for me. In writing it, I came to realize it is my greatest epiphany and, in fact, has been an awakening, a new direction, a healing, a miracle, a coming of age, and a calling. It's been an absolutely amazing ride, and one I know would not have been completed (at least in one piece) without the support and encouragement of *so* many people.

First and foremost, I must thank all the people who gave me interviews when *Epiphany* was just an idea—before I had developed a project, before I had an agent or a book deal, before I knew anything, really. Because they gave their precious time and stories without hesitation, I was able to build a project. In order of their involvement, these early supporters were Sam Gosling,

Michael Roizen, Joel Harper, Larry Wright, Elizabeth Avellán, Mary Bruton, Stephen Bruton, Mehmet Oz, Roly Gosling, Baraka Victor, Michala Rose, Christopher Lee, Ariane de Bonvoisin, Cory Booker, Rabbi Shmuley Boteach, Alexis Minko, Tracy Matthews, Frank Desiderio, Bart Knaggs, Linda Biehl, Julie Horton, Orian Williams, Sam Danniels, Caroline Moody, and G. W. Bailey.

Other very special people I'd like to thank who touched my life with their stories are Ali Afshar, Angelica Aragon, Grace Ballard, Herb Ballard, Geraldine Baron, Vin Di Bona, Cherise Fisher, Matt Flannery, Bronagh Gallagher, Brad Hirschfield, Jusstine Kenzer, Kristen Kemp, Jeff Lamb, John Lockley, Harry Mastrogeorge, Yolanda Pedraza, Sue Schachter, John Scott, and Mark Thornton.

To all the people who "got" this project and me, and then helped make it happen, I am forever grateful, especially to Linda Loewenthal, and Julia Pastore, my gracious, sublime editor. I also thank Shaye Areheart, the lovely publisher who ushered me in and wrote a poem after we met about epiphanies that I will always cherish; Tammy Blake, for all her input, enthusiasm, and care (nothing like bonding over laughter and pain in Joel Harper's studio!); and Domenica Alioto, Campbell Wharton, Jennifer Robbins, and everyone else on the team at Harmony for their hard work and for being such dreams to work with. My deep gratitude to Noel Nicholas, my godsend assistant—I'll miss our interview-landing victory dances; Monty Bass and David Scott, my Web interview editors; Christopher Baldi, who edited the original video for the book and website and refused to let me pay him, prompting me to donate to his favorite charities (Operation Smile, Smile Train) instead; Elora Dorini, for her terrific transcription work and feedback; Deena Kalai, my outstanding attorney; the incredibly talented Sean Taylor, who has helped me in countless ways over the years; Robin Kressbach, Rogers McInnis and Emily Parliman for their invaluable assistance; W. G. Snuffy Walden for his genius, inspiring music; and Sergio

Carvajal, Marc Hulett, Fran Berry, and "Chief" Carolyn Rangel for all their help and belief in the project.

I must give a huge extra-special thanks to my magnificent sister, Faye Ballard. From acting as a production assistant on a Wiener Dog shoot, to laughing (instead of crying and/or killing me) about being locked in storage units while assisting me with moving, to helping me enormously with this book, she is always getting me out of scrapes, and I am forever indebted. Also to John Zmirak, for his splendid editing skills and humor. Having them on my team made me feel safe and supported, and certainly made everything more fun.

My gratitude to all my friends for their love and support throughout the years knows no bounds. There are some distinctive players I want to especially thank who were always there for me during this particular journey and kept me laughing no matter what.

One is Joel Harper, to whom so many roads lead. Without his endless support and always having my back, I don't know where I'd be. Mary Bruton is my soul sister and confidante who always makes everything better, and she and the late, great, lovely Stephen Bruton were my family in Austin. Clive Davis's unbelievable generosity and guidance made the hardest time in my life beautiful and adventurous and has led me to so many fantastic people and experiences. Others include my dear friends Kelly Korzan, my insanely creative editor and partner-in-crime on many projects, and the brilliant Tim French; Mitchell Welch, brother, producer, and wingman extraordinaire; the fabulous V. A. Stephens; Jeff Moll, my incredible Africa travel companion; the exuberant Kesha Dirkson; and the uber-talented Merrilee McCommas. My intense thanks also goes to Judy and Bill Moore, whom I will always consider family; to John Blaylock, for always being rock-solid and for utilizing his excellent recon skills on my behalf; to Sam Gosling, for his advice, generosity, and for always showing up just when I need him; and to Roly Gosling, for being my gracious, hilarious host during my visit to Tanzania, making possible one of the most awe-inspiring adventures of my life. I thank Jusstine Kenzer for all the encouragement and excellent recommendations; Ann Knight-Swartzman, for helping me get settled and grounded in LaLa Land; Marco Perella, for forcing me to play Lola; John Capruzzo; and The Circle Girls, especially Anjika McElroy, Leslie Murray, and Cheryl Hamada. I am also extremely appreciative to Mehmet and Lisa Oz for their wisdom and friendship and whose early support for this project was absolutely pivotal in getting it off the ground.

Big thanks to my friends who jumped through hoops and worked their connections to get me interviews: Amy Steinman, for all the songs and lattes and always supporting me in any way she can; Amy Wollman, who never fails to come through; Brian Braff, a true gentleman through and through; and Sue Schachter, for always believing in me and my endeavors and promoting this project from the start.

I am deeply grateful to my phenomenal friends and healers: Lisa Norman, who initially sent me on my way; Mary Schneider of the Austin Holographic Repatterning Institute; Bo Olszewski, for helping me through my crazy writer's block; and Heather Jelks, the most incredible life coach there ever was.

To my extremely generous and loving parents, Faye and Marshall Ballard, I give tremendous thanks for their patronage and for who they are and for all they have done and do for me. I don't know where I'd be without their support and belief in me and this project. Also to my wonderful siblings Marshall and Katherine Ballard, and Erica and James Reiss; and to my nieces, Brooke and Tatum Reiss, who gave me brilliant five- and seven-year-old epiphanies.

I also have to give a very special thank-you to Frank Desiderio, the original champion of *Epiphany*. I'm not sure it would have happened without him wanting to develop it, and he definitely gets credit for sparking the idea for the book.

Throughout the years, I have had the good fortune of having several unique and gifted teachers who have made all the difference. Because of their seeing and believing, I was able to. My sincere gratitude goes to Carol Lanning, Linda Raya, Joe Paradise, and Harry Mastrogeorge for being this kind of great teacher to me.

To my majestic, magical teacher and friend Geraldine Baron, I owe so much. She was an invaluable influence and support in my life and in so many others'; it was a true privilege to know and experience her mastery and share in the love, wisdom, and light she brought to this world.

I also must thank the ever-inspiring, connector-extraordinaire, and beauty hunter, Jennifer Pastiloff, and the brilliant Beth Karlin for their undying support, input and love. Without them and their example and encouragement, it is quite probable that an *Epiphany* workshop would not exist. Leslie Conliffe, Eric Handler of PositivelyPositive.com, Danielle Boonstra, Sherry Mills and Lyn Girdler have also been instrumental in urging me forward and helping me get the word out on epiphanies.

Finally, and most of all, my deepest gratitude, respect, and heartfelt thanks to each and every person in this book and everyone else who has shared and are sharing their stories with me. They all have taught and continue to teach and show me that we can all be teachers to each other.

*A teacher affects eternity; he can never tell
where his influence stops.*
—HENRY ADAMS

65246345R00176

Made in the USA
Charleston, SC
19 December 2016